# DR. CARLTON FREDERICKS'

# NEW & COMPLETE

# NUTRITION HANDBOOK

MAJOR BOOKS • CHATSWORTH, CALIFORNIA

**MAJOR BOOKS**
21322 Lassen Street
Chatsworth, California 91311

PRINTED IN THE UNITED STATES OF AMERICA

ISBN 0-89041-079-8

Originally published as
**The Nutrition Handbook.**
Copyright © 1964
Library of Congress Catalog Card Number: 76-9381

# CONTENTS

To the physicians of the
International Academy of Preventive Medicine,
who long ago realized that Alexis Carrel
was prophetic when he remarked that
the physician of today will be
the dietitian of tomorrow—or
the dietitian will be the physician.

# AUTHOR'S NOTE

What we call modern nutritional science is in part based on rediscovery. The ancient Italians fed burned sponge to goiter patients, successfully treating the thyroid disorder with what was essentially a source of iodine. The Bible clearly anticipates our discovery of Vitamin A when it remarks that the eyes of the cattle failed, for they had no green grass. The primitive Indians of Canada treated scurvy by administering the adrenal glands of the deer, now known to be one of the most highly concentrated sources of the vitamin in the body. Though the term "vitamin" was originated in 1912, by Dr. Casimir Funk, for whose laboratory I was a nutrition educator, the concept was anticipated by the Sumerians, whose gods included one whose duty it was to enter the mouth with the food and to escort it to its proper destinations in the body—surely, a fair working definition of a vitamin. Part of the treatment of rickets employed by the distant ancestors of the British, was to pass the naked child through a fork in an ash tree, under the full glare of the sun—an interesting anticipation of our modern knowledge of the method by which the body receives the anti-rickets vitamin, Vitamin D.

This book reflects some of that ancient knowledge, updated and amplified by the findings of thousands of qualified workers in the field of nutrition, both contemporary and long ago, as published in the competent scientific journals in biochemistry, nutrition, and medicine. Those papers have passed over my desk in the tens of thousands, for I am the editor of a medical newsletter, and a regular contributor, in clinical notes, to a medical journal.

Another source of the information in this book derives from the research findings, published and unpublished, made available to the author by his colleagues—not only workers in the field of nutrition itself, but those who are ap-

9

plying nutrient therapies in fields ranging from ortho-molecular psychiatry to obstetrics, gynecology, opthalmology, dermatology, neurology, and all the other "ologies" which attempt to reassemble the whole man from the sick man.

Still another is the author's personal research in myoneuropathies (nerve-muscle) disorders, derangements of carbohydrate metabolism (particularly, diabetes and hypoglycemia) and obesity.

Inevitably, in so broad a cross section of sources of information in nutrition, conclusions will be gathered which collide head-on with those of the establishment in this highly polemical field. When this occurs, it is often a reflection of the cultural lag—the gap in time between findings, their acceptance, and their application to the health problems of man. This book makes an effort to shorten that lag.

Carlton Fredericks, Ph.D.

# CHAPTER 1

## TO YOUR (REALLY) GOOD HEALTH

MY COPY OF FUNK AND WAGNALLS DICTIONARY DEFINES health as "an optimal state of functioning of the organism—never achieved."

One of my colleagues in a medical society with a deep and abiding interest in nutrition as a preventive and a therapeutic modality, Dr. Roger Williams, a great biochemist and nutritionist, has remarked that optimal nutrition is never achieved, that all nutrition is a compromise.

We tend to accept compromises which are not compulsory. For instance, the medical definition of good health is the absence of disease. And that definition is flexible enough so that an insurance company will accept you as healthy if you have nothing more than a little sinus trouble with postnasal drip, six colds per year, indigestion, heartburn, flatulence, constipation, dry hair, a couple of allergies (so long as they don't give you asthma), decayed teeth, periodontal disease, irritability, fatigability, insomnia, and difficulty in concentrating. Which means that the popular definition of health is any state of well-being that allows you to walk on the street without falling flat on your face—if the wind is blowing in the right direction. If that's your philosophy, you have as little reason for reading this book as you have for changing your diet.

Your response to all this is predictable. Like the man who has jumped off the roof of a tall building and not yet reached ground level, you're doing all right—so far. Do stop and think for a moment: When the day comes that your physician scans a report on your blood and urine tests, and announces that you're diabetic, or prediabetic, your first question will be: "Doctor, what should I eat?" Ask that question *now*, before disaster strikes, unless you have fallen in love with the system of "crisis medicine" to which we have been gradually conditioned.

We accept a host of minor ailments as "average" health, which we then consider normal because it's average. We tolerate major diseases as a dispensation of an irate Providence, when many of them can be prevented or mitigated through proper nutrition. We undergo surgery for pathologies which could have been avoided with good nutrition, or which could be treated, sans the scalpel, with nutrients alone. (Take slipped disks, as an example, which are often treated successfully with large amounts of Vitamin C, but more often, invite surgery.) We endure a record in reproductive inefficiency—failure to conceive, failure to bear normal, healthy babies—which breeders of thoroughbred horses and pedigreed dogs would not tolerate in their animals. In short, as the United States Department of Agriculture puts it, we manage to remain unaware that about 90 percent of our sicknesses could be banished or their ravages significantly reduced, just by changing our diets for the better.

*We must begin by redefining good health. It isn't the mere absence of disease, and it isn't an "average" collection of minor symptoms. To a nutritionist, good health is a positive state of well-being. It is a composite of good intellectual and physical functioning, of good appetite, digestion, and elimination; of good muscle tone, of heightened resistance to infection and fatigue; of that wonderful feeling of buoyancy which makes each new day a new adventure, to be savored and enjoyed to the full.*

Let it be clearly understood that there are no miracles in nutrition. Poor diet is not the explanation of all disease, although every disease ultimately and inevitably involves nutrition. Good diet is not the answer to all disease, although overcoming deficiencies can be extremely helpful. Happily, however, our new knowlege of the action within the body of protein, fat, minerals and vitamins gives us in nutrition a weapon which can free man from much unnecessary sickness and bestow upon him the capacity to respond better to medication when he does become ill. Good nutrition cannot carry you beyond the limits set by heredity; but many people never achieve these limits, and it is the errand of the nutrition educator to help people to realize their full potential.

As you read and learn more about the sheer drama of vitamin chemistry and its importance to your health, do not be led into over-emphasis on this phase of nutrition. Many kinds of dietary imbalance and deficiency exist and will continue to exist so long as man eats for pleasure rather than for good nutrition. Do not, however, be equally guilty of under-emphasis. There are so many astonishing rewards in good nutrition that it is wise to remain open-minded.

Nutrition makes us what we are. It is our "internal environment." The food we eat today is banging a typewriter tomorrow, frowning over a newspaper, scolding a child, quarreling with a husband. Today's nutrition determines your life-span, affects your personalities, regulates your working efficiency, builds or tears down resistance to shock, infection and fatigue. The intelligence of your children will be affected by their diets; their reproductive efficiency will be molded by their food; the strength of their bones and teeth will be determined by what they eat.

In a lifetime you eat as much as 150,000 pounds of food. That impressive tonnage includes everything from the proverbial soup to nuts but, fundamentally, it is made up of protein, fat, sugar, starch, water, vitamins, minerals, and fiber. Improperly selected, that diet will permit you to remain alive, but you may be only half alive. Properly selected, the same tonnage of food will help give you glowing health—the nutritionist's not-so-Utopian concept of positive buoyant health.

*Dr. Carlton Fredericks' New and Complete Nutrition Handbook* aims at no compromise. The author wishes you to have the best of health. This, of course, demands the best of diet. You will, therefore, find that the nutritional requirements set forth in this book are rather higher and more stringent than those specified by the average text. Even if you do not achieve all the goals herein delineated, you will be better

13

off for trying. Every change in the right direction is an improvement and will manifest itself in feeling better; for if you take three steps forward and fall back two, you are still one step ahead!

## ARE YOU NUTRITIONALLY DEFICIENT?

Check yourself as a nutritionist would. He notices whether your body is undersized or whether you appear to be underweight. This is not an exclusive index, however, because you may carry normal or even excess weight and still be badly fed. Poorly nourished overweight people usually have flabby and very soft fat.

If you are not eating properly, your muscles are likely to be small and soft; your skin will have a very significant looseness and pallor and may be waxy or sallow. Middle-aged persons, after years of poor diet, may have premature wrinkling because of a lack of subcutaneous fat to pad the skin.

Lips and eyelids are telltale of poor nourishment. Because mucous membranes are intimately affected by diet, these will appear thin and tautly stretched. There may be some crusting about the lids, also some redness. Hair will be rough and lusterless, with the property of coarseness but without the virtue of being manageable. Dark hollows or blue circles may be apparent under your eyes, and your facial expression may be drawn or worried, making you look older than your years. Or, so contradictory are the signs of deficiency, you may be falsely animated on the surface, but with an indefinable air of strain about your face.

Characteristic of people who subsist on a bad diet for a long period of time is the fatigue posture—head thrust forward, flat chest, round shoulders, protruding abdomen.

The malnourished are likely to tell the nutritionist that they are irritable, overactive and fatigued; or they may go to the other extreme and be phlegmatic, restless, depressed, unable to concentrate. They will say that they have difficulty in getting to sleep, and, when sleep comes, it is restless. They complain about low resistance to infection, lack of endurance and vigor, nerves, indigestion, constipation, a finicky appetite. They usually present a long list of foods which they feel "disagree" with them.

Other symptoms of deficiency are more specific—such as cracks at the corners of the mouth, running parallel with the lips; a purple or very shiny tongue; over-sensitivity to bright lights; a feeling of weakness or irritability, or inability to concentrate if a meal is delayed.

These symptoms are warning signals, but the absence of them does not necessarily mean that you are well fed. For if you eat a diet which is neither truly deficient nor truly optimal, you will live in the shadowland where one is neither truly sick nor truly well.

An average woman's menstrual cycle is a classic example of the prices for living in that shadowland. She accepts a five-day menstrual flow because, being average, it's considered normal. She endures a premenstrual week with depression, anxiety, hysteria, dizziness, water retention with weight gain, backache, cramps, sensitivity of the breasts, and cravings for sweets, because these, too, are average symptoms, and thereby considered normal. Yet when we make a few simple changes in women's diet, the five-day menstrual will shorten to three days in more than 50 percent of the subjects for whom we try the experiment, and premenstrual tension and other symptoms lessen or totally disappear. If we are to appraise the nutrition of American women by the changes in the menstrual disturbances when nutrition is bettered, we must come to the conclusion that most of them are poorly fed.

If you are not yet convinced that a "healthy" American may not be, and that a "good average diet" may well be average, but not good, consider the Japanese. Before World War II, they considered themselves to be people whose short stature was dictated by heredity. With an improvement in the national dietary, post-war, the Japanese children began to grow taller than their parents. Obviously, their potential for growth had been restricted by suboptimal nutrition, but they never realized it, and considered themselves to be well-fed. To what extent is your capacity for good health and improved functioning restricted by your diet? You'll never know whether you are in the position of the pre-war Japanese, unless you explore the potential benefits of a better diet.

# CHAPTER 2

## ATTACK THE MAN—DON'T DISCUSS THE ISSUE

THE ESTABLISHMENT IN NUTRITION WIELDS THE POTENT leverage of an income of 120 billion dollars a year. It is an economic tide that sweeps over the mass media, allowing the food processors subtly or blantantly to persuade the public that puffed rice is an excellent breakfast, white bread a nutritional bonanza, and white sugar a desirable source of energy. (Never mind that the medical journals are filled with articles on the diseases primitives develop when newly exposed to such foods—the diseases that fill our hospitals, at that. The public doesn't see such articles.)

Those who command both the agriculture and food processing industries are able to lean heavily on our universities, via gifts and grants. Through the medical establishment, they are able to punish physicians who desert harmful medications in favor of the physiological approach of good nutrition. They silence professors of nutrition who have the courage to criticize their overmilled, overpriced, and overused foods. And when they are particularly threatened, these giants of the nutrition field fall back on the ancient ploy of attacking the man when the issues can't comfortably be discussed. So arise the cries of "food faddism." It is the rallying term for dietitians who have been indoctrinated, rather than educated. It is the almost unanswerable charge hurled via the mass media, when the establishment wishes to pretend that we Americans live in the best of all possible nutritional worlds. Unanswerable because it is most difficult, and I write from personal experience, to persuade reporters that an independent laboratory, or an isolated medical worker may be more objective in the approach to nutrition than the spokesman for General Mills or Kellogg.

This is not to say that food faddism is nonexistent, but that it is a term very frequently used in lieu of a competent reply to competent criticism of American foods and food habits. Were our foods not subjected to overprocessing, not vehicles for dubious additives and questionable pesticide residues, we should still be hard-put to achieve good nutrition, for the best-balanced diet supplies barely more than the maintenance requirements of most of the nutrients—for a healthy person.

For the sick, where requirements for nutrients may soar, maintenance intake is simply not enough. Thus, although pellagra is definitely a dietary deficiency disease, it can't be cured with diet alone. That is why Tom Spies, pioneer in the nutritional treatment of deficiency disorders, treated his pellagrins not only with a high-calorie, high-protein, high-vitamin-mineral diet, but with large amounts of brewer's yeast, desiccated liver, and vitamins, taken both orally and by injection. And what that medical researcher learned to be necessary in the treatment of deficiency disease, is a principle which must be invoked in maintenance diets for healthy people.

As much as it outrages a dietitian, who somehow can accept added vitamins in cornflakes, but balks at them in a capsule, the realization must be accepted that there are people with high nutritional requirements whose needs can't be satisfied with ordinary foods alone, because it would demand that they overeat. For such people, brewer's yeast, wheat germ, and vitamin-mineral supplements are not optional, but mandatory, diet insurance. Since the existence of such people is interpreted by the dietitian and the home economist as a negation of everything they were taught, they bring social pressure on those unfortunates by labeling them as "food faddists." Better a healthy food faddist than a "normal" unhealthy American.

To give you an example of the workings of the orthodox mind in nutrition, a victim of indoctrination masquerading as science, consider a review of my cookbook by an American Medical Association dietitian. Too much emphasis on "faddist foods" was the damning verdict. This referred to recipes in which wheat germ is an ingredient. The fact that wheat germ is rich in essential nutrients is unimportant. The fact that wheat germ is removed from 94 percent of the public's bread is not a threat. The restoration of it to the diet, though, becomes socially, technically, and professionally taboo. Yet a concentrate of a factor in wheat germ oil has been observed at the University of Illinois, in their physical fitness department, to help reverse part of the aging process in flabby, middle-aged men. And a higher concentration of the factor has been helpful to children with cerebral palsy, and to patients with multiple sclerosis. Explicit in these responses is the obvious conclusion: We'd be better off if they restored wheat germ to our bread, or, still better, if we ate nothing but whole grains with the germ (embryo) intact. But that would crucify the thousands of recipes released by dietitians and home economists, based solidly on degerminated flour, garnished with cupfuls of white sugar. Rather than discuss *that* ominous possibility, it becomes felicitous to write about "faddist" ingredients in cookbook recipes.

The mention of sugar brings up another point. If we outlawed the use of more than twelve pounds of sugar per person, per year, we'd reduce tooth-decay without fluoridating our reservoirs, cut down on the incidence of diabetes, and prevent many cases of hypoglycemia (low blood sugar), a disease with symptoms so closely resembling neurosis that many patients are supine on psychiatric couches who should be vertical at lunch counters. (See Chapter 5 for a discussion of the mischief caused by excessive use of sugar.) But if we put a ceiling on sugar intake, we'd decimate the recipes in the average cookbook, and eliminate most of those published in the mass media.

There is a corollary to all this: Those who drown common sense in a sea of hyperbole, by labeling wheat germ, brewer's yeast, and other special-purpose foods as "miracle foods." That kind of exaggeration is as regrettable as the abuse of the term faddism. Factually, special-purpose foods are concentrated in vitamins, minerals, and other nutrients, and, in proportion to these high values, they are low in calories. Thus, they are helpful in reversing the direction of a food technology which tends to concentrate calories at the expense of nutrients—white rice, white sugar, and white flour being prime examples. In practical terms, we can obtain from a few teaspoonfuls of wheat germ—with 150 calories—vitamin-mineral values which white bread—with 1,200 calories per loaf—doesn't give us at all, or yields in unsatisfactory amounts. Since we live in a mechanized age which places a calorie ceiling on our diets, the special-purpose foods like wheat germ are useful in permitting us to achieve dietary adequacy while maintaining normal body weight.

So it is with vitamin-mineral supplements, the use of which also has been swept under the encompassing label of food faddism. These supplements exert no penalty in excessive intake of calories; they protect us against our errors in selection and preparation of foods for retention of these values, and they raise our intake high enough to take care of individual differences in requirements. But that last phrase is also anathema to the orthodoxy in nutrition, for it is basic to their philosophy that tables of nutritional needs can be drawn up, which will serve as a standard for adequate diet for all 200 million Americans. Thus we are equated biochemically and nutritionally, as carbon copies of each other.

Yet the medical profession, which issues these generalizations, is the first to warn us never to use the medicine prescribed for another patient, even if our symptoms (and disease) are identical—for reactions to drugs are so very highly individual. Just as individual are our nutritional needs and tolerances, with our dissimilarities more marked than our similarities. Nutritional needs in animals, for various nutrients, can vary by a factor of up to forty, depending on what nutrient you are discussing. There is no reason to suppose that man's requirements are not equally varied, and the limited evidence we have gathered does, indeed, asseverate our individuality. Man's calcium requirements may vary by a factor of five; his need for amino acids, similarly, may differ by a factor of three to five; his requirement for nitrogen may require that he eat as little as two ounces of meat or other animal protein daily, or as much as ten ounces—to arrive at the same nutritional equilibrium.

So it is with vitamins. Linus Pauling has accumulated data indicating that our need for Vitamin C may range from 250 mgs. daily to about 2,500, the latter being the amount of the vitamin a person would synthesize daily, had he not lost the capacity for its manufacture, somewhere in the course of evolution. There are psychotics who remain sane only if their intake of pyridoxin (Vitamin B6) is 500 times as great as the R.D.A—the table of recommended dietary allowances which is based on the nonexistent "standard reference American." There is no place in the Washington scheme of matters nutritional for those whose needs are great. There *is* a place where such needs can be fulfilled, though—in a diet carefully selected, and in vitamin-mineral supplements well chosen.

The next time you encounter the legend "R.D.A." on a vitamin or food label, mentally equate it with a proposal to make bras and false teeth in one size, for manufacturing economy. Which would make about as much sense.

# CHAPTER 3

## BEAUTY FROM WITHIN

IT WAS YEARS AGO THAT ONE OF MY RADIO LISTENERS remarked that her beauty parlor operator was the first person to notice that she had changed her diet for the better.

better. Her hair, he pointed out, was more manageable, less wiry, and had a better sheen. The manicurist echoed him: My listener's nails, she remarked, showed less tendency to split and were growing faster. No veterinarian would find these comments, applied to an animal, startling, for veterinarians know that an animal's coat is a mirror of its diet.

By the same token, when you complain about leathery, oily, or dry skin, or coarse skin with large pores, it is time to remember that beauty starts from within. No cream, oil, soap, or astringent can create what is not there. External care is important; so is simple cleanliness, to the complexion; but a coat of paint on a disintegrating surface is a waste of materials and energy.

Actually, there is no special dietary recommendation for healthy hair, and another for strong, fast-growing nails, and yet another for a good complexion. For that matter, nutrition isn't the only factor affecting skin, nails, and hair.

If your thyroid is underactive, your troubles will range from constipation to dry skin, from too many colds to dry, brittle hair, from fatigability to slow-growing nails. Your doctor can check thyroid performance very easily—there is a simple, under-arm temperature test which is surprisingly sensitive. And, if you're trying to be a more vital and attractive person, that test is worth pursuing. You might remember that a diet chronically low in iodine is not the only nutritional pathway to thyroid insufficiency. Lack of Vitamin B1—chronic and mild—will drag down thyroid function, too. Eating too much sugar, which most Americans do, attacks your beauty in two different ways: via thyroid deficiency—caused by lack of Vitamin B1, caused in turn by excess intake of sugar; and via a direct effect of sugar on the skin, which concentrates the sweet more rapidly than the blood does. A sugar-filled skin is an invitation to infection, as diabetics painfully learn.

Dietary deficiencies which impair nail growth and strength do not point only to lack of calcium and Vitamin D, though that is the popular belief. Nor is gelatin a panacea for splitting nails, though it appears to be helpful when the nails tend to split, layer by layer. Of first importance is high-quality animal protein, to supply the sulfur-containing amino acids, which are building materials for hair and nails. Eggs are a rich source of these types of protein acids. The Vitamin B Complex affects both nails and hair, and concentrates high in choline are occasionally quite helpful. Calcium intake can, of course, be maintained with milk, cheese, and yogurt, but if calories are a large consideration, calcium orotate supplements can be used, this being a particularly assimilable form of the mineral. Brewer's yeast is also helpful as an adjunct source of protein and Vitamin B Complex.

Adequate total protein intake is critically important and can be easily maintained if you make it a point to take an animal protein—these being of the highest efficiency—at every meal even if portions are modest. This yields other dividends, in terms of the menstrual cycle, and in warding off hypoglycemia (low blood sugar) as you will learn later.

Remember that persistent anemia, circulatory disorders, and systemic disease have an impact on the nails, and sometimes, on the hair, which means that you should be cleared medically before you ask for miracles from nutrients.

## HAIR

Thickening hair nutritionally, stopping hair loss, and growing hair on bald heads are as yet impossible dreams. Consider that the prisoners rescued from German concentration camps were starved to the stage of being walking skeletons, but many of them still had full heads of hair. There is but one observation in nutrition which offers any clue to hair growth: the report that the inositol (a B-Complex vitamin) content of falling hair is about 50 percent below the level in healthy hair. However, I have never seen inositol cause hair growth on bald spots, though a few diabetics, dosed with it for reasons other than their baldness, did report that a "fine fuzz" appeared. I suspect that this was lanugo—like the very temporary hair of the newborn, not destined to stay. If you wish to experiment, inositol is available in tablet form. Since it is a vitamin of the B Complex, it should be taken together with the entire group, in the form of a Vitamin B Complex supplement. Many of these supplements, however, do not supply significant amounts of inositol, which explains the recommendation that this vitamin be employed separately.

The recommendations made for dietary care of the nails will, of course, apply to hair, with an added proviso: If dandruff is present, it must be brought under control. If the numerous shampoos, employing zinc or selenium salts, do not prove effective, a dermatologist should be consulted. There are fungus infections of the scalp which mimic dandruff, and a deficiency of Vitamin B6 (pyridoxin) can cause a type of dandruff (actually, a seborrhea) which can contribute to hair loss. Pyridoxin supplements are available, but it is a good idea not to self-treat until a dermatologist has checked your scalp under a Wood light and ruled out fungus and other infections.

A few years ago, in an interview on the Merv Griffin program, I remarked that I have less gray hair than the average person of my age because I use a vitamin supplement which deters graying, and in some cases, reverses it. This information was so "old hat" to me that I was astonished by the mail seeking the exact identity of the vitamin formula I was using. Having thoroughly educated the public in the use of such a formula in the first edition of this very book more than thirty years ago, you can understand I was not under the impression I'd said something the public would regard both as new and fascinating. At any rate, the vitamins for gray hair are not a panacea—not all subjects respond—and the formula is better used to slow down graying, than to try to reverse it. But behind the formula there is a considerable amount of research—both my own, and as reported in the scientific literature.

It was some thirty years ago that Dr. Agnes Faye Morgan reported that a group of laboratory rats had turned gray-haired on a diet deficient in vitamins. Moreover, they developed the graying at an age corresponding to a ten-year-old child. At the time, heredity was supposed to control hair coloring (and loss of it), and Dr. Morgan was at a loss to explain how dietary deficiency could be involved. Autopsies of the animals revealed that their adrenal glands showed signs—in internal bleeding—that the vitamin deficiency had seriously affected them. With a second group of animals, Dr. Morgan again produced gray hair with vitamin deficiency, then restored the color to the hair by restoration of the missing vitamin, and with autopsies demonstrated that the adrenal glands showed signs of internal damage, which had subsequently been repaired. So it was that the California nutritionist had stumbled upon the realization that these glands are heavily dependent on pantothenic acid. Decades later, Dr. Esther Tuttle showed that large doses of pantothenic acid relieved signs of adrenal stress in humans.

The research led to an experiment with human beings in Boston, where Benjamin Sieve, M.D., gave the same vitamin to a group of prematurely gray men and women, and eight months later, displayed photographs showing three-fourths of the subjects had normally colored hair. Dr. Sieve, however, didn't confine his research to pantothenic acid. He later added paba, which is chemical shorthand for para-amino-benzoic acid, had a significantly stimulating effect on infertile women, implying an interaction with the pituitary gland. Since this gland is believed to be involved in hair pigmentation, addition of paba to the dose of pantothenic acid became logical.

Still another scientist entered the gray-hair arena. He was working with a group of life-term convicts in a New York State prison. The popular belief was that long-term confinement in a punitive institution caused premature graying of the hair, but his research indicated that it might be prison diet and its inadequacies, rather than prison life which was responsible, for he, too, displayed photographs, which showed darkening of the hair in some of these men.

At this point, the inquiring mind might wonder what the fuss is all about. Unless we in nutrition are minded to go into competition with the beauty parlors and hair-dye purveyors, what's the point of all this?

There *is* a valid point. This gray-hair research confirms the nutritionist's view, so well voiced by the early German researchers who said that between the vitamins and the hormones there is a state of co- and counter-play, the effects so inextricably mixed that a deficiency of one might show up only as an imbalance of the other. And *that* is important, for it adds a new dimension and opens new therapeutic avenues in our effort to help those whose glands do not work at full efficiency. The effect of paba on fertility is a case in point. I once held a luncheon for several hundred children, born to parents who had been infertile until we changed their diets, and gave them vitamin supplements—paba and pantothenic acid included. Which explains why Mike Douglas, to the mystification of his audience, once introduced me as "the father of several hundred children"—and then refused to explain.

I realized all the vitamins in the experiments came from the Vitamin B Complex— the group found in liver, yeast and other natural sources. We decided that the sensible way to use them would be to combine them with their original source. Consequently, we decided on a formula and proceeded, with the co-operation of some medical friends, to test it.

Our first subject was a little girl, only seven years old. She not only had gray hair—she had a condition called "vitiligo," a disease in which the color of the hair and the color of the skin disappear simultaneously. On her little body were oyster-white patches of decolored skin, sharply contrasted against her normally olive complexion. Some months after the family physician had begun to give the vitamin formula to this child, her mother wrote us that little freckles of color made their appearance, merging into larger patches until finally the entire body resumed its normal color, as did the hair. Such results in "vitiligo" were reported by Sieve but occur rarely.

Stimulated by this experience and by success in other cases of premature gray hair, we released the formula to the public. We have since been deluged with letters from thousands of women, expressing their gratitude. Some of these commented shyly on the fact that their skin, too, appeared to be less wrinkled. They seemed surprised. It is well known to vitamin technicians that certain of these B Vitamins have the effect of redistributing body fat. When this phenomenon occurs on the face, it might well mean that some of the wrinkles are ironed out.

## THE ANTI-GRAY HAIR FORMULA

The author's objective in presenting this tested and occasionally successful anti-gray hair vitamin formula is not a cosmetic one. Gray hair can be quickly recolored in the beauty parlor or at home with dyes and tints. It has been our experience, however, that the gray-headed, when fortunate, can not only recolor their hair with vitamin supplementing, but also reap the benefit of systemic well-being. Thus, while this formula certainly does not presume to offer the prospect of eternal youth, it does offer some interesting possibilities in prolonging the characteristics of youth far beyond the "normal" period.

The dosages of vitamins recommended here have been tested and found to be nontoxic. (Allergies to vitamins, or intolerance, are possible. If you have allergies or food sensitivitism, always check with your physician before you try something new.) It is offered in two parts: dietary, first; supplementing, second. The diet should particularly emphasize the following foods:

| | | |
|---|---|---|
| Milk | Liver | Wheat germ |
| Oysters | Sweetbreads | Brewer's yeast |
| Shrimps | Whole Wheat | |
| Clams | Whole Rye | |

I personally use paba in a special form—the potassium salt, which is available only on prescription. It is more efficient than ordinary paba because it's more soluble. (It's interesting that this preparation is advertised in the medical journals for the treatment of bursitis and certain arthritis conditions, when one remembers that the public has been told that vitamins have no effect on arthritis. Apparently, the medical men who read these journals don't remember that paba is a vitamin.) But ordinary paba can be used, too, though its relative insolubility requires a higher dose; 200 to 300 mgs. of paba daily will be an adequate trial. This should be accompanied by 100 mgs. of calcium pantothenate, and by a concentrate of all the B Complex vitamins in a natural base, such as liver, yeast, or rice polishings.

Percentages of failures in recoloring gray hair are high; successes in retarding graying are more frequent. If you fail, you may still earn a dividend, for nutrients which support activity of the glands must help in slowing down the aging process. And paba is, after all, the prime active ingredient in the so-called "rejuvenation treatment" pioneered by Dr. Anna Aslan, Rumanian specialist in reversing the tolls of senility.

## ACNE

Many years ago, a well-known medical nutritionist, Dr. Norman Jolliffe, published a recommendation that Vitamin A, in large doses, be used in the treatment of acne. That recommendation today collides head-on with the illusion, created by medical societies and government agencies, that Vitamin A is toxic. This statement is meaningless, since *anything* is toxic—even water, if you swallow enough, even blondes, as some men have discovered. (I've been trying to desensitize myself with frequent, small and increasing doses—of Vitamin A, that is.)

The cases which "prove" Vitamin A to be toxic are based on the experiences of children, primarily, and moreover, very young children who were vastly overdosed with the vitamin. One four-month-old was given 240,000 units daily; a three-year-old was plied with even more. But these doses were one hundred times the recommended allowance of the vitamin. And if you multiplied your daily intake of coffee by one hundred, *it* would be toxic, and your intake of salt, multiplied by one hundred, would *kill* you. Yet no one is screaming about the toxicity of caffeine and salt, and no one has urged that prescriptions be required for their purchase. The limitation of Vitamin A potency to 10,000 units per capsule is simply an aspect of the propaganda drive against vitamins, which will become clear when I remind you that our fathers and mothers took cod-liver oil, in childhood, with 33,000 units of Vitamin A per spoonful. They showed no toxicity, and lived to sire us.

Nonetheless, when I followed Jolliffe's recommendation, which was based on actual clinical experiments with high Vitamin A doses in the treatment of acne, I was promptly accused of inflicting neurological toxicity on my readers. The charge was made by a superannuated physician, whose services were engaged by a group of manufacturers of overprocessed foods whose products are forbidden to sufferers with acne. The doctor, apparently teetering on the edge of senility, was astute enough not to tell the public that my recommendation was based on a paper by one of his medical colleagues, and that I suggested that *high vitamin doses should always be used under medical direction.* So goes the cause of propaganda, masquerading as science—but Vitamin A, in water-soluble form (or water-dispersible), which are forms making for better utilization, still remains a helpful treatment in some cases of persistent acne. So does the application of Vitamin-A-acid, which is used locally. It is available on prescription only, and like the high Vitamin A doses, *should be employed under your doctor's direction.* Not at all incidentally, Vitamin A's toxic threshold rises when Vitamin B Complex is taken with it.

In any case, the average teenager has sometimes seen improvement in his acne when his physician has prescribed supplements of Vitamin A, in the aqueous form mentioned, in potencies up to 100,000 units daily, accompanied by the Vitamin B Complex and lecithin, the latter a factor helping the utilization of fatty substances, such as Vitamin A.

Though dermatologists differ about the contribution of sugar to the troubles of acne sufferers, removal of as much sugar as possible from their diet does help some acne patients—and less sugar intake is desirable for us all, anyway. Iodine may trouble the skin, and the physician may want the patient to forego iodized salt, use of kelp and other iodine supplements, and limit the use of fish and whole fish-liver oils. When sugar intake is to be reduced, honey and molasses are forbidden, too, and high-sugar fruit intake must be curtailed. (Orange juice, for instance, is about 10 percent sugar.)

A daily supplement of Vitamin B6, from fifty to one hundred mgs. daily, has been reported to help reduce the oiliness of the skin in acne. This should be accompanied by a source of the whole Vitamin B Complex, from dried liver, wheat germ, brewer's yeast, or a commercial concentrate of the vitamins, accompanied by a concentrate of the natural B Complex source. It is possible to purchase such a supplement as an all-in-one formula, from numerous companies.

Proper use of a sun lamp is often helpful. Your physician will tell you that it should be used only to the point where the skin turns a little pink—never to the point of blistering and burning. If you reflect on the improvement in acne, which often occurs in the summer months, you'll realize the basis for this recommendation.

Don't squeeze pimples and abscesses. Do keep your face scrupulously clean. Do maintain adequate calcium intake—a gram daily, yielded by a quart of milk, or four ounces of cheese, or the equivalent amount of calcium from bone meal or calcium orotate.

There is considerable help to be had from intelligent use of a low-sugar diet, free of chocolate and cocoa, with moderate amounts of starch, generous protein value—from meat, fish, fowl, eggs, cheese, and milk—with about five teaspoonfuls of polyunsaturated fat daily, in the form of salad oils (free of BHA and BHT), or wheat germ oil taken as a supplement. Some cases require that the physician, in addition to controlling the diet and the supplements, administer endocrine (glandular) therapy, and, in very aggravated acne, antibiotics. No case is hopeless.

## TROUBLE WITH TEETH: THE FIRST WARNING

In repeated endorsements of fluoridation, the heavily subsidized Harvard nutrition department remarked: "In the fluoridated cities, the children need not give up their sticky sweets." Behind this complacent licensing of an excessive intake of a bad food—sugar—is the bizarre belief that a diet which wrecks teeth has no adverse effect on other organs of the body. Substituting fluoridation for dietary education is a pathetic proposal, when you realize that the sugar which causes tooth decay also contributes to periodontal disease—pyorrhea and weakening of the structures supporting the teeth. This means that you harvest the dividends from fluoridation when the teeth which loosen and fall out don't have any cavities.

The experience of primitives who shift to our diet, high in sugar and other overprocessed carbohydrates, should warn anyone—with or without training in nutrition—that tooth decay is but the tip of an iceberg. When, for instance, the natives of Africa desert the diet dictated by the inherited wisdom of the centuries, dental caries are only the first price. They are followed by other problems, though the period over which they develop is much longer, and the association with the change in diet wasn't appreciated until extended medical observation was possible.

Among the prices for a diet high in sugar and overprocessed cereals, grains, and flour: constipation, hiatus hernia, diverticulosis, diverticulitis, appendicitis, varicose veins, hemorrhoids, and that dreadful killer—second among the causes of death from cancer in the U.S.—bowel cancer. Accordingly, the Harvard nutritionist was not being good to little children when he promoted fluoridation with the promise that it would take the curse off candy.

The African primitives with their experience with our diet

30

and the diseases which follow it, offer eloquent testimony to the fact that a diet which rots the teeth can't be good for the body. Those who have fallen prey to this kind of unthinking should reflect on the fact that the mouth shares circulation with the body—it doesn't have a separate circulation; it has the same nutritional needs; and it reacts very sensitively to the nutritional insults which damage other organs. So sensitively, that dentists are cautioned to remember that the mouth is a mirror of the body, placing the dental practitioner in a unique position to be the first to recognize nutritional deficiencies.

The evidence from the primitives is too formidable to be brushed aside by scientists intimately linked with the processed food industry—though they try. Coronary thrombosis is virtually unknown in native Africans who pursue the primitive diet. Obesity and heart disease are curiosities in the hospitals which service them. When an African appears as a victim of a heart attack, he is studied intensively, for he is the rarest of rarities. So is the native African who manages to develop one of our formidable diseases of the stomach, colon, and blood vessels. And these rarities inevitably turn out to be primitives who have fallen prey to the appeal of our "convenience," high-sugar, overprocessed carbohydrate foods.

When we export our diet, we export our sicknesses—and tooth decay is the first warning. Accordingly, if you or your family display many decayed teeth, you may regard the process as a warning red flag: All is not well with your diet. If you ignore the flag, many decades may pass before its meaning will become apparent to you—but it will. Based on insurance company statistics, your chance of developing a degenerative disease—cancer, high blood pressure, heart disease, arthritis, hardening of the arteries, or diabetes is about one in three. If you'd rather not play the game of Russian roulette, mend your dietary habits *now*.

The penalties for our high sugar intake, and large consumption of other processed carbohydrates, are ubiquitous—so common that we consider their sum total as "average" health. Reflect on the fact that the appearance of tooth decay in primitives is followed, in the next generation, by the initial appearance of interrupted heredity: The children have high, narrow, arched palates, which interfere with tooth-spacing. Now they have crowded mouths, with the teeth erupting in and out of the gum line, like a crooked picket fence—and they are ready to import the orthodontists whom we keep too busy for foreign travel. Not long after this, the primitive will begin to bring defective children into the world—with club feet, cleft palates, and spinal deformities. Do they recognize that these disasters, so new in their experience, are somehow linked to their new, palatable, and so convenient white man's foods? Why should they—do you?

Incidentally, none of the preceding statements is unsupported theory. If you'd like to learn more about the manner in which your diet twists primitive health into the pattern of ours, read Dr. Weston Price's *Nutrition and Physical Degeneration*, published by the Price-Pottenger Foundation, Los Angeles, California. If you want immediate and convincing evidence that our overprocessed sugars and starches begin the mischief, talk to the pediatricians who treat childhood diabetics. You will find that juvenile diabetics usually have less tooth decay than children on uncontrolled diets.

This chapter began with the supposition that pro-sugar nutritionists seduced you into the belief that fluoridation is a complete antidote for the harmfulness of sugar. For many mothers, this will raise the question of the toothpastes with fluoride. I know the principle is endorsed by an impressive scientific community, and the endorsement is probably not weakened critically by the fact that at least one scientist who helped to create the fluoride toothpaste is among the endorsers—*but* there has been a thorough study of the amount of fluoride *swallowed* by children using such pastes. You and I well know that the younger the user of the paste, the less likely he is to brush thoroughly, or to rinse thoroughly. A painstaking study of fluoride ingested through such habits revealed that the children from this one source—swallowed fluoride toothpaste—may have a considerable overdose of the chemical—and that is without consideration of the amount in water and, which is rarely considered, in food.

I used to endorse the local application of fluoride pastes to the teeth, performed by the dentist, until a practitioner sent me the statistics concerning the percentage of the children who, from this source, swallowed enough fluoride to cause vomiting. Which reminded me in turn of the fluoride tablets, often suggested as a means of voluntary self-fluoridation, to escape forced mass medication. But Dr. Reuben Feltman, a long-ago friend of mine and a fine dental researcher, elicited bloody vomiting in pregnant women, with fluoride tablets which supplied the same amount of the chemical supposed to be the daily dose in water.

So it is that I present the ANTI-TOOTH DECAY DIET:

Daily Intake: One pound of vegetables, mostly green.

One-half pound of fruit.

One quart of milk.

One to two eggs.

One-quarter to one-half head of lettuce—preferably, when available, an equivalent quantity of loose leaf lettuce, chicory or escarole.

Eight ounces of orange juice, unstrained, in addition to other fruits.

Meat once daily.

Whole wheat bread and whole grain cereals exclusively.

For dessert—puddings made with milk and eggs, fruit, gelatin, dates and figs.

Sweets never more than twice a week. This classification includes pie, cake, doughnuts, candy and drinks made with artificial flavoring.

The supplements to this diet contain Vitamins A, B1, B2, B Complex Factors, Niacinamide, C, D and E fortified with eight essential minerals—calcium, phosphorous, iron, copper, zinc, magnesium, manganese and iodine. The effect of the supplements is two-fold. It protects the children against variations in the natural vitamin-mineral content of the food and it simultaneously increases the efficiency of utilization while raising the vitamin-mineral intake to the optimal point without straining the capacity of the child for eating food in quantity.

This diet may be followed by both adults and children and, as the reader may surmise, will be conducive to general health as well as to dental health. (Still doubt it? Look up the papers by E. Cheraskin, M.D., of the University of Alabama Medical School, Department of Oral Medicine, who has demonstrated that a diet low in sugar and processed carbohydrate will in less than ten days demonstrably tighten loose teeth.)

# CHAPTER 4

## THE *PRE*-CONCEPTION DIET FOR *BOTH* SEXES

## SEX

THE NUTRITIONIST IS CONCERNED WITH REPRODUCTIVE efficiency, with the ability to conceive and to bring into the world, healthy, normal children. The average man, though, equates reproductive efficiency with a high level of sexual performance. And the public has problems in all three areas. Our men suffer not only with impotency, but a low sperm count. One young man in six is unable to father children, and nobody knows the percentage of men who are, whether fertile or not, impotent.

There is the corollary, in women: Frigidity is a common complaint, and inability to conceive is a problem in at least 10 percent of our marriages, with the responsibility for failure equally divided between the sexes. The woman usually accepts the total responsibility, and trudges from one gynecologist to another, from one fertility clinic to another, and is never asked the first question the veterinarian, faced with an infertile animal, will always raise: How was she fed? (Incidentally, if you think the population explosion means that I am exaggerating our reproductive inefficiency, ask yourself why there is a black market in babies for adoption.)

## POTENCY

In an effort to sustain or stimulate sexual potency, both sexes—with men predominating, since the burden of performance falls primarily upon them—have plied themselves with an unbelievable assortment of foods, drugs, vitamins, irritants, and even poisons. It is strange that they haven't given more attention to total diet, instead of stressing the imaginary aphrodisiac effects of Vitamin E or oysters. It is still stranger that we demand perfect sexual performance from bodies which are often less than healthy. The flame of love is fragile and easily extinguished. As the wrong circumstances, or a coupling of the wrong personalities or the wrong "electricity" can dampen ardor and ability, so can any systemic disturbance. Consider, for instance, hypoglycemia—low blood sugar. One of our common disorders, it causes frigidity in about 44 percent of the women patients, and impotence in about 29 percent of the men. Considering that a change in diet is often all that is needed to control hypoglycemia and its symptoms, it is astonishing that hypoglycemia is not more frequently investigated when loss of libido or potency is part of the patient's problems.

There is but a pair of nutrients for which aphrodisiac effects have been reported. *Paba*—the vitamin previously mentioned as sometimes helping to recolor gray hair—has been reported *occasionally* to stimulate male potency and female libido. If it does, there is a price: Paba also stimulates fertility, particularly in the female. One researcher gave it to twenty-two women with a history of infertility, as demonstrated by five years or more of unsuccessful efforts to conceive. They reaped a harvest of twelve babies, within two years. The other nutrient is *manganese*, known to affect the pituitary, too, because of its action in stimulating maternal behavior in animals. *Occasionally*, in the use of manganese in orthomolecular treatments for neurosis and psychosis, an aphrodisiac effect has been encountered.

It shouldn't need stressing, but most of the causes of impotency in the male are located above, rather than below, the collar line. This explains an occasional action from Vitamin E in impotency. The vitamin is *not* the middle letter in the word sex and has none of the reputed actions in frigidity or impotency. But it does exert a dampening effect on the transmission of anxiety from the emotional to the thinking brain, so much so, that its use has been proposed as a substitute for ECT (electric convulsive therapy) in the depressed and anxious. And relief of anxiety often makes a positive contribution to sexual performance, both in the male and the female. It would be a better choice than tranquilizers, for while these dampen anxiety more effectively, among their side reactions, paradoxically, may be lessening of the sexual drive, and loss of both potency and the ability to ejaculate.

The Vitamin B Complex, because of a general, rather than a specific effect, is sometimes helpful to the sex drive, merely because people who feel better, tend to perform better. Lethargy, anxiety, a feeling of something terrible about to happen (with no justification), irritability, difficulty in concentrating, and hair-trigger temper are some of the symptoms of mild deficiencies in thiamin and niacin. So is loss of a sense of humor. The symptom complex certainly must subtract from sexual performance, for it closely resembles that which used to be called neurasthenia, which is often accompanied by loss of interest in the opposite sex.

Applicable to the female is the interaction between certain nutrients and estrogenic (female) hormone. Both paba and folic acid (which contains paba) interact with this hormone. Raising estrogen levels—or increasing reactivity to estrogen—has demonstrably increased the libido in some women, as indicated by their reactions to birth control pills, containing estrogenic hormones.

None of these provides "instant sex." Unlike drugs, nutrients exert their actions gradually. And no supplement of any nutrient will yield full dividends, if it is used as a license to continue a bad diet.

## CONCEPTION AND PREGNANCY

I have pointed out that our record of reproductive inefficiency wouldn't be tolerated in any kennel breeding valuable dogs. I'm not going to recite the details of the dismal record. Just remember that five babies in every one hundred are premature, and may be handicapped by it, which is deplorable when you realize that mere changes in prenatal nutrition have lowered the incidence of prematurity by more than 80 percent.

There is one misconception I must mention: The belief that a defective baby is always the total responsibility of the mother—her genes, her pregnancy. This is simply not so. My good friend, Dr. Wilfred Shute, demonstrated this, many years ago, in treating with Vitamin E the *husbands*—not the wives—in families with a record of bringing defective babies into the world. In pregnancies subsequent to the treatment (remember that the women themselves remained untreated) the number of defective babies born was reduced to the vanishing point. Subsequently, some of these men discarded the use of the vitamin, after which, in those families, the percentage of defective babies born rose to its former level. Case closed: The father has pre-conception responsibilities rivaling those of the pregnant woman. There is a case for copying the primitives, who insist that for six months (or a year) prior to attempting conception, both marital partners eat a carefully selected, high-nutrition diet.

Despite such evidence, it is striking that my paper on nutrition in reproduction was the first of its kind in the twenty years of existence of my host—a society for the study of infertility and reproductive failures.

It is dismaying that a large percentage of nutritional failures to support good reproduction are iatrogenic: caused by the physician himself. I have reference to an obstetrical pregnancy diet which is prescribed by thousands of practitioners, which itself contributes to complications in pregnancy, such as toxemia, eclampsia, and other serious problems. The diet is significantly restricted in calories; it is likewise deliberately restricted in salt; and it is accompanied by the use of a diuretic, to promote excretion of fluid.

Dr. Tom Brewer, a dedicated medical man, has spent years in attempting to persuade his colleagues that this nutritional regime actually promotes, rather than prevents, pregnancy complications. He is vitally concerned with the fact that pregnant women need salt; that diuretics cause mineral deficiencies, and that attempts to restrict pregnancy weight-gain accomplish nothing helpful. The purported reason for such restriction of weight-gain, that of reducing the baby's dimensions to make birth easier, is a fallacy. What is more likely to be restricted is not the baby's width, but his length, which lends nothing to ease of delivery. But the diet does promote complications for both mother and child.

In my own pregnancy diets, women are restricted in weight-gain, but this is accomplished without depriving them of a rich supply of essential nutrients, including protein, the two types of fats, and all the essential vitamins and minerals. Thanks to the research of Dr. Brewer and the organization to which his philosophy gave impetus—the Society to Protect the Unborn Through Nutrition (SPUN)—I have lost my concern about excessive weight-gain during pregnancy, and accept with equanimity gains which in the past I would have feared made for prolonged labor. I have also lost my caution about salt intake, though I never restricted it excessively, since my diets encouraged consumption of milk and other animal proteins, which supply significant amounts of the nutrient.

In presenting the diet which follows, let me explain again that this is a diet for two, to be used before conception and during pregnancy, by both partners. The husband's pregnancy diet may seem a capricious thought, but I want him well-fed, even after he has delivered well-nourished germ plasm to his bride, for pregnancy is, to me—as the father of five—harder on the man than the woman. (*He* doesn't send *her* out at three in the morning of a midwinter gale, at below-zero temperatures, in search of raspberry sherbert, without which, she promises, the child will be born with raspberry birthmarks.)

Another area of concern, though little attention is paid to it in most diets for pregnancy, is the period of early-pregnancy morning sickness, which, in some women, may last four months or even longer. There is a tendency on the part of the prospective parents and, unfortunately, the obstetrician, to consider the nutritional requirements as minimal for the first 120 days, because, runs the conventional explanation, the fetus is so small that his needs must, perforce, be satisfied—even if the expectant mother is living largely on olives, popcorn, and ginger ale.

Actually, during the first few months of conception, the matrices (the framework, the blueprint) for all the baby's organs are being created, and nutritional factors must be present in adequate amounts, at the right place and at the right time. (Remember that as TAP—time, amount, place.) Time becomes important because a nutrient supplied on the fifteenth day, when needed on the thirteenth will not be present when it is needed in the formation of cells, tissues, and organs, and the moment of need having passed, it cannot be recalled. (You might remember that thalidomide harmed babies when the drug was taken in the first few months. Doses later in pregnancy had no such effect.)

This doesn't mean that a day without food will prejudice the baby's normalcy. It does mean two important things: The diet for pregnancy should begin before conception, to build up reserves as much as possible. The body's capacity for storing certain nutrients is quite limited, particularly when they are water-soluble, such as Vitamin C and the B vitamins. Second: It means that every effort should be made to help the nauseated pregnant woman to eat and retain what food she can, rather than to dismiss her plight as of no importance.

Useful hints: One type of morning sickness is caused by lack of Vitamin B6 (pyridoxin), utilization of which seems almost universally disturbed during the first trimester in most pregnancies. In such a morning sickness, as little as ten or twenty milligrams of the vitamin, by mouth or given by injection, can be prescribed by the physician. If deficiency in it is in fact responsible for the nausea, it disappears with remarkable speed.

Another hint which helps the queasy mother-to-be is separation of beverages from solid foods—dry meals interspersed with interim liquids. And one final hint: Hopefully, your physician will agree that no drug of any nature should be used in pregnancy unless it is a matter of life or death. Thalidomide, if you didn't know it, was prescribed as a sedative. Enough said? Many drugs cross the placental barrier, and many of them are capable of causing harm. For example, we hear a great deal about the unfortunate girls who developed vaginal cancer because their pregnant mothers were dosed with synthetic female hormone. We don't hear about the boys emerging from such pregnancies, who are less masculine, less aggressive, less athletic, as their response to the potent medication. The pity of it all lies in the fact that the drug was given to avert threatened abortion, which has been accomplished, without risk to mother or child, with simple doses of harmless wheat germ oil. Considerations like this are behind the recommendation that the preconception and pregnancy diet which follows should be supplemented with vitamins and minerals, as described.

## THE DIET FOR EFFICIENT REPRODUCTION

*Daily Intake*

One eight-ounce glass of unstrained fruit juice, preferably orange or grapefruit.

One serving of fresh fruit, unpeeled. (Wash thoroughly.)

Two cups of cooked vegetables—undercooked rather than overcooked.

One cup of salad made with dark green leafy vegetables, with a dressing of vegetable oil (without BHA or BHT) plus any other seasonings desired.

Three squares of butter.

One serving of oatmeal, whole wheat or other grain cereal, plus one teaspoon wheat germ, and one tablespoon fine bran.

Two eggs.

Six ounces of lean meat, fish, or fowl—emphasis on liver, kidneys, sweetbreads, and other organ meats.

Four slices of whole wheat, whole rye, or whole corn bread. This does not mean commercial rye bread or pumpernickel, which are overprocessed.

For dessert: whole gelatin desserts, junket, custard, stewed fruit, fruit whip, Betty's cookies or similar good foods. No conventional pastries; no commercial ice cream.

Conventional spaghetti, macaroni and noodles should not be used. Buy high-protein spaghetti, made with added gluten and wheat germ, which is high protein.

Brewer's yeast, wheat germ, dried skimmed milk, and soyflour can be added to appropriate recipes.

Newcomers to nutrition, unfamiliar with the techniques of converting everyday recipes into high-nutrition meals, while retaining palatability, should consult the *Carlton Fredericks Cookbook For Good Nutrition*, published by Grosset and Dunlap, or the paperback version, published by Bantam. There are also excellent good-nutrition cookbooks by Beatrice Trum Hunter, and by Adelle Davis.

*Supplements*

Wheat germ oil, which can be added to salad oil or taken as is—in liquid form or in capsules.

A Vitamin B Complex supplement, preferably in liquid form; this allows the manufacturer to supply significant quantities of the natural B Complex sources, which a capsule can't contain.

Multiple vitamins and minerals, in low potencies. Extra calcium may be prescribed, too, in supplements providing an added intake of a gram of the mineral.

Vitamin E, in the form of mixed tocopherols with the potency measured in terms of the alpha tocopherol content. Do not accept any form of alpha tocopherol alone. Low potency should be used.

If in the absence of disease to explain the process, swelling of the ankles or face should develop, consult the physician for recommended supplements of Vitamin C and the bioflavonoids, which by reducing capillary permeability, may reduce the tendency for fluid to accumulate in the tissues. Do not do this unless medically cleared to be sure a pregnancy complication or a disorder is not responsible.

Three teaspoonfuls of bran daily, added to recipes or taken in 500 mg. tablets (six daily, in divided doses, with meals, will help minimize the constipation many pregnant women experience when the pressure of the baby interferes with elimination).

## LACTATION

The preceding diet is adequate to support lactation. If extra help is needed, consult your physician for added supplements of paba, for the pituitary-stimulating effect of this nutrient has been reported to stimulate the production of milk. Don't be talked out of nursing your baby. Try to avoid the supplemental bottles of formula, so urgently suggested during temporary periods of lessened milk production, for this becomes a vicious circle: Loss of the stimulation of lactation by the baby's nursing still further reduces milk production. Of course, many mothers must surrender when their children are not thriving, for lack of enough milk, but some of the surrenders are obviously premature. The important point: No formula ever devised is as good for a baby as the nourishing milk you, a well-fed, healthy mother, produce.

## BABY'S DIET

There is really no way in which to generalize about babies'

diets, for the dietary needs and tolerances of the little ones differ as much as those of the adults. Your pediatrician can tell you that the calorie needs of two infants of the same body weight may be quite different—if one is a long, thin baby, and the other a shorter, fatter one. Requirements for other nutrients vary similarly. Within those limitations, a few generalizations are permissible.

You've already been urged to raise your baby on the breast. Let no one even try to persuade you that boiled cow's milk, modified with a processed carbohydrate, and fed through a nipple supposed to simulate the mother's equipment, is any kind of a facsimile of the natural way of nourishing babies. Breast milk isn't overheated, unless mother takes awfully hot baths, and there is evidence that heated (and sometimes, twice or three-times heated) protein does not support optimal health, as raw protein does. And don't underestimate the dividends a baby receives from intimate, close contact with his nursing mother. No bottle, propped up on a folded diaper, is remotely a substitute for that procedure, which has far-reaching bonuses for the baby, in maturing as a healthy, properly developed infant. Even the shape of the mouth and palate may be unfavorably affected by the bottle, with its rubber imitation of the breast. If for any reason you can't nurse, a formula modified with lactose (milk sugar) probably will make more physiological sense and be less costly than the proprietary modifiers.

It's not my field of interest, but let me divert here to urge that you lose—if you have any—fear of treating the baby for anything but what he is: a small human being. I read much twaddle about correct methods of exercising baby's legs and arms, and remember the American Indians whose infants are tightly bound, up to their chests, for the first year or two of life—and are riding horses expertly, a year or two later. I know that in bygone centuries, when a mother was without milk, and wet nurses were not available, the baby was fed on balls of baked dough, soaked in beer. I'm not recommending the diet—just reminding you that babies are surprisingly adaptable. This doesn't argue for abusing their resilience. It is just to underscore the fact that a baby who thrives on the bottle, sweet desserts, and other undesirable foods is not an endorsement of the diet but a testimonial to the adaptability of the human organism. And that leads to the important point, with regard to vitamin supplements and mineral supplements for babies.

Professionally and as a parent, I have long taken a dim view of the fish-liver oils (or concentrates of them) which your pediatricians have been persuaded constitute the only necessary supplements for babies. Yes, babies may thrive with such supplements, but that doesn't mean that they're optimal, any more than was the emergency diet of charred dough and beer.

I recall years ago, a paper by Hoobler, a pediatrician who traveled widely in South America, where he saw many malnourished infants. When he returned to this country, he was suddenly stricken to realize that in "well babies" he could pick up symptoms, in a mild degree, of the deficiency disorders he had observed abroad. Accordingly, he began to feed brewer's yeast to babies, which in the 1940s represented a kind of medical nihilism. Here is one of his comments on the responses of the infants: "Thin, weak, crying, cranky babies changed into happy, rosy-cheeked, smiling infants, whose appetites were never satisfied." Yet the medical establishment of that day assured pediatricians then, as they do now, that supplements of Vitamins A and D, nothing more, are needed by babies.

Finding nothing satisfactory in more complete vitamin-mineral supplements for infants, I created my own for the remarkable, if impossible, Fredericks children. They all matured on a multiple vitamin syrup and a multiple mineral syrup, which we gave in water, juice, or from the spoon, beginning with very small amounts, and gradually increasing the dose until the correct intake—a teaspoonful of each syrup—was fed. To this day, though the product (which was then commercialized by a vitamin laboratory) is probably no longer available, I still meet adults who tell me they were fed "April's syrups" when they were children. Equivalent products are available under many labels. It is my hope that your pediatrician will permit you to use such formulas, rather than the two-vitamin supplement stipulated by the orthodoxy—who probably never read Hoobler.

And while we're on the subject, let me add that brewer's yeast and wheat germ still benefit baby, and can be added to solid foods, early in the institution of such feeding. Which brings up another point: Don't engage in a horse-power race, so that you can boast of how early your baby was placed on solid foods. The time for that varies from one infant to another. I recall one Fredericks baby who was on strained meat—mixed with juice or certified raw milk—before he was six weeks old. Without it, he howled with constant hunger, despite a generous supply of breast milk. Which is a good point at which to remind you that breast milk, while the best possible food for infants—the only substance on the face of the earth which we can say dogmatically was intended as a food for man—was *not* intended by Nature to be a child's sole nourishment for an indefinite period. Even breast milk has its deficits. That is why some pediatricians have added strained meat to the formulas for some infants, in the sixth week of life, thereby avoiding some of the anemias common in the newborn.

I used to recommend the commercial baby foods, and I've stopped. To make them safe, the processors give them very intensive treatment. To make them palatable—to you, not the baby, because he couldn't care less—the processors use too much salt and too much sugar. Here is created the basis for possible hypertension, later in life, and for the sweet tooth which characterizes (and harms) so many American children. But the processors know that *you* taste baby's food, and aim at pleasing the adult palate.

I also don't like the manner in which starch is modified in baby foods. This term, "modified starch," translates as: We have deliberately lowered the digestibility of this ingredient. The purpose: to keep the baby's saliva from "digesting," and rendering inedible, what is left after a feeding. Buy a food mill, and make your own good strained vegetables and strained meats. Your baby will gratefully respond. If you have a reliable source of unsprayed (organic) foods upon which to draw, spend the premium dollar for it. No baby ever profited by a food additive or a pesticide residue. And you'll save money.

Having stressed the individuality of the baby's nutritional needs and tolerances, it is obviously with reluctance that I give you a sequence in which the infant's diet is gradually expanded. Just keep in mind that the baby will tell you what he is ready for, and when. The Fredericks baby previously mentioned—who is now over six feet tall—who *had* to have strained meat in the sixth week, was also fed mashed banana in the second week. Others of our children didn't raucously demand such early feeding of solid food. Baby does know more about his needs than you suppose. Just try strengthening a formula by, let us say, 10 percent before the child is ready for it, and he will take 10 percent less, in his subsequent feedings. So you judge your time table by the baby's responses. If he's not satisfied, he'll let you know. If what he's being fed stirs intolerance or allergy, he'll tell you plainly.

The supplements can be started by the third or fourth week, for many babies. So can fruit juices, half and half with boiled water. You begin with one teaspoonful, and increase to two tablespoonfuls or more by the third month. By that time, some infants will want as much as three ounces of fruit juice daily, which is subtracted from the day's water allowance. If there is a history of allergy in the family, orange juice, which is highly allergenic, should be on the deferred list. In that case, you begin with grapefruit or apple juice, the latter enriched with Vitamin C.

Eggs may be added to the diet in the second month. New foods are introduced in the company of other, familiar (and liked) foods. (This works for husbands, too.) Mix coddled egg yolk with fruit juice or milk, using only a drop of yolk the first day; two drops, the second; three, the third; and so on until the eleventh day, when a half of a yolk may be fed. This gradual method avoids foreign protein reactions, or minimizes them. If babies are allergic to eggs, and the pediatrician, aware of the added resistance they create to rheumatic disease, still wants to feed them, he may order you to hardboil the eggs. (Here is a token recognition of the changes in protein when it's heated.)    Cereals may enter at four months, or earlier for some babies. For constipated babies, whole wheat or oatmeal; diarrhea calls for whole barley or brown rice. Cereals should be prepared in a double boiler, sieved, and thin enough to run off the end of a spoon. Bran may be introduced for normal and for constipated babies, but not, of course, for those with diarrhea. The tip of a teaspoonful, gradually increasing to a half teaspoonful daily, may be added to cereal. The objective is not laxative action, but promoting normal stool transit time—essential to avoiding bowel cancer, appendicitis, and numerous other digestive disorders common in America and missing among primitives who consume a high-fiber diet. (Those interested in more details concerning the benefits of bran and other dietary fiber should read *The Carlton Fredericks High-Fiber Diet,* published by Pocket Books.) The primitives also escape constipation, hemorhoids, varicose veins, polyps, diverticular disease, and hiatus hernia, indicating that starting the bran habit in infancy is good use of the prophylactic values of fine nutrition.

Green leafy vegetables and legumes are frequently introduced by the fifth month—again, earlier for some babies. Start new foods in small amounts, and remember that a baby judges his meals by texture, perhaps more than taste. Be guided by your physician as to the timing of the introduction of vegetables and meats and other animal proteins—fish, and fowl, for instance. If no doctor is available, remember that most babies are ready for meat at ten months, though some, as I've indicated, profit by it earlier. Offer raw greens, such as succulent romaine lettuce, at eight or nine months, so that your baby grows up accustomed to a healthful habit of salad greens. If you accustom your baby to whole grains, and don't offer white flour or sweet baked products, he'll never miss these foods. Our Fredericks children never saw white bread until they were about four, and thought, at the time, it was cake.

Be adamant about friends and doting grandparents who come bearing gifts of candies, commercial ice cream (make your own, and avoid the additives and excessive sugar) and other "goodies" which start the bad nutrition habits. After his first birthday, the baby should be able to participate in the kind of nutrition and menus with which this book is identified. This is to say, he should be able to eat at the adult dining table. If he can't, *you* are eating improperly.

# CHAPTER 5

## IT ISN'T ALL "PURELY MENTAL"

*Psychosomatic Disorder—Depression, Anxiety, Insomnia—Hypoglycemia—Alcoholism and Drug Addiction*

IN BYGONE YEARS, PEOPLE HAD NERVOUS BREAKDOWNS, or suffered from "neurasthenia," which translates as "weak nerves." If their families could afford it, such patients went to a sanitarium, were bedded in a peaceful atmosphere, and catered to by an attentive professional staff, and came home minus their weakness, timidity, nervousness, irritability, difficulty in concentrating, and shortness of memory span. Their recovery was attributed to rest, peace, and quiet, and no one noticed another possible and potent factor: They were fed carefully prepared, nourishing meals. So, as one medical nutritionist put it, it wasn't only devoted nursing, peace, and quiet which brought them back to mental and emotional normalcy. It was also good nutrition.

That lesson has been forgotten. Patients are now no longer called neurasthenic, and nervous breakdowns are described in other terms. The sanitariums are used largely for other purposes, and the patients who, in bygone years would have gone to them, now visit psychiatrists who are not interested in their eating habits.

Yet what we now term neurosis can be caused by faulty nutrition alone, in some cases. Full-blown symptoms of psychosis, we now know, can be produced by a diet too high in sugar and caffeine, coupled with a life situation involving too much stress. And mental diseases presently palliated with tranquilizers and antidepressant drugs are being treated successfully with goodly doses of vitamins, minerals, and other nutrients, which are *not* given because of deficiencies in the patient's diet.

Let's begin our journey through mental and emotional disturbances, which are "not all in the mind," by considering what happens to the nervous system and the brain when the vitamins and minerals needed to burn sugar—the only fuel acceptable to the brain—are not adequately provided. Here is the language used by a researcher who found that deficiencies in a few vitamins can cause severe personality disturbances—with *no* visible physical symptoms at all:

"The functional activity of the central nervous system is dependent upon its respiratory metabolism. Its respiratory metabolism is limited almost exclusively to the oxidation of carbohydrates. This oxidation of carbohydrates requires a number of specific entities which act as intermediaries or catalysts, and without which oxidation cannot take place. Some of these specific chemical substances cannot be formed within the human body as they can be in some lower organisms, but must be supplied pre-formed."

Translated into nontechnical language, this means that the central nervous system must "breathe" to carry on. In its breathing processes, starches and sugars are burned up (oxidized). To burn these starches and sugars, certain chemicals are needed by the body. Among these necessary chemicals are several which the body cannot make for itself. These are vitamins, which should be provided by the diet. If they are not present in the diet, the burning of the starches and sugars will be interrupted, and the central nervous system will call its activities to a standstill.

Here is an actual case history of how this breakdown occurs in the human body, and how it is repaired: A forty-nine-year-old woman comes to a hospital in a state of mental confusion. She does not know where she is, or what day of the year it is. She is restless and frightened. She thinks people are trying to poison her; she sees imaginary insects and snakes. Her history is one of gradually developing and progressively increasing nervousness, marked by insomnia and personality changes. She has been experiencing difficulties in elimination. For about a year, she had subsisted largely on sweet and fatty foods, with only occasional green vegetables, very few eggs, practically no milk, no meat. For three months there had been a sharp loss of appetite, and for two weeks she had refused all food.

In the hospital, this woman's treatment included five daily administrations of the vitamin niacin. On the third day, she was mentally clear, entirely rational. She became oriented, no longer had delusions or hallucinations, was cheerful.

"Oh, well," the average reader will probably say in reaction to the foregoing account, "I don't eat a diet like that. That woman was very deficient. She must have had pellagra."

True enough. Here, however, is the report of the physician who cured her: "It has long been recognized by most physicians who studied pellagra that many patients had minor, vague and indefinite complaints that usually existed for years before the classical symptoms of pellagra appeared. Mild mental disturbances are almost always the first evidence of chronic partial deficiency of nicotinic acid—or niacin."

Our patient had a complete deficiency—and a complete collapse. If you make one side of the equation a partial deficiency, the other side is partial collapse. The careless observer would call such a partial collapse "being nervous." An overworked, all-encompassing and dangerous word!

Of what do people with early or mild deficiencies complain?

50

How does the central nervous system voice its grievance, make known its need of vitamins? The commonest symptom is "nervousness." This is not a definite status; it is a vague, blanketing term. The mildly deficient and nervous patients are easily upset or disturbed by trivial things. They are easily startled, excited or irritated. They are likely to be sensitive to noise, and they are disturbed by children and the radio. They are sensitive in the sense of being easily offended or hurt, and they grow angry or cry with very little provocation. They are easily frightened, and they worry a great deal.

These are the protests of the central nervous system, complaining because the diet does not provide enough of some of the B vitamins. Anxiety is a striking symptom of this deficiency. It ranges from feelings of uneasiness and apprehension to severe and clear-cut attacks of anxiety, with marked heart and breathing symptoms and fear of impending death. Such anxiety-beset persons have heart disturbances severe enough to cause concern. They frequently wake from sleep with fear, a sensation of smothering, choking palpitation. They may imagine things—someone coming up the walk, someone calling them, someone in the room. They are often melancholy without knowing why, and cry without cause. They prefer to avoid crowds, noise and company. Similar symptoms can be caused by low blood sugar—made *worse*—like Vitamin B deficiency—by eating sugar.

Insomnia is one result of the central nervous system's deprivation of vitamins. In the lonely hours of the sleepless night, the sufferer worries about his health, his heart, his sanity. Memory is impaired, and attentiveness or concentration becomes difficult. Thinking goes into slow motion, decisions become fraught with conflict. The patient feels sluggish and complains of lack of alertness. His common phrase is—"I don't feel like myself." Dizziness, headache and restlessness appear. It is interesting that in these chronic, mild, pre-pellagrous deficiencies, the restlessness is present concomitantly with marked fatigue. Fatigue is the great and ever-present accompaniment, and the degree of fatigue is likely to be the degree of the other symptoms.

Let us follow another actual case history, this time of a thirty-four-year-old housewife. She comes to the nutrition clinic of a hospital, complaining of nervousness. Please note that this patient has come of her own volition, and is not being treated for disease. She says that she is very tense and restless, wants to be up and going all the time but cannot stand any excitement. She states: "I get scared to death over nothing, and stay scared all the time." She worries about riding in a car, for fear that it might turn over. She worries about her family, fearful that something may happen to her children. She worries about losing her mind. "I feel swimmy-headed," she says.

The rest of the clinical report of this woman's history is almost a routine recital of symptoms kicked up by an outraged central nervous system badgering the management— in this case, our patient—for more vitamins. Her memory was poor. She could not make up her mind. She had headaches most of the time and felt drowsy and tired all of the time. Noise bothered her. Her eyes ached.

The patient traced the onset of her symptoms back to a bout with influenza, after which she lost her appetite. Perhaps it was the reduced food intake. Perhaps the flu left her with bacteria in her intestinal tract which raided the vitamins in her food. This would deprive her of the benefit of those vitamins, and, by removing her appetite, remove also the opportunity of replenishing her vitamin reserves. A physical examination showed little. She was underweight— as thousands of normal though nervous women are who do not regard themselves as being vitamin deficient. She was undernourished—as thousands of men and women are who are aware of their own apprehensiveness but not of their imbalanced diets. She had a slight tenderness of the calf muscles.

The patient was given a large dose of multiple vitamins and thiamin chloride (B1). That night, the doctor's report states, she slept well. When she awakened she did not feel scared, tense or jittery. Her dizziness and headache had disappeared. The second dose brought further improvement.

Two days later the vitamin dosage was stopped, and the patient experienced a return of her symptoms. She once again felt tense, restless and nervous. After a few days, the patient was given a dose of distilled water by injection. No improvement showed. On the following day the vitamin injections were resumed, and the improvement was prompt and marked.

Does it seem amazing to you that such a simple-seeming step as the injection of vitamins could banish so many symptoms of distress? It is no more amazing than the recovery of a diabetic from coma when a dose of insulin is given. Function returns when the body has all the factors it needs to carry on.

As these lines are written, the author has before him the detailed record of a group of female patients who volunteered to eat a diet low in Vitamin B1 in order to allow physicians to investigate the nervous and mental disturbances which originate with such deficiencies. The diet used in the experiment is as deceptive as that eaten as a matter of course by millions of Americans (who consider themselves well fed, thank you).

Severe Vitamin B1 deficiency was produced in this group of women on a diet plan which allowed plenty of lean meat, cheese, skimmed milk, fruits and vegetables. The diet was supplemented with brewer's yeast *from which the Vitamin B1 had been removed,* plus Vitamin C, plus fish-liver oil to provide Vitamins A and D. It is a deceptive food plan; it looks adequate, but it is deficient in Vitamin B1. Here is a condensation of the doctor's diary, which detailed the record of a typical patient:

Prior to the experiment, this patient had no symptoms. She was well adjusted, congenial, industrious, efficient and vigorous. She was not anemic, and her basal metabolism was normal. After two months on the deficient diet, the doctor notes that she worked slowly and negligently; she followed instructions inaccurately and became forgetful, irritable and quarrelsome. Her appetite flickered, and her basal metabolism dropped to minus 23. Ordinarily, these symptoms would be labeled "under-active thyroid." They were induced by a deficiency of Vitamin B1.

The doctor's diary records that at the end of five months, "this woman wept and laughed alternately. She was critical of herself, displayed apathy, confusion and fatigue. She complained of indigestion and numbness of hands and feet."

By the seventh month of Vitamin B1 deficiency, this patient was unable to work because of dizziness and weakness. She described herself as "feeling helpless." She was confused and bewildered and found it difficult to make decisions. Her complexion paled and her blood pressure dropped. The basal metabolism was still low. There was no weight loss recorded. The diet supplied sufficient *calories*.

At this point, the researchers began to administer Vitamin B1 in small doses. At the end of two months, the doses were increased. The doctor's diary notes: "The improvement was gradual. Patient still tired easily, and was alternately cheerful and apathetic. She slept badly, but her appetite was good. At the end of four months of correct diet, during two of which the intake of Vitamin B1 had been appreciably increased, the patient became congenial, cooperative and industrious. She no longer complained, and showed no physical defects."

After the subject had eaten a correct diet for six months, the doctor closed his diary with this note: "Patient free of symptoms. She is agreeable, efficient and vigorous, but still anemic; her basal metabolism still abnormal."

The reader may draw his own conclusions from this factual narrative. Medical science does. It is now known that a deficiency in Vitamin B1 or niacin can make you a mental, emotional and nervous wreck. This is not surprising, for the functioning of the brain and the nervous system leans heavily on the vitamins. What is surprising, however, is the number of people who allow themselves to be driven into fatigue, nervousness, indecision, mental and emotional uproar because of a rigid rejection of vitamin therapy. They belong to the "what-was-good-enough-for-Grandpa" school.

If you re-read the preceding discussion, you arrive at

several conclusions which collide head-on with popular (and professional) concepts of nutritional deficiency. When one writes about inadequate diets, the medical men tend to think in terms of outright deficiency, and the full-blown, classical deficiency diseases they studied: xerophthalmia, beriberi, scurvy, rickets, sprue, and pellagra. This is the all-or-nothing principle: Either a diet is good enough to support good health, or it is bad enough to cause clear, easily recognizable symptoms of deficiency disease. But in between those extremes, there is a middle ground: The diet good enough to prevent pellagra may still not supply enough niacin to support proper function of the brain and nervous system. The diet adequate to prevent beriberi may not supply enough Vitamin B1 (thiamin) to protect the patient against inexplicable feelings of anxiety, stemming from a brain chemistry deranged for lack of a requisite supply of thiamin. The diet which is protective against scurvy may still not supply enough Vitamin C to protect against bleeding gums or other signs of capillary fragility.

In re-reading the patient histories in this chapter, you should also notice that the mental and emotional symptoms of partial lack of the B vitamins tend very much to overlap. This is perfectly understandable, if you realize that *anything* which interferes with the "burning" of carbohydrates by the brain will ultimately cause nervousness, irritability, maniacal outbursts of rage, and other symtoms referable to the disturbed functioning of starved brain cells. So it is that low blood sugar produces symptoms indistinguishable from those caused by partial lack of Vitamin B1 or niacin. What difference does it make whether the brain is short of fuel, or is adequately supplied, but can't burn it?

Some of the symptoms of specific deficiencies do not, of course, overlap. Thus we can distinguish between beriberi and pellagra, in a patient displaying symptoms which might be attributable to either deficiency disease, by telling him a funny story. If he laughs, the dominant deficiency is in thiamin—leaning toward beriberi, for lack of niacin causes, as its first effect on brain metabolism, loss of a sense of humor. (Have you been amused by any of the small jokes in this book?)

This specificity of deficiency symptoms of various nutrients has led to some fascinating discoveries. Take, for instance, the case of an amino acid (one of the building blocks of protein foods) called tryptophane. This is an essential amino acid, meaning that the body can't manufacture it, as it does some others, and the factor must be supplied, preformed, in the diet. The government and medical agencies which deal with the "standard reference American," and who have presumed on that basis to set up nutritional requirements which are absolutely uniform for 220 million Americans whose biochemistry *isn't*, assure us that 500 mgs. of tryptophane daily is an adequate allowance for all mankind. But there are insomniacs who sleep much better if we raise their intake of the amino acid to 1,000 mgs. daily, and a percentage of them who profit even more by 1,500 mgs. Not only that, but since insomnia is often a symptom coexistent with depression, it is striking that the higher intake of tryptophane relieves the depression in some of these people who can't sleep properly.

Another example is Vitamin B15—pangamic acid, which, though discovered by an American chemist, is in wide use abroad, but unrecognized by the FDA in this country. In Russia, the vitamin is used in the treatment of cardiovascular diseases, in which it is found helpful. Yet psychiatrists who have experimented with the factor in the treatment of children who do not communicate vocally have reported an occasional improvement—sometimes, a striking one—in the speech of children treated with Vitamin B15.

Still another example is found in Vitamin E. A deficiency disease attributable to lack of this vitamin has not been recognized, save for a tendency for red blood cells to die prematurely. But the vitamin has been used successfully in the treatment of depression in menopausal women, and it has been found that their vasomotor disturbances—"sweats and flushes" often improve. It has also been used successfully in the treatment of types of heart disease, and in intermittent

56

claudication, a painful condition of the limbs, which interferes with walking.

A number of such specific actions of specific nutrients have been identified. As a result, depression is treated with large doses of Vitamin B1, and, sometimes, with large doses of Vitamin B2 (riboflavin). Confused thinking is treated with goodly amounts of niacin or niacinamide. And that lets us arrive at three important conclusions:

First, a deficiency of an essential nutrient need not cause *all* the textbook symptoms of the classical deficiency disease. Pellagra, stemming from lack of niacin and protein, is a disorder in which, classically, there are three symptoms: diarrhea, delirium, and dermatitis (skin rash). But *your* niacin deficiency, particularly if mild and chronic, may skip the skin, leave the digestive tract unscathed, and zero in on brain function alone. Now you are a neurotic.

Second, deficiency for you may be adequacy for me. A "normal blood level" of a nutrient is a meaningless statement. *Normal for whom?* is the question which must be answered.

Third, a nutrient may be used to treat a disorder not caused by deficiency in that dietary factor. You don't take aspirin or tranquilizers for aspirin or tranquilizer deficiency. You may take large doses of Vitamin C because you're allergic, and high levels of Vitamin C have an antihistamine (anti-allergy) action.

There is still another question which must be considered, as we contemplate the role of nutrition in disorders which are considered "purely psychiatric" or "all in the mind." There is such an entity as "relative deficiency." This is a way of stating that your dietary intake may be adequate in terms of the requirements of that standard reference American, but your own requirement may be so high that there is no feasible way to satisfy it from food alone, however carefully selected. Such a contingency may be created by a quirk of your brain chemistry, which is the situation with some normal and some schizophrenic people, or it can be induced by something you are taking, a drug, for instance.

The woman who uses birth control pills is an example of the latter: The pill itself causes deficiency in a number of B vitamins. As for the rise in requirement arising from the peculiarity of your own chemistry, consider what is called in psychonutrition the "Sara syndrome." This is a type of schizophrenia which not only causes delusions of persecution and distortions of reality, but also induces stretch marks in the skin, white spots in the nails, disturbances of the menstrual, amnesia, convulsions, and maldevelopment of the knee joints. The patient is synthesizing a chemical alien to the body, which has the capacity to interfere with the availability to the body of a vitamin and two minerals—pyridoxin, which is Vitamin B6, and zinc and manganese. By raising the intake of these factors high enough, the interference is overcome, and the patient returns to sanity, the physical symptoms also disappearing or reducing in severity. Maintaining that sanity calls for continued ample dosage of the vitamin and the minerals. Reducing the intake to the "recommended dietary allowances" set by the government throws the patient back into the unreal world of insanity.

This, incidentally, is the field called "orthomolecular psychiatry," which means "the right molecule," and which is practiced with nutrition (as well as other modalities) rather than with psychotherapy, tranquilizers, and the psychoanalytic couch.

Drugs *are* used in orthomolecular psychiatry, but only as temporary crutches. Similarly, in other types of schizophrenia, doses are employed of niacin, niacinamide, Vitamin E, Vitamin C, Vitamin B6, lithium, and a hypoglycemia (low blood sugar) type of diet.

Lithium is also employed in manic-depressive conditions, where the patient's mood shifts from unwarranted elation to equally unjustified despair. This metal, unlike the antidepressive drugs, restrains the wide swings of the emotional pendulum without choking the creativity of the individual. It is, as you have gathered from the preceding discussion of the use of manganese and zinc in psychiatric conditions, one of a number of minerals employed in ortho-molecular psychiatry.

Calcium is frequently used, particularly for those who have anxiety caused by elevation of lactic acid in the blood. Magnesium is used, with Vitamin B6 and Vitamin E for children who are bed-wetters. Treatments of this kind are helping not only the sufferers with schizophrenia, but the retarded, the emotionally disturbed, the hyperactive, the autistic, and the withdrawn.

## HYPOGLYCEMIA (Low Blood Sugar)

Americans eat an unbelievable amount of sugar. We manufacture and import about a hundred pounds per person, per year, but averages being what they are, and babies, reducers, diabetics, and the sensible not eating their share, the average intake of sugar per year rises to about 120 pounds, or a teaspoonful and one-third, every thirty-five minutes, twenty-four hours per day. This inflicts on the body a burden of processed carbohydrates with which it is not well equipped to deal, for it is impossible to consume this much sugar in natural foods. (You wouldn't eat twenty apples at a sitting, but you will easily consume the equivalent in sugar by guzzling soda pop, eating apple pie, and chewing candy.)

The problem with sugar lies, then, not only in the fact that it is a very poor food, but that we are taking it in unphysiological amounts, placing an enormous strain on the sugar-regulating mechanism of the body. Three reactions to this stress are possible: We may ride with it, and escape consequences; we may exhaust the capacity of the body in managing so much sugar, and wind up with diabetes; or, which brings us to the topic of this discussion, we may become oversensitized to sugar, overreact to it, and burn it too fast.

This latter condition describes hypoglycemia, or low blood sugar. Paradoxically, it is not caused by a deficit of sugar in the diet, for we have an oversupply. It is a deficit of sugar in the blood, or the opposite of diabetes, caused by excessive production of insulin, the sugar-burning hormone, in response to sudden rises in blood sugar levels.

When airline pilots were examined for low blood sugar, 44 men out of 177 were found to have the condition. This is understandable, for the factors, other than high sugar intake, which make us susceptible to hypoglycemia include excessive use of caffeine—in coffee, tea, cola beverages, and chocolate, and stress; and the airplane cockpit certainly is a center for all these influences. Examination of five thousand young, healthy soldiers, newly inducted into the armed services, turned up more than seven hundred cases. Examination of many groups of schizophrenics revealed an average of 60 percent of them to be suffering from hypoglycemia. Tests of patients receiving orthodox psychiatric therapies invariably show more than half of them to be hypoglycemic. It is apparent that our life-style, our menus and snacks, and our beverages have placed an unbearable load on our sugar-regulating mechanisms.

The most common type of low blood sugar is caused by excessive production of insulin. This in turn may reflect tributary causes—imbalance of the autonomic nervous systems, excessive stimulation of the adrenal glands, which try to raise the blood sugar when the insulin has too drastically lowered it, or a deficiency of the hormones which raise blood sugar, including adrenal hormones, glucagon, and a pituitary factor.

All this technical verbiage may be useful in giving you a picture of the complexities of the processes by which we may be stuffed with sugar, and paradoxically, suffer from an inadequate supply in the blood. It tells you, too, why eating sugar is obviously not the remedy for hypoglycemia, since more sugar would simply perpetuate excessive reactions to it. But it doesn't tell you what hypoglycemia does to a person's mental and physical functioning. The best way to appreciate that is to take a close look at a chart which was assembled by a physician who treated eleven hundred patients with low blood sugar, recording not only their symptoms, but the percentages of the patients complaining of them:

60

| | |
|---|---|
| Nervousness | 94% |
| Irritability | 89% |
| Exhaustion | 87% |
| Faintness, dizziness, tremor, cold sweats, weak spells | 86% |
| Depression | 77% |
| Vertigo, dizziness | 73% |
| Drowsiness | 72% |
| Headaches | 71% |
| Digestive disturbances | 69% |
| Forgetfulness | 67% |
| Insomnia (awakening and inability to return to sleep) | 62% |
| Constant worrying, unprovoked anxieties | 62% |
| Mental confusion | 57% |
| Internal trembling | 57% |
| Palpitation of heart, rapid pulse | 54% |
| Muscle pains | 53% |
| Numbness | 51% |
| Unsocial, asocial, antisocial behavior | 47% |
| Indecisiveness | 50% |
| Crying spells | 46% |
| Lack of sex drive (females) | 44% |
| Allergies | 43% |
| Incoordination | 43% |
| Leg cramps | 43% |
| Lack of concentration | 42% |
| Blurred vision | 40% |
| Twitching and jerking of muscles | 40% |
| Itching and crawling sensations on skin | 39% |
| Gasping for breath | 37% |
| Smothering spells | 34% |
| Staggering | 34% |
| Sighing and yawning | 30% |
| Impotence (males) | 29% |
| Unconsciousness | 27% |
| Night terrors, nightmares | 27% |
| Rheumatoid arthritis | 24% |

| Phobias, fears | 23% |
| Neurodermatitis | 21% |
| Suicidal intent | 20% |
| Nervous breakdown | 17% |
| Convulsions | 2% |

With the traditional but regrettable resistance of the medical orthodoxy to new ideas, the establishment in medicine has tried to label hypoglycemia as a "fad disease," implying that there are actually few genuine cases of it, and that most of those who claim to suffer with it are hypochondriacs. This is more than somewhat tragic, for many hypoglycemics, as you might imagine from the description of the symptoms, wind up labeled as neurotics, psychotics, psychopaths, "a little queer," or "constitutionally inadequate." As a result, there are many patients chattering from the psychiatric couch who should, instead, be sitting at a dinner table, eating well balanced, low-sugar meals.

By way of arguing that the disorder obviously doesn't exist and *can't,* the incompetent point out that no single disease could cause so many symptoms of so many types, involving so many different systems in the body. If this criticism isn't a product of ignorance of the impacts of low blood sugar on the organism, I am at a loss to explain its basis, for a deficit of sugar strikes directly at the thinking brain, the emotional brain, and the nervous systems. One need not be a neurologist to understand that disturbances in every organ and system of the body would flow from such a process. I'm not really at a loss for other explanations of resistance to the concept of hypoglycemia. (One medical antagonist who has bitterly resisted the concept is intimately associated with a "foundation," which is actually subsidized by processors of coffee, makers of cola drinks and candy, and manufacturers of baked products and sugar—the foods which are forbidden to hypoglycemics.)

Since I have devoted an entire book to hypoglycemia (*Low Blood Sugar and You,* published by Grosset and Dunlap), it's obvious that in this brief review, I can't cover the entire subject. Suffice it to say that the necessary treatment, other than reducing sugar intake to the lowest level possible, consists of:

1. Nutritional help for the liver, which is even more important to regulation of blood sugar levels than the pancreas, to which most attention is usually devoted, the emphasis being placed on insulin production.

2. Relief for the pancreas from constant over-stimulation by excessive intake of sugars and starches. We hold the starch intake to about 60 mgs. daily.

3. With the intake of sugar greatly reduced, and the starches held down to about 60 grams daily—more for some patients, and sometimes, less for others—we raise the protein intake—from meat, fish, fowl, eggs, cheese, milk, and dairy products, and the intake of polyunsaturated (vegetable) fats. We use about five teaspoons daily of a vegetable oil, free of additives, in this diet. This is not only a contribution to the needs of the body, but it helps the overweight hypoglycemic to lose weight.

4. As important as the composition of the meals is, of equal importance is their timing. Low blood sugar is most easily controlled with six small, rather than three large, meals daily. In each of these, some protein is taken.

5. The diet is supplemented with multiple vitamins, multiple minerals, and a Vitamin B Complex concentrate. Special purpose foods high in vitamins and minerals are also used, to bring in supplies of the natural factors which can't be provided adequately in small capsules: wheat germ, brewer's yeast, and desiccated (dried) liver. The liver should be vacuum dried or solvent extracted. If the latter, avoid the hexane-extracted type.

There are, of course, other types of help which the physician may provide—oral medications, injections of adrenal hormones (needed by about 10 percent of hypoglycemics), biofeedback, vitamins by injection, supplements of glycerin, and numerous other therapeutic modalities.

Be wary of the professional man who tests for hypoglycemia by examining one drop of blood. Nothing about low blood sugar can be learned from this procedure alone. Be wary of any test for low blood sugar which requires less than five or six hours; many cases do not reveal their troubles in a shorter test. And avoid any "treatment" for low blood sugar which includes doses of sugar, candy, honey, or any other sweet. The treatment sounds logical, but from what you have read, you realize that it can do nothing except provide temporary relief, with a marked worsening of symptoms as the ultimate price.

Some other notes of interest: Many women who do not suffer from hypoglycemia at other times, develop it in the week before the menstrual, with consequent fainting spells, dizziness, and craving for sweets. They should stay on the hypoglycemia diet, if they wish to avoid these episodes. Avocados contain a type of sugar which not only does not stimulate insulin production, as ordinary sugar does, but tends to depress it. This is a good food, which should be a fairly frequent choice for the hypoglycemic.

Tobacco makes hypoglycemia worse. So does liquor. Allergies may touch off hypoglycemia. Hypoglycemia may touch off or worsen allergies. (See the following discussion of asthma, as an example.) Allergies may also cause all the symtoms of hypoglycemia, without a change in the blood sugar levels. The symptoms disappear when the offending foods or environmental triggers are bypassed.

When there is strong suspicion of hypoglycemia, and the six-hour test does not reveal it, the symptoms can sometimes be elicited if the physician places stress on the body, asking the patient to run on a treadmill, or hyperventilate briefly.

It becomes obvious that a high percentage of patients visiting physicians and virtually all those visiting psychiatrists and psychologists should be cleared for hypoglycemia before treatment. Untreated, hypoglycemia may be a prelude to diabetes, which is to say that the overactive, oversensitized pancreas ultimately becomes exhausted. Prophylactic moral: Don't stay as sweet as you are. Excessive sugar intake spells nothing but trouble. And no form of sugar—from fruit, from honey, from the sugar bowl—whether white, yellow, or brown; in the form of molasses or other syrups—is exempt. This doesn't forbid use of such sugars. It does, sensibly, limit intake.

## ALCOHOLISM

*All* alcoholics are hypoglycemic, for it is an inevitable result of substituting whiskey for food. Some alcoholics *begin* by becoming hypoglycemic, and at the point where the low blood sugar would ordinarily cause a craving for sweets, they pervert the craving into an appetite for alcohol. *That* group in the alcoholic population can be *cured* of alcoholism by adopting and staying on the hypoglycemia diet. The heavy consumer of sweets who becomes an alcoholic is suspect of being in this group. So is the drinker who, when drying out, eats large amounts of candy. This paragraph is *not* based on theory. Let me quote from one of hundreds of letters:

"I didn't make any vows, pledges, promises. I didn't ask for the intervention of the Almighty, and I did no praying. I didn't call on fellow alcoholics or exdrinkers for aid. I had already been through A.A., Antabuse, shock treatment, and psychotherapy without results. I just went on the hypoglycemia diet, and a few months later, suddenly realized two things: I hadn't had a drink in weeks, and I didn't want one."

Let me make it clear again that I am not proposing hypoglycemia as *the* cause of alcoholism. I *am* proposing it as a cause for a type of addiction to alcohol. And the establishment in the field has remained deaf to the suggestion and blind to the evidence for the twenty years in which we've researched the problem.

There is another putative cause of alcoholism in nutrition, proposed by the eminent biochemist, Dr. Roger Williams. Briefly stated, it is based on the theory, which animal and human research corroborates, that some alcoholics begin with an exaggerated requirement for certain nutrients, failure to satisfy which is then expressed, again in a perverted way, by a craving for alcohol. It has repeatedly been demonstrated that animals on a poor diet will become alcoholics; given a good diet, they stop their drinking. It has also been demonstrated, by Dr. Williams and others, that alcoholics who are treated with supernutrition may spontaneously stop drinking, or even recover the ability to take a single drink, and stop. This research has received exactly the same unhealthful neglect accorded the work in the field of hypoglycemia.

## DRUG ADDICTION

There is a stage of addiction to some of the hard drugs in which an intense craving for candy develops. (The addicts call it the "Chunky" stage, referring to the foil-wrapped chocolates they crave.) No research, to my knowledge, has been performed to fix or expunge the possibility that hypoglycemia may be caused by the drugs, which would, of course, help to perpetuate the habit, for the symptoms of low blood sugar are so devastating that anything even remotely helpful in escaping them is likely to be tried. No research has been, to my knowledge, performed to determine if drug addiction can be initiated by a preceding hypoglycemia.

In both drug addiction and alcoholism, there is another role for good nutrition, for both groups suffer from the impact of their self-chosen, poor diet, and both can be helped both physically and mentally by a high-protein diet of the hypoglycemia type, supplemented with multiple vitamins, multiple minerals, and the Vitamin B Complex—the latter both in concentrated form, and from the special-purpose foods previously cited—desiccated liver, wheat germ, and brewer's yeast.

# CHAPTER 6

## STAYING YOUNG

### Prolonging the Prime of Life

TIME DOESN'T AGE US, OBVIOUSLY—AT LEAST, IT ISN'T the clock and it isn't the calendar that take the spring out of the step, put the silver in the hair, and settle the arthritis in the joints. Time is but a measure of duration—both tapes and clocks measure, but they don't cause anything. Do we not see sixty-year-olds who are young, and fifty-year-olds who are senile? Aging is not only a highly individual phenomenon, but is capricious in choosing its targets, not only as persons, but as organs, for the forty-year-old may have aged kidneys, and the seventy-year-old may have a heart like that of a young man.

There is a scientist—I interviewed him on one of my television programs—who studied the capacity of human cells to regenerate. He identified a cellular calendar, a kind of biological clock with a finite life, for all the human cells he tested could reproduce for not more than fifty generations. You could, of course, "use up" the fifty generations in a few years or in many, so that the internal clock wasn't necessarily synchronized with the external one. And how fast your body runs through those fifty generations would, in part, be determined by your life-style—including your nutrition. Accordingly, the scientist's discovery didn't negate the importance of eating properly. The discovery also omitted an important consideration: The life of the cell in the last generation, after the capacity to divide and regenerate had been exhausted. This—the cell's post-miotic life—wasn't investigated.

Later, there came a discovery which should have received more attention from the public and the professions than it did. Researchers discovered that the test cells had reproduced for only fifty generations because of limitations on the nutrients available to them, and not because of an internal clock which had run down. They showed that with an increase in the amount of Vitamin E provided to the cells, the number of generations could be increased to 120. Considering the contempt many scientists have exhibited for the "Vitamin E faddists" as they put it, it was amusing that the researchers who made the discovery also made the following comments:

(a.) Research with a group of cells can't be extended to the entire, complex organism of man. What prolongs cell life, in short, may not prolong human life.

(b.) Notwithstanding these reservations, both scientists announced that they are now supplementing their diets with Vitamin E.

Apropos of the disdain many physicians and nutritionists exhibit for those who "waste their money by taking Vitamin E," or who, to use the pungent phrase of a prominent scientific cynic, are "enriching the sewers with Vitamin E," isn't it remarkable these critics never comment on the fact that this vitamin is removed from virtually all the starches eaten by the public—starches which comprise 50 percent of the American diet? Removal is fine; restoration is the concern only of the little old ladies in tennis shoes . . .

Actually, the observations of the beneficial effects of Vitamin E on the capacity of cells to regenerate have received insufficient attention from both the professions and the public. Here is underscored a vital action of the vitamin in retarding the aging process, one which was understood long before the studies of the limiting effects of Vitamin E deficiency on cell mitosis. This is the antioxidant effect of the vitamin, which translates as helping the fat in our cells to resist rancidity. This is an oversimplification, but the story is too complex and too long to be told here. Suffice it that we are exposed to cosmic radiation, or some unknown factor like it, which disturbs the exquisitely balanced chemistries and the sequence of enzyme actions within the cell. The talk of Vitamin E as an aphrodisiac is nonsense, and if it weren't, the action of the vitamin as an antioxidant would still be of first importance, for this is our most effective protection against premature aging of our cells.

Interestingly, the forms of Vitamin E which the public considers unimportant are the ones most effective in protecting the cell fats against oxidation. The public is buying *alpha* tocopherol, which is vital to the energy processes within the cell, but has very little antioxidant effect. Protection against the damaging actions of peroxides—the superactive form of oxygen created by the irradiation effects—derives from other forms of Vitamin E—the beta, gamma, and delta tocopherols. Therefore, if you want both the effects of Vitamin E on intracellular chemistry, and as a protection against the premature aging process initiated by activated oxygen, you do not buy alpha tocopherol alone, but *mixed* tocopherols, meaning that the alpha form is accompanied by the beta, gamma, and delta tocopherols. The potency will be stated in terms of alpha activity, this being a policy dictated by the ancient (and mistaken) belief that the helpfulness of Vitamin E derives entirely from the alpha form alone. Someday, the manufacturers should be persuaded to tell us not only the alpha tocopherol activity of a supplement, but the amounts present of the beta, gamma, and delta forms. Part of the confusion derives from the pioneering research of my good friend, Dr. Wilfred Shute, who, as a cardiologist, is interested only in the alpha tocopherol form of the vitamin. But Dr. Shute, obviously, is not administering Vitamin E with a thought to slowing down again. Emerge from this discussion with the simple understanding that intelligent use of Vitamin E as a supplement, with consideration of both its effects on intracellular energy processes and on retardation of the aging mechanisms calls for a concentrate of mixed tocopherols, offering not only the alpha, but the beta, gamma, and delta forms.

There is also some confusion about the use of milligram measurements versus units of Vitamin E. Figure 400 mgs. of alpha tocopherol to be equivalent to 268 units.

The amounts of Vitamin E to be used are difficult to specify, since measurements of potency are always stated in terms of alpha activity, and we are vitally interested in adequate intake of the other forms. I shall therefore suggest dosages in terms of alpha tocopherol, cautioning you again to be sure that the preparation supplies this as part of the tocopherol complex—as a mixture of alpha, beta, gamma, and delta tocopherols.

For the person with heart disease—particularly, in the early stages—Vitamin E therapy *must* be supervised by a physician, for there are, in these circumstances, distinct dangers in improper use of the vitamin, a warning Dr. Wilfred Shute himself has repeatedly uttered.

For those who take Vitamin E because they are well, and want to stay that way, or young, and want to retard aging, the amount of the vitamin needed will be predicated on the dietary history. If you've eaten like the conventional American, as if determined to commit biological (attenuated) suicide—the only legal kind—you may need 400 mgs. daily.

If you're over fifty, when the aging process brings with it progressively impaired efficiency in the utilization of fats, and thereby, fat-soluble vitamins, you will profit more if that intake is in the nonoily, emulsified, or water-dispersible form of the vitamin. An alternative would be the use of a supplement of lecithin, taken with the vitamin.

If you're a young adult, 100 mgs. daily should suffice. There are no laboratory tests which supply guidance. Your subjective reactions, your feelings of well-being, are as good a weather-vane as any. Please note that responses to Vitamin E take months. Tests have shown that individuals depleted in the vitamin, and then generously supplied with it, do not recover from the deficiency for six months or more. Older persons may find from 400 to 800 mgs. daily to be ideal; the need varies.

There are other antioxidants in nutrition, which help in slowing down or reversing aging. These include certain amino acids (from high-quality proteins) from foods such as eggs, meat, fish, fowl, milk, cheese, and dairy products, other than cream and butter.

Other antioxidants include selenium, and Vitamin C, which is, of course, supplied by citrus and other fruits, and vegetables and salads, but if you seek an amount which will yield maximum protection against the mischief of activated oxygen in your cells, you'll have to rely on tablets. This is one of the rarely mentioned dividends from Dr. Linus Pauling's thesis. And don't discount it: Postmortem studies have shown that the age at death is in linear relationship to the Vitamin C levels in the blood: The higher those levels, the older the person was when he died.

The optimal requirement of Vitamin C for this and other purposes will range from 250 mgs. daily up to 2500 or more, for some individuals. It may sound like a great deal, but the top figure—2500 mgs. is no more than the amount of Vitamin C man would be synthesizing in his own body, if he hadn't lost the ability, somewhere in the evolutionary process. (Incidentally, animals which *can* manufacture the vitamin will, when placed under stress, increase their output to the equivalent for man of 14,000 mgs. daily, which says something for our heightened need for the vitamin when the body has heavy demands upon it.)

Selenium is supplied by many foods; brewer's yeast and liver are among the good sources. Torula yeast, incidentally, doesn't supply this mineral, which is essential to proper utilization of Vitamin E, and which is an antioxidant in its own right. Be sure, therefore, that the yeast you buy *is* brewer's, and if the label is silent on the subject, write to the manufacturer. Selenium is part of a compound called "Factor 3."

These anitoxidants, however, don't exhaust the arsenal of the nutritionist in prolonging the prime of life. Since nutrition prevents or mitigates what it alleviates or cures, the favorable responses of the aged and senile to high potency doses of Vitamin B Complex offer a clue to the kind of nutrition which will retard the process of growing old.

I have seen remarkable changes in the senile aged when vigorously treated with the Vitamin B Complex, which is an understandable and logical response. This group of vitamins is essential to proper utilization of food, to proper synthesis of the enzymes which make possible our low-temperature kind of life, to proper employment of oxygen in releasing the energy values of the diet, and even to the synthesis of the RNA and DNA which monitor and control cellular chemistry. Later in this text, you will find a description of effective formulas for Vitamin B Complex supplementing. Don't debate their value. You didn't debate when the processing mills removed the Vitamin B Complex from 50 percent of your foods—which they did and still do.

Among the B Complex vitamins, as one example, is the para-amino-benzoic acid, or paba earlier discussed in the context of retarding or reversing graying of the hair. That vitamin has actions which interlock with those of hormones critical to the retention of youth: It is synergistic, or works with insulin, estrogen, and the cortisol (cortisone) types of hormones. I cite this to give you an example of the effect of just one vitamin of the B Complex. You will find a more detailed discussion of the actions of others, in Chapter 12.

The emphasis placed on these individual factors should not be allowed to obscure the importance of totally balanced nutrition. No supplement will yield maximum dividends, if it is added to an inferior diet. A visit to a medical nutritionist to determine, so far as the present state of the art permits, your individual dietary needs and tolerances is a good investment, if you'd like to invoke fully the action of good nutrition in prolonging the prime of life. No chart of food requirements, generalizing about the needs of the entire public, can possibly be accurate for *you*, as an individual.

Injections of procaine (Novocaine or KH3) are also helpful in retarding the aging process. The response is not only to the paba, which is part of the molecule of this familiar local anaesthetic, but to the solvent with which it is chemically linked. A series of injections of 5 cc's of procaine, intramuscularly, several times weekly for a period of ten or twelve weeks, with another series, a month or two later, may accomplish an unbelievable reversal of signs of aging. Choose a physician familiar with the therapy. For those of you who can't afford the process, there is the less-effective, but still useful, device of taking paba in the form of the potassium salt, which, as I mentioned earlier, requires a prescription. Ordinary paba, sans the potassium, is available, over the counter. See the discussion of the anti-gray hair formula in Chapter 3 for quantities.

I am wary of the eulogies regarding doses of RNA and DNA, and the sweeping claims made for the Niehans cellular therapy. I have seen the first produce no demonstrable effect, and some bad side-effects from the second. This doesn't say that some people may not benefit. No generalizations in nutrition are possible, and certainly none concerning these off-beat techniques.

The diet to retard aging has no separate identity, really. It's the diet to help preserve good health, and that is the total diet, the total nutrition offered in this book. Don't discount that, either. The next time you look at Bob Cummings or Gloria Swanson or Hildegard, remarkably young, all of them, for their ages, please realize that it didn't happen as a dispensation from Providence. They took care of their nutrition, and their nutrition took care of them. I know because I've listened carefully to what they've had to say, often with the advantage of personal conversations with both Bob and Hildegard. I could name a thousand others who are young and active at what the public considers an advanced age. They don't surrender to the concept that time itself is toxic, but you, if you're an average American, do. Why else would you speak of a "senile cataract"? Question: Is the other eye any younger?

I am aware of other influences on the aging process, among them, the emotional and psychological outlook of the individual. You've commented on that obliquely, when you've wondered why men who retire without plans for retirement seem to age so suddenly, and sometimes, to die so quickly. Let me put the situation in a single sentence: The outwardly turned mind is self-healing, stays young, and helps to keep the body young; the inwardly turned mind abscesses, and brings down the temple in which it is housed.

We tend to overlook the influence of the brain on the processes of growing prematurely old, but have you ever noticed how disintegration accelerates when a stroke occurs, with its damage to brain circulation and tissues?

## THE "GOLDEN YEARS" TOO OFTEN AREN'T

With all the eulogies of growing old, too often it is a period in which you feel fine, thank you, but the house in which you are living is falling apart. Some of those reminders that no one is immortal or goes unwounded all the way do *not* originate with poor nutrition, but are the cumulative toll of many types and kinds of insults you and the organism have endured, over the decades. Some of them, though, are distinctly the product of eating a diet low in essential nutrients.

While deficiencies can reach the point of no return—in which the tissues seem to have "forgotten" how to respond to improved nutrition—it is also true that many of them can be reversed. I am flatly saying that many of the symptoms mistaken for senility are actually the long-deferred bill for sixty or seventy thousand improperly selected meals. Moreover, lifetime food habits are difficult to change—the old-dog-doesn't-learn-new tricks-easily theme and some of the tolls of aging have direct effects on the person's nutrition.

Changes in the structure of the mouth may prevent dentures from fitting properly, impairing the ability to chew. Enzyme activities decline—sometimes because of poor nutrition, always contributing to impaired utilization of foods, and thereby to a vicious cycle. Production of saliva may go down, with the amount of starch-digesting enzyme thereby lowered. Pancreatic activity may be reduced, lowering the efficiency of utilization of all food—protein, fat, carbohydrate, vitamins, and minerals. At least one old person in four has little or no hydrochloric acid in the stomach, which deficiency lowers the ability of the body to break down proteins.

All these deficits can be rectified. There are concentrates of pancreatic enzymes available, taken with meals, three

74

times daily. There are supplements of hydrochloric acid available, coupled with betaine or glutamic acid. Fat-soluble vitamins can be taken, as previously noted in the discussion of Vitamin E, in the nonoily, emulsified, or water-dispersible forms, or lecithin can be used when Vitamins A, D, E, or K (the fat-soluble factors) are ingested.

The dietary recommendations for the aged include cutting down on caloric intake—it is better, in old age, to be a little underweight. The protein requirement requires attention—a half gram of protein per pound of body weight is the average need. Animal proteins are important to the elderly. (It should be remembered that an average portion of meat supplies nineteen or twenty grams of protein.) Protein deficiencies in old age are responsible for some of their tiredness, anemias, and swelling of the ankles. Many old people are reluctant to eat meat because they think it damages the kidneys or raises the blood pressure; others have trouble chewing meat. Nevertheless, protein sources can be fish, flesh or fowl; organ meats such as liver and sweetbreads; milk, cheese and eggs. The aged are benefited by the milk nutrients (non-fat milk powder is the best buy for protein, calcium, vitamins, and other minerals) and by the use of wheat germ, brewer's yeast and rice polishings. If there is difficulty in chewing, there is no reason why the animal food should not be pureed, minced, scraped or flaked. Strained baby meats are useful, as well as baby vegetables and soups. Many of the baby meats incorporate animal organs and make excellent sandwich spreads.

The carbohydrate needs of old people are best served in the form of oatmeal, wheat germ, whole wheat bread, fruit, juices and vegetables.

The low-cholesterol diet for the aged makes no verifiable sense. The body still requires fats, although the fat intake should be reduced. Homogenized milk and whipped butter are easier for the elderly to utilize; and the addition of lactic acid to milk, or the use of yogurt, acidophilus milk, protein milk compound and buttermilk is desirable.

To no group of adults are vitamins and minerals more important than to the aged; they respond quickly, dramatically and hearteningly to high-vitamin, high-mineral intake. Supplements should include multiple minerals, multiple vitamins, a B Complex concentrate (preferably in liquid form) and Vitamin E. When aging has progressed too far and is too rapid, a series of injections of the Vitamin B Complex and separate injections of Vitamin B12 will sometimes halt or even reverse the process, giving the patient a momentum in recapturing youth, which supplements and good foods can subsequently maintain.

To summarize: the old should get enough calories to maintain normal weight for age, sex, and height. They should have a half gram of protein a day for each pound of body weight. They should use fats, but use them sparingly. They should eat foods which are rich in vitamins, minerals, and protein. The diet should be supplemented, as previously outlined. A dietary framework for the basic needs of the aged would be as follows:

One pint of milk or its equivalent. The equivalent of one pint of milk is approximately 2½ ounces of yellow cheese. Part of the milk may be utilized in creamed soups, puddings, and the like. Skimmed dried milk may be added to recipes to reinforce the milk intake for those who do not take sufficient milk from other sources.

There should be one serving daily of orange, grapefruit, tomato, or their juices. Raw cabbage or salad greens are desirable, provided the aged are able to tolerate these foods. There should be one serving of green or yellow vegetables, some of them raw, daily. One serving of potatoes or other vegetable or soup. One serving of whole grain cereal, reinforced with wheat germ; or oatmeal, or whole wheat cereal. One egg daily, or at least four a week.

One serving of meat, poultry, seafood, or other protein-rich food daily, with emphasis on organ meats.

All breads and flours should be whole grain or enriched with wheat germ as well as with vitamins. Both butter and margarine should be used.

By intelligent use of enzyme supplements, of vitamins and

minerals by mouth, of injections of the Vitamin B Complex when needed, coupled with a highly nutritious diet, I have seen remarkable recoveries in "senile dements," and gratifying responses in the prematurely aging. The program must be competently mounted and supervised, and not administered on the familiar lay basis that a little being good, a lot more will be better. This doctrine often works for vitamins, but may go awry with, for instance, protein. The very old tend to excrete protein (nitrogen) faster than they can ingest it, and need special help—such as the use of Vitamin B6, as one example, in achieving better nitrogen balance. Which all adds up to a recommendation which by now should be familiar: Eating intelligently and using supplements intelligently is your domain; treatment for special nutritional problems calls for a medical nutritionist.

# CHAPTER 7

## NUTRITION IN SICKNESS

IT IS A CLICHE TO SAY THAT THOSE WHO MEDICATE themselves for illness—whether with drugs or nutrients— have an incompetent doctor. It is a catch phrase which understandably irritates the public, for the majority of medical schools do not offer courses in nutrition, and yet many physicians will not disqualify themselves in this field, as they willingly do in others which probably are beyond their scope of expertise. Which is to say that warnings against self-medication in nutrition are likely to be ignored by those who have experienced difficulty in finding qualified medical nutritionists. Yet supervision by such competent practitioners is a must, when nutritional therapies are employed.

It is not that nutrients are dangerous medications, but that there is the real risk that the layman will be unaware of limitations on his knowledge—or that of the authors of books on which he is relying, and worse than that, of the complicated factors which enter into human illness. To give a quick example: Surely the use of paba in an effort to repigment the skin in vitiligo, and rid one's self of disfiguring white patches is a harmless application of our knowledge of nutrition. *But* vitiligo is sometimes a warning that stomach hydrochloric acid is threateningly low, and this the layman is unlikely to comprehend. For all these reasons, this chapter is not an invitation to self-medication, but will serve, rather, to illuminate some neglected areas where nutrition may join hands with medicine, for the benefit of mankind.

## ALLERGIES

We have known about allergies for many decades, and yet still don't understand them. They are described as "individuality gone berserk." They are described as a perversion of a normal defense mechanism, in which substances normal to the body—such as food—evoke defensive reactions which, directed against the foreign protein of bacteria, are useful, but perverted, become a source of hives, eczema, frequent colds, and other phenomena lumped under the title of "allergic reactions."

The phychoanalysts, as usual, have glib explanations for the process, but fail to explain how a newborn baby manages to come into the world with dozens of allergies to mar his chances for health. The allergist talks about antigens, which touch off the allergic reaction by stimulating antibody production, and the price when the production of antibodies is too great. Which doesn't explain injections for desensitization, since such injections should produce antibodies, too—unless we settle for antibodies which battle antibodies, and at that point, explanation leads to need for more explanation. Then there are allergists who reject the antigen-antibody theory.

This leads us exactly nowhere, so let's try a new approach:

Where do allergies start? My own hypothesis begins with an obvious assumption: Man throughout history has had allergies. There is evidence for that, but both the incidence and the seriousness of the condition must have increased in recent years, for it is impossible to visualize the caveman as surviving in his hostile environment if tortured by hayfever, choked with asthma, or scratching with eczema. The turning point, to me, came when formula feeding was introduced; cows' milk is high on the list of allergenic (allergy-causing) foods, and breast milk is practically blameless, unless mother is eating (or taking) something which (a) reaches the milk, and (b) is a potent allergen. This book being a nutrition handbook, and not a text on allergy, I can't explore the subject in depth, but will try to bring you up to date on some aspects of allergy which are ignored, overlooked, or little understood.

Undoubtedly, some allergies begin in childhood, when new proteins are introduced in the baby's diet. That is why pediatricians often advise you to feed new foods to babies gradually, increasing the amounts as you go along, giving the small body an opportunity to learn to tolerate the new protein. This immunity is created exactly as the doctor does it with injections of ragweed pollen for hayfever, or cold vaccines—in small and steadily increasing doses. In lieu of gradual easing of a food into the diet, the pediatrician may choose to alter the food's protein thereby decreasing the risk of a reaction to a highly allergenic protein food. An example: introducing eggs in the hardboiled form, where high heat has altered the egg protein, reducing the chance of touching off a sensitivity. Conversely, when the allergist is searching to identify the foods, which are disturbing an allergic person, he is very likely to scan most closely the list of foods of which the patient is fond, and which he eats most frequently and in the largest quantities. These are the most likely troublemakers—though not always, for it is possible to be violently allergic to elephant meat or some other exotic food you never or rarely encounter.

To say that the foods of which you are fond are most likely

to be the triggers for an allergic reaction brings up the question of the addictiveness of allergenic foods and beverages. There is actually an addiction involved in many a craving for a favorite food. When a patient says he simply must have a chocolate bar, or a cigarette, or a glass of milk, the neuroallergist (a new type of specialist) pricks up his ears, for this is addiction which implies that the patient *unconsciously* is using repeated doses of food to delay (as long as possible) the allergic reaction. The process roughly goes like this: The glass of milk (or the cigarette, chocolate bar, slice of bread, or whatever) initiates a reaction which includes stimulation of the autonomic nervous systems—those that function without your control. (That is why acceleration of the pulse is a symptom of allergy in some people.) The first effect of the allergy then, is pleasurable. An hour, or two, or three later, the undesirable effects of the allergy will appear—in headache, stuffed nose, irritability, fatigue, or any of the pleomorphic forms in which the body expresses its discomfort in an allergic reaction. Now begins the craving for the next dose of the offending food, drink, smoke, or whatever: It will serve as a means of deferring the bad reaction, for it will induce another stimulation of the nervous system, and a new "high." This process not only explains addiction to the very substances which are causing your troubles. It also explains why the drunk, with a terrible hangover, craves a morning dose of "the hair of the dog that bit him," for reactions to whiskey (or to its grain source) may be allergic in nature.

This type of allergic reaction is but a first cousin of what the allergist evokes when he gives you a scratch or patch test, and watches for reddening, swelling of the skin, or itching. For these addictive allergies will frequently express themselves as "mental" or "emotional" disorders. With the briefness of this explanation, you may find it difficult to accept the truth that allergy to foods or other environment factors may cause suicidal depression, neurotic symptoms, or even a full-blown paranoid psychosis. It will also worsen the condition of children with learning difficulties, and intensify the symptoms caused by low blood sugar. Hypoglycemia (low blood sugar) invokes allergy in two ways: Allergies may cause low blood sugar or the symptoms attributed to it; low blood sugar may cause allergies. With regard to the latter: There are cases of asthma which have been cured by treatment of an underlying hypoglycemia. With regard to the former: There are people with low blood sugar who faithfully follow the prescribed low-sugar diet, but do not recover until the foods to which they are allergic are removed from the diet.

It is interesting that the foods most frequently blamed by the patient for his allergic outbreak are innocent of blame. In a list supplied by two specialists, thirty-seven foods are mentioned most commonly in patients' complaints; but very few of the foods known to be common offenders are included among the thirty-seven. In actual testing, the foods which are most frequently found to be allergy producers are: wheat, eggs, milk, chocolate, cabbage, tomatoes, oranges, walnuts, strawberries, bananas, potatoes, cauliflower, oats, rice, oysters, salmon, celery, lettuce, squash, apricots, apples, cantaloupe, grapefruit and peaches.

It must be remembered, also, that cooking or other processes may alter the allergic nature of foods. There are people who cannot eat onions without an attack of asthma, but who have no ill effects from eating onions soaked in vinegar. Some people can eat cooked cabbage, but not cole slaw. Very frequently, the person who is allergic to milk has no difficulty when he drinks milk which has been boiled and subsequently chilled. By this process the nature of the protein in the milk is slightly changed, removing the source of allergy for some individuals.

An allergy can wear more disguises than Sherlock Holmes. Everyone is familiar with "strawberry rash," but many of us do not know that allergy can cause hives, skin rashes, swelling, abdominal distress, constipation, diarrhea, colitis, sores on the lip or in the mouth, constant headaches, hay fever, asthma, bronchitis and sinus trouble. Allergy may be reflected in epilepsy, housemaid's knee, kidney disturbances, fever, and difficulties in menstruation.

When the allergist tests for food allergy, he has many techniques on which to draw. He may use scratch or patch tests, previously described. He may feed very small amounts of suspected foods, and ask for a record of your reactions. He may place you on a basic (elimination) diet, in which all highly allergenic foods are eliminated, and keep you on it until your symptoms subside, after which he will have you add one new food at a time, carefully recording your reactions. In lieu of this, in serious cases, he may place you on a total fast, with nothing but pure spring water, and then break the fast with a single food, and, at intervals, add others, one at a time. (This invokes no magic "detoxifying" power of fasting. It is simply a method of ridding the body of allergens.) He may choose, instead, which is a likely possibility, if your allergies are not too severe, to give you neutralizing doses of Vitamin B6, Vitamin C, calcium, and bioflavonoids—factors in nutrition which combat allergy, offset histamine, and reduce the excessive permeability linked with the allergic reaction when it affects the cell walls, thereby contributing to swelling and other symptoms. Or he may elect to try large doses of Vitamin B Complex and predigested protein, a combination which has been shown (many years ago) sharply to reduce the severity of allergic reactions, both in animals and in man.

A new dietary technique to control very severe, multiple food allergies that are not responsive to treatment is the rotation diet, which is simpler to pursue than to describe. Each day, one single protein source is used at all meals—beef, for instance; and the same vegetables and fruits are drawn on at all meals, that day. If it is a wheatless day, the bread will be made from rice, rye, or corn. The next day, the protein may be fresh-water fish, at all meals, and so on. By means of this rotation pattern, in which the "beef day" will not be repeated for at least four days (or more, if the physician so elects) intractable allergies can often be controlled, if not eliminated. Unfortunately, this avant-garde method is not used by allergists, and the procedure does need competent supervision by a practitioner experienced in administering it.

Neuro-allergists, interested in the impact of allergy on the brain and nervous systems, use another method of testing. Employing a concentrated solution of the food or other test substance—which may be anything from tobacco to fungi— they place a few drops of the solution under your tongue, where the rich vascular network promptly absorbs it. Your reaction will not be itching or redness, but neurological and cerebral. If you have a tendency to schizophrenia, such a test may elicit some of the symptoms. Or it may bring on distortions of perception, in which people appear to be yellow dots, floating on a purple background, or their faces seem to grow larger or smaller. If you have a real hostility toward your spouse, this learned reaction may be triggered by the systemic allergic reaction, explaining why you're more homicidal toward your mate when you've eaten something to which you're allergic. Such tests have become an important aspect of orthomolecular psychiatry, for allergy may frequently be part of the problems of the depressed, the suicidal, the paranoid (who suffer delusions of persecution when they've eaten something they're allergic to) and those with autism, schizophrenia, metabolic dysperception, and learning difficulties. The reaction may be offset with a neutralizing, quite dilute solution of the same food which initiated the symptoms, or with massive, one-gram doses of Vitamin B6 and Vitamin C. Readers interested in deeper exploration of the subject should see the author's *Psycho-Nutrition* text.

Nutritional treatments often yield surprising benefits in some cases of allergy. I've seen a child's asthma disappear with injections of Vitamin B12. I've seen hayfever, in patients who didn't respond to Vitamin C, markedly mitigated by supplements of Vitamin E. I've seen eczema of a type supposed to originate with allergy, disappear with feedings of unsaturated fat, Vitamin B6, and Vitamin E. And I've seen "negative" dividends: Intermittent deafness disappeared when the patient stopped drinking tomato juice, of which he was fond.

# SINUSITUS

Sinus trouble is often a challenge for the allergist. It may be emotional. I saw a violent case develop in a girl who was jilted at the altar, and disappear when finally, she married someone else. (*He* has a postnasal drip now, but that's another story.) Sinusitis may be caused by foods to which you're allergic, by dust, which is present twelve months per year, unlike pollen—or by allergy to one's own bacteria. Dust vaccines are available, and can also be prepared from the dust in your own household, which is logical—that's what you're likely to encounter, and to which you're likely to react. A vaccine (autogenous) can be prepared from your own bacteria, on the basis of the same logic, and you can build resistance with small and gradually increasing injections of dust, the autogenous vaccine, or, if you need them, both.

In addition to relieving the patient with sinus infections from the aggravating factors of allergy to dust, bacteria, and food, the physician may elect to place the patient on a low carbohydrate diet, of the type used in hypoglycemia (though it may here be offered in three, rather than six meals daily.) A typical diet for sinusitis, not aimed at weight reduction, follows:

## SINUSITUS DIET

### BREAKFAST

Fruit, 10% ................................... 1 serving
Bacon ....................................... 3 slices
Egg .............................................. 1
Bread (toast) ............................. 1 thin slice
Butter ...................................... 1 square
Cream, 20% ................................... ¼ cup
Beverage—coffee or tea

## LUNCH

| | |
|---|---|
| Meat, fish or fowl ................................... | 1 |
| Vegetable, 3% ............................... | 1 serving |
| Salad: | |
|    Vegetable, 3% ........................... | 1 serving |
|    Salad dressing with oil ................. | 1 tablespoon |
| Bran soy muffin ................................... | 1 |
| Butter .................................... | 2 squares |
| Fruit, 5% ................................... | 1 serving |
| Milk ....................................... | 1 glass |

## DINNER

| | |
|---|---|
| Meat ....................................... | 1 serving |
| Vegetable, 6% ............................... | 1 serving |
| Salad: | |
|    Fresh vegetable, 3% ...................... | 1 serving |
|    Salad dressing with oil ................. | 1 tablespoon |
| Bran soy muffin ................................... | 1 |
| Butter .................................... | 2 squares |
| Fruit, 5% ................................... | 1 serving |
| Milk ....................................... | 1 glass |

In many of the diets recommended throughout this book, the carbohydrate content of permitted fruits and vegetables is specified. For this reason, the following reference chart is given:

## CLASSIFICATION OF FRESH VEGETABLES AND FRESH FRUITS
### According to Percentage of Carbohydrate Content
#### VEGETABLES

| 3% | 6% |
|---|---|
| Asparagus | Artichokes—French |
| Beet Greens | Beet |
| Broccoli | Carrot |
| Brussel Sprouts | Celeriac |
| Cabbage | Dandelion Greens |
| Cauliflower | Kale |

## 3%

Celery
Chinese Cabbage
Cucumber
Eggplant
Endive
Green pepper
Lettuce
Marrow
Mustard Greens
Okra
Radish
Sauerkraut
Sorrel
Spinach
String Bean (tiny)
Summer Squash
Tomato
Watercress

## 6%

Kohlrabi
Leeks
Onions
Parsley
Pea (tiny)
Pumpkin
Rutabaga
String Bean (mature)
Squash
Turnip

## 15%

Parsnip
Pea
Salsify

## 20%

Corn
Garlic
Horseradish Root
Potato
Shelled Bean

## FRUITS

## 5%

Avocado
Honeydew
Muskmelon
Rhubarb
Watermelon

## 10%

Blackberry
Cranberry
Gooseberry
Grapefruit
Lemon
Lime
Orange
Papaya
Peach

## 15%

Apple
Apricot
Blueberry
Cherry
Currant
Grape
Guava
Huckleberry
Nectarine
Pawpaw
Pear
Plum
Quince
Raspberry

| 10% | 20% |
|-----|-----|
| Pineapple | Banana |
| Fresh Prune | Fig (fresh) |
| Strawberry | Grape Juice |
| Tangerine | |

## COLITIS

Colitis is another disorder which may be of psychosomatic origin, but it also may be initiated or aggravated by allergy, with milk and wheat frequent offenders. Because of the frequency of defecation of these patients, and malabsorption of nutrients from the colon, nutritional deficiencies, caused by the disorder, may aggravate it. Multiple vitamin, mineral, B Complex, Vitamin E, Vitamin C, and bioflavonoid supplements are often helpful to these patients. More than helpful—sometimes lifesaving, in severe and in ulcerative colitis, are supplements of dried stomach or dried colon tissue. This is given on the grounds that the healthy colon doesn't digest itself, and thereby, such tissue must have within it, a protective factor. Whether the explanation is valid or not, the material is often curative in colitis. When my readers mention this to physicians, they sometimes encounter a blank stare of outright cynicism. I know not why; such tissues have been advertised in medical journals for at least twenty-five years. Perhaps I'm the only reader of those journals. Colon tissue is not the only "organ" preparation of benefit in colitis. Combinations of various organ meats—desiccated liver, kidney, pancreas and similar meats have been beneficial, too, though not quite as specifically. These all may be helpful, together with the use of bran, in diverticular disorders.

## THE COMMON COLD

Returning to an earlier topic: Since the common cold often has an allergic component, one wonders about the controversy concerning Vitamin C and colds. High doses of the vitamin were recognized in 1940 to be antihistamine. If that action has no effect on the common cold, why is it that all the drugs for common colds, which you've seen advertised on television, contain antihistamines? Are they all fraudulent—or is the controversy a contrived one by the implacable enemies of what they think of as "food faddism"? It is because of this antihistamine effect that Vitamin C, in one gram or larger doses, taken a few times daily, has helped many a case of pollen allergy (hay fever—which doesn't come from hay, isn't a fever, but often responds to the vitamin).

I have observed helpfulness from Vitamin C in building resistance to colds, shortening their duration, or decreasing their intensity. (I've seen all three.) Those who criticize Dr. Linus Pauling will not shake him, for he began his investigation of the vitamin after using it to shake off a lifetime personal history of marked susceptibility to colds, which ended when he raised his Vitamin C intake, he personally told me. Since I published the same observation in this very book, in its first edition, January, 1942, it's obvious that I agree with him, but with a reservation or two.

The common cold isn't common. It's a number of disease entities, combined under one title. Among "common colds," there are those which are amenable to Vitamin C (or other vitamin) therapy, and those which are not. There are also people who are Vitamin C responders, and those who are not. And finally, there are people who respond to Vitamin C by dropping the cold from the head to the chest, thereby introducing a persistent bronchitis, as a substitute for a head cold. Many of these people will break colds more successfully with Vitamin A. When a Vitamin C responder takes Vitamin A for a cold, nothing happens. When a Vitamin A responder takes Vitamin C for a cold, he may initiate a chest cold. When you don't know which type you are, therefore, you begin with Vitamin A—the dosage as outlined by my good friend, Dr. C. Ward Crampton, who described the therapy in the *New York State Journal of Medicine,* many years ago: 250,000 units of Vitamin A in one dose, taken daily for five days. (I'm aware that the FDA has made this difficult to do, by limiting the potency of Vitamin A capsules. Would that they were as zealous with the tranquilizers which cause tardive dyskinesia, and Red #2, which causes deformation of the unborn young, and is present in ice cream, lipstick, soda pop, and even white cake icing.) If you swallowed the story about Vitamin A toxicity, remember that your mother swallowed cod-liver oil—with three times the Vitamin A potency now permitted, and not having the FDA around, was too ignorant to develop toxicity. In any case, the period of dosage is too short, in using Vitamin A to abort colds, to warrant any discussion of toxicity. I *will* pause to point out the nature of the cases cited by FDA to "prove" Vitamin A is toxic: A four-month-old baby, who showed signs of toxicity after being dosed with 240,000 units of Vitamin A daily, for three months. (In the same scale of overdose, table salt will kill, but FDA hasn't moved to limit the size of salt containers, or to put an RX label on larger ones.)

## ASTHMA

In controlling asthma, the preceding notes concerning the common cold assume heightened importance, for in many asthmatics, an upper respiratory injection is prelude to an attack. Control of alergies is likewise vital in the type of asthma (there *is* more than one type) in which food allergies are involved. The rotation diet, the use of Vitamin A or C to abort colds, the employment of an autogenous vaccine to raise resistance to colds, and desensitization of the patient to molds, pollen, and dust may be critical in helping some asthmatics. I have already commented on the type of asthma which appears to be directly linked to an underlying hypoglycemia, and which is controlled (or even disappears) when the low blood sugar itself is brought under control. We don't have space or time to describe the evidence behind these remarks about hypoglycemia, but you might remember these points:
1. Hypoglycemia triggers or intensifies allergic reactions.
2. Diabetics (unless they simultaneously have low blood

sugar, which coincidence does occur) virtually never have asthma.

3. Asthma has been known to disappear when diabetes has developed.

Those nutrients which are involved helpfully in allergies will often be useful to the physician in management of the allergic type of asthma. Included would be multiple vitamins and minerals, and the Vitamin B Complex, as general supplements to the diet. Important are those nutrients which help to normalize the permeability of the cell walls: Vitamin C, bioflavonoids, Vitamin E, Vitamin B12, and calcium. (There are a few cases on record where administration of Vitamin B12 not only has spurted growth in undersized children, but mitigated or eliminated asthma.) Of special interest is the action of nutrients important in pituitary-adrenal function. These would include calcium pantothenate, Vitamin C, Vitamin E, and paba. It should be noted: *Paba, being synergistic with insulin, can't be used in large amounts by hypoglycemics, who already are overproducing insulin.*

The restricted diet in an asthma based on food allergies may induce deficiencies which will worsen the patient's disorder. In addition, the allergic do not absorb and utilize foods as efficiently as those free of allergies. Malabsorption, malutilization, and a restricted diet are debilitating factors of prime importance, correction of which is essential to many asthmatics, and, for that matter, for many with other types of allergy.

## ANEMIA

Anemia, to the average reader, is a simple disorder which occurs in two forms: iron-deficiency, easily rectified with doses of iron, and pernicious anemia, for which one takes Vitamin B12. If matters were so ordered, there would be no such medical specialty as *hematology*. There are anemias caused by lack of nutrients other than iron, associated with lack of certain of the B vitamins, for instance; and there are serious and even life-threatening anemias which involve degeneration of the bone marrow; and pernicious anemia, though it does involve a need for Vitamin B12, is a disorder with a complex of possible causes, among them a lack of hydrochloric acid, a deficiency in an internal factor which is needed as a "conveyor" for Vitamin B12, and, in some cases, a deficiency in biochemical vehicles (transcobalamins) needed for proper utilization of that vitamin. There may also be involved a deficiency in folic acid, and, in fact, there is little logic in taking Vitamin B12 without accompanying doses of folic acid.

Beyond all this, there is an overriding compulsion on the physician to be sure that the anemia, rather than involving dietary deficiency or a breakdown in blood cell manufacture, or an interference with transport of nutrients, does not originate with hidden hemmorhaging. Which all adds up to the familiar warning: Don't try self-diagnosis. Your simple "iron-deficiency anemia" may be anything but simple, and your protection may require a great deal more than supplements of iron. If you do need iron supplements, it is well to remember that simultaneous use of Vitamin C will help iron absorption, and that both folic acid and Vitamin B12, even when the anemia is not pernicious, may be useful in helping iron utilization. The scope of the problem, whatever the type of anemia, goes beyond "tired blood." Anemia can make you prone to infection; and infection may tend to make you anemic. That's a vicious cycle you'll do well to avoid.

None of the preceding should let you forget that there are many people who do suffer from iron-deficiency anemia, which is a totally unnecessary debilitating factor. Not only that, but before the blood reveals the lack of iron, you may show the deficiency (in lowered activity of two iron-containing enzymes) with the kind of fatigue and irritability ordinarily attributed to anemia itself. Another misconcept has to do with Vitamin B12. To read most medical papers on the subject is to come to the conclusion that only pernicious anemia is an excuse for taking doses or injections of Vitamin B12. This is simply not so, for two good reasons: You may be deficient in the vitamin, not show any sign of anemia, and yet be suffering from degeneration of the nervous system or brain, for lack of the vitamin. Here the only symptom may be paranoid behavior (delusions of persecution). It is estimated that at least 1 percent of the "senile paranoids" tucked away in institutions and sanitariums could be rescued with injection of Vitamin B12.

Another relevant observation: Vitamin B12 has been used successfully in the treatment of herpes simplex and herpes zoster (cold sores and shingles), neither condition having anything to do with anemia, and neither, in fact, caused by deficiency in the vitamin. This is an excellent example of the fallacy of the statement that only a person deficient in a vitamin profits by doses of it. The vitamin has also been used in orthomolecular psychiatry, in the treatment of weak, tired, irritable, and indecisive patients. Some of them have responded beautifully, even though their blood levels of Vitamin B12 were within "normal range." Normal for whom becomes again the critical question.

Iron deficiency anemia is much more common in women than in men. This, obviously, is a distinction based on the loss of iron in the menstrual cycle. For this reason, an iron deficiency anemia in men is likely to spur the physician into a search for hidden hemorrhaging, since men conserve and recycle their iron supplies without the monthly loss. That loss in women raises their iron requirement to eighteen mgs. daily, a figure which will have no meaning to the average woman until I tell her that it requires 1,000 calories of well-selected foods to supply six mgs. of iron. How many women can consume 3,000 calories daily? Given a choice between obesity and anemia, the average woman will unhesitatingly choose being anemic. Here is a classic example of the need for supplements; eighteen mgs. of iron in tablet form, as part of a multiple mineral supplement, exacts no calorie toll at all.

While liver is a source of all the known blood-building nutrients, it should be emphasized that dried brewer's yeast has a significant amount of the antipernicious anemia factor for which liver became famous. It is a cheaper source, and one which, in a palatable form—which does exist—more people are likely to use regularly. Your health food store carries numerous brands of brewer's yeast. Select one labeled *primary*, which means it is not a byproduct of brewing, but grown specifically to be used as a dietary supplement, in which case it is likely to offer higher potencies of its natural vitamins and other factors. And do select a brand which is palatable. People don't profit by what they refuse to swallow. Dosage recommendations, if that is the proper term to use for this good food, will be on the label. If they aren't, try two to three teaspoonfuls of brewer's yeast daily, or the equivalent in tablets. It can be blended into drinks, baked into bread (not for leavening, but for food value) or incorporated in recipes for meatloaf, hamburger, and similar dishes. Start with small amounts, and test as you increase the concentration, so that you protect flavor and palatability of your recipe.

Brewer's yeast should remind us that blood is not built from iron and vitamins alone. Blood is a protein substance, and sizable amounts of protein are needed to raise hemoglobin. Brewer's yeast averages from about 40 percent protein to high in the 50s. Other types of protein sources should, of course, be used. Pork liver is excellent—an inexpensive form of the organ meat which happens to be more nutritious than that which the public prefers, such as calf's liver. Other foods rich in blood-building properties will be listed for you at the end of this section.

Chelated forms of iron and other blood-building metals—copper, for instance—are available. In these, the metal is "wrapped" within a protein blanket, which, because of the electrical charge carried by such a compound, promotes better absorption from the digestive tract.

Here is the promised list of blood-building foods:
MEATS:
    Liver—all kinds, but particularly pork liver; one large serving (three ounces) should be included in the diet three or four times a week.
    Kidney

Beef
Chicken—gizzard
Lamb
Pork
EGGS
FRUITS:
Apricots
Peaches
Prunes
Raisins
Two or three servings of fruit selected from this group
should be included in the diet daily.
VEGETABLES:
Beet greens
Lettuce

It is often difficult to induce anemic individuals to eat
some of the distasteful foods recommended, especially since
to be effective they must be repeated over and over again in
the diet. Here are a few suggestions, which the ingenious
housewife can add to the diet:
Ground dried apricots, prunes and raisins may be soft-
ened with lemon juice and used as a spread on whole
wheat date and nut bread.
Using the same fruits, plus nuts and lemon juice, form the
mixture into balls or squares and dip into brown sugar.
To make liver—even pork liver—palatable, bake covered
with tomato juice, onions, green peppers and celery.
Grind small amounts of liver into meat loaf and meat
balls.

## KEEPING BLOOD VESSELS YOUNG

Arteriosclerosis—the "normal" hardening of the arteries,
and atherosclerosis—hardening of the arteries in a degree
threatening health or life itself—are subjects of great controversy in both medicine and nutrition.
Those satisfied with very simple explanations of very com-

plex phenomena have "solved" the problem of atherosclerosis by changing the diet to reduce intake of cholesterol, a fatty substance involved in hardening of the arteries, and dropping the level of animal fat in the diet. To justify this, they point to studies of various nations and ethnic groups who eat much cholesterol and animal fat, and have serious problems with diseases of the blood vessels and the heart. Seldom does the public (or, for that matter, the profession) realize that this evidence is handpicked, at the expense of ignoring nations and ethnic groups who eat such diets, and yet escape blood vessel and heart disorders. Quick examples: the Masais, in Africa, who eat gargantuan quantities of meat and consume large amounts of blood, both rich in cholesterol and fat. Yet hardening of the arteries and coronary heart disease are *not* problems for the Masais. This is an example—and there are many others—of ugly facts which are ignored by enthusiastic theoreticians. A celebrated heart surgeon has remarked that he has opened innumerable arteries, but has never been able to find a significant correlation between the level of blood cholesterol and the condition of the artery walls. Any statistician will tell you that a correlation is at best no proof of a causal relationship; and an insignificant correlation has no meaning at all.

Despite all this, the anticholesterol drive among the professions has reached levels which, obtained in any scientific cause involving the public, would be called faddism. Meat production is being revised to place emphasis on lean meat. Small babies are being deprived of butterfat. Egg sales have been sharply depressed. The public, never overfond of organ meats, is wary of such good foods as liver, condemned because it is a rich source of cholesterol. The scientist is appalled by this—if only because he knows that the first invader of the artery wall isn't cholesterol at all—it is an abnormal molecule of sugar combined with protein—a glycoprotein. Nor is cholesterol the sole constituent of the subsequent deposition, for calcium figures in the deposits, too.

Nor is this series of observations the sole basis of the thinking of those who are less than enthusiastic about the cholesterol theory and the anticholesterol school of diet. The proposition is deceptively simple: This obstructive fat, cholesterol, deposits on the arterial walls; therefore all you need do is eat a diet which eliminates, or at least minimizes cholesterol intake. But this simple approach can be negated by another (and simple) observation: Most of the cholesterol in the body doesn't come from the diet, but is synthesized by the body itself. Moreover, should the dietary supply be reduced to the point where the body's need for cholesterol is not being satisfied, internal production would undoubtedly be increased. Which emphasizes a point too often overlooked: Cholesterol is needed by the body for the manufacture of sex hormones and many other vital factors. It is *not* merely a mischief-making fatty substance; it is vital to life itself.

To get rid of cholesterol in the diet requires tabooing not only foods containing it, but those supplying the animal fats from which cholesterol is manufactured by the body. The taboos would fill several pages: You would have to eliminate all fatty meats and minimize your intake of the less fatty. Butter would be banned; likewise, cream, and cheeses, other than those with a low-fat content, such as cottage cheese (uncreamed). All organ meats would be deleted. Eggs would be a particular no-no. Even olive oil would be suspect, since its oleic acid reacts more like animal than like vegetable fat. Shrimp and other types of seafoods would be eliminated, in favor of the white-fleshed (less fatty) types. Milk would be forbidden, unless defatted. Cakes and other baked products made with butter or eggs would be eliminated. Which brings us to the point: The high-cholesterol foods almost invariably turn out to be foods which are also rich in essential nutrients. They can be partially replaced, if one has the expertise to make proper selections, but only by use of more knowledge of nutrition than the average consumer possesses. Some of the high-cholesterol foods have unique and irreplaceable values; there is really no animal protein that gives you what liver does, for example. Thus the net result of a low-cholesterol diet may be low (poor) nutrition, which helps no one. Yet there are scientists who seem willing to sacrifice every organ in the body in an effort to protect the arteries against atherosclerosis. What profit if you die young, with healthy arteries?

In order to understand why I have described the low-cholesterol diet as an oversimplified and unsatisfactory answer to a very complex problem, let's assume that I am practicing preventive medicine, and you come to my laboratory for the specific purpose of protecting yourself against hardening of the arteries and the heart disease associated with it. The following are some of the questions to which I would be compelled, in justice to you, to find answers:

1. What is the condition of your thyroid? This gland controls blood cholesterol levels, to some extent, and it is known that thyroid-treated patients rarely have heart attacks.

2. What kind of water flows from the taps in your home—hard water or soft? It is known that heart attacks are significantly higher in soft-water areas than in hard-water areas. This is true, regardless of levels of blood cholesterol.

3. What does your blood chemistry show in uric acid levels, triglycerides (which are manufactured from sugar and which may be more threatening than cholesterol), high-density lipoproteins, fasting insulin levels, and responses to a sugar-tolerance test? (The last because both diabetics and hypoglycemics may be more susceptible than normals to blood vessel and heart disease.)

4. What is the blood-pressure response to immersing your wrists in cold water? To exercise?

5. Is your profession one that demands adherence to deadlines, and resistance to constant pressures? And are you a hard-driving personality or one who attempts to substitute the power of money for the power of love? (Don't laugh: These personality characteristics have been meaningfully related to increased likelihood of heart attacks.)

6. To what extent does stress change your blood chemistry?

The list is partial, and could be amplified, but even this short presentation must lead to grave doubts concerning the competence of those who would have you believe that reducing egg consumption to three per week (a fine example of numerology) is the key to flexible arteries and a healthy heart.

There *are* those whose bodies mishandle cholesterol. That group in the population may benefit by restriction of intake of fat (animal) and cholesterol. But one does not forbid strawberries to the entire public because some people get a strawberry rash. And one does not tinker with the dietary habits of hundreds of millions of people on the basis of the idiosyncrasies of a population subset. Particularly when such manipulation of the diet can and often does lead the public into even poorer nutrition than it usually consumes.

Years ago, physicians prescribed a drug which interrupted the synthesis of cholesterol in the body. So many people developed falling hair, skin disorders, and eye disease that the lawyers representing them, in suing the pharmaceutical manufacturer, formed a national association, to avoid duplication of legal effort. Surely the incident should emphasize how far into the unknown we go when we tell people that the diet on which, over millions of years, they evolved, must abruptly be drastically changed. For man's evolutionary diet was that of the hunter and the herdsman, who had no puffed rice, no bread, no sugar bowl, but a generous intake of cholesterol and animal fat, associated with a high protein diet.

When the cholesterol theory was first proposed, many observers turned to the Eskimos to demonstrate that a high intake of this fat didn't necessarily cause vascular (blood vessel) and heart disease, for these primitives, eating great quantities of blubber, are largely immune to such disorders. The cholesterol faddists responded by pointing out that Eskimos die young—too young, it seemed, to allow the atherosclerosis to develop. Entirely apart from the fact that there are no reliable statistics on the lifespan of the truly primitive, this claim was actually negated by another one made by the anticholesterol group, for they told us that even our young men show advanced atherosclerosis. Why, then, were the Eskimos spared? There came the ultimate answer: The problem lies not in cholesterol alone, but in the amount of animal fat accompanying it. It is the combination, they said, which is lethal. And that led us into our modern-day emphasis on margarine, salad oil, and other sources of vegetable (unsaturated) fat. Which in turn led inevitably to another of the extremes to which faddism takes us. A group of patients were placed on a diet in which all fats were of vegetable origin. Their heart-attack rate did go down, but their cancer rate rose, as a sharp reminder that all this tinkering with the diet can take us into uncharted areas, and bring unexpected hazards.

Meanwhile, thoughtful nutritionists were pointing to the importance of specific dietary factors which help us to utilize fats. These include many of the Vitamins—B6, choline, inositol, and Vitamins E and B12. Emphasis was placed on the usefulness of lecithin, in helping the body to transport and utilize fats. Many of these nutritionists—myself, included—observed patients whose blood cholesterol, in the face of a generous dietary intake of the factor—fell when these nutrients were supplied in generous amounts. And those are some of the reasons for the repeated suggestion in this book: It is sane to supplement your diet with generous potencies of the Vitamin B Complex, which would include pyridoxin (B6), Vitamin E, B12, choline, and inositol; and with a half-dozen nineteen-grain capsules of lecithin, daily. I have seen abnormally high levels of cholesterol sharply reduced by this procedure, sans any change in the diet, and the reduction increased by moderate curtailment of cholesterol intake, with a moderate increase in intake of polyunsaturated fat, such as cottonseed oil, safflower, corn oil, etc. "Moderate intake" of vegetable oil means what it says: about 20 percent of the total fat intake derived from such oils—not more.

For those who already have mild cases of atherosclerosis, therapeutic doses of these nutrients may bring significant benefit. For those who also have a history of heart attacks, such therapy may likewise be helpful. In either case, the treatment should be medically supervised.

When hardening of the arteries is advanced, these nutrient therapies may be helpful, but they are unlikely to reverse the condition. When atherosclerosis is markedly interfering with circulation, to the point of causing senile behavior, for example, the prime therapy is chelation—a technique by which the doctor may actually be able to strip significant amounts of the deposits from the vessels. Chelation is—like all medical treatments—not 100 percent innocuous, and must be administered by an expert specializing in that type of treatment. Your physician can obtain information from the American Academy of Medical Preventics, Suite 207, 11311 Camarillo Street, North Hollywood, California. The information will not be sent to laymen, but those who do not have physicians can obtain from the Academy lists of practitioners who are experienced in such therapy. When chelation is performed, the nutritional treatments usually accompany it. Remarkable benefits have been achieved, some of them in very advanced cases of atherosclerosis and heart disease associated with it.

All of the preceding statements have taken you, the reader, far away from the simplistic statement that cholesterol is *the* mischief maker in vascular and heart disease, with animal fat as its helper. Which is as it should be: The body is a complex organism, and its problems very rarely susceptible of simple solutions.

## ARTHRITIS, RHEUMATIC FEVER

Numerous special diets have been proposed for arthritis. But the term "arthritis" does not describe a single disorder, and it is highly unlikely that any one system of diet would prove healing for all types. There is osteoarthritis, wrongly labeled as a "wear and tear" disease—wrongly, because it reflects a metabolic disturbance, which, unlike wear-and-tear, can be corrected. There is rheumatic arthritis, an entirely different type of disorder. There is hypertrophic arthritis, and menopausal, and traumatic, and Marie Strumpel, and one which is associated with psoriasis. For these good reasons, I back away from authors who claim to have the secret of diet in arthritis. That, though, doesn't detract at all from the benefits of corrected diet for arthritics, even though the Arthritis Foundation has assured the public that nutrition has nothing to offer in these diseases—that poor nutrition doesn't cause, and good nutrition doesn't yield benefits in arthritic disorders. (I know of two vitamins markedly helpful in types of arthritis, for example.) In any large group of arthritics, one will find the usual distribution of dietary histories—ranging from atrocious, to fair, to good nutrition; and correction of inadequacies in nutrition *always* yields dividends, in arthritis or any other disorder. It is time that the establishment in arthritis research paid some attention to the nutrition of the patients whose treatment they influence.

As an example of progress which has been neglected, consider the term "hypertrophic arthritis." It refers to a crippling type, in which the hands and fingers are likely to be deformed and useless. Dr. John Ellis, pioneer in vitamin research in this kind of arthritis, thinks the term "hypertrophic arthritis" to be a misnomer. He labels the condition as resulting squarely from deficiencies in Vitamin B6 and in potassium, and has demonstrated repeatedly that function can be restored to crippled hands with doses of these nutrients—Vitamin B6 in tablet form, potassium from oranges, bananas, tomato juice, and other foods rich in the mineral. His evidence includes photographs, taken before and after such treatment, pictures the establishment manages to ignore. Those interested in Dr. Ellis' research in hypertrophic arthritis will profit by reading *The Doctor Who Looked at Hands,* available in paperback.

There are very few scientific papers and competent textbooks offering evidence of direct relationships between poor nutrition and the onset of arthritis, or direct therapeutic benefits from nutritional treatment of this group of diseases. This fact does not negate such relationships; it simply points to the neglect of this subject by a drug-oriented medical establishment. Equally neglected is the indirect evidence. For example, we know that nutrition may favorably or unfavorably influence the functioning of the adrenal glands, and we know that adrenal function in rheumatoid arthritis is obviously not normal. No one has put these two isolated facts together, and arrived at a synthesis which might—and from my observations would—be of benefit to patients with this disease. This chapter will record some of this evidence.

Low protein intake, and particularly, failure to eat eggs, has been found to be a frequent characteristic of patients with rheumatic fever and rheumatoid arthritis. Ironically, such patients, sometimes because of poverty, sometimes because of ignorance, sometimes because of allergies, have bypassed the protein foods, and emphasized the carbohydrates: starches and sugars. This is ironic, for many of these sufferers manifest a disturbance of carbohydrate metabolism, i.e., they are preferring the type of food their bodies are least able to utilize properly.

During the First World War, trench fever—which was probably rheumatic fever—was as frequent among American troops, plied with doughnuts and coffee, as it was infrequent among British troops, who complained about their monotonous diet of bully beef. It has been observed that children with rheumatic fever more often than not have a history of not eating eggs. It has also been observed that extra eggs in their diets proved therapeutically more beneficial than the customary treatment with antibiotics, such as penicillin. Yet no one has followed up this lead, and no one has investigated the added dividends which might accrue if the medical treatment were combined with the nutritional therapy. At any rate, in the medical literature is a record of children with severe rheumatic fever, who were treated with two extra eggs daily, over and above their accustomed intake, and whose progress was compared with that of children with mild cases of rheumatic fever who were treated with penicillin. The egg-consuming youngsters improved so much that, by the end of the trial, their cases were relatively lighter than those of the children given the antibiotic. Whether this was a response to added intake of high-quality protein, of which eggs are the best source, or to a unique constituent of eggs was never determined.

Processed starches and sugars, such as white flour, white rice, white sugar and other unnatural foods eaten in great quantities by the public, act as a stress upon the pituitary and adrenal glands. The use of adrenal hormones, such as cortisone, in rheumatoid arthritis reminds us that adrenal function is critical in this disease. Eating foods which burden that glandular system is therefore obviously prejudicial to the recovery of rheumatoid arthritic patients. The disease itself is a stress on the organism; adding a second stress, from improper diet, often proves to be the proverbial added straw, for it is a characteristic of the body's stress-resisting machinery that it is geared to cope with only one insult at a time. When distorted diets are reported to be helpful in this type of arthritis—such as a seafood diet—one wonders whether it is the presence of the seafood or the absence of the processed carbohydrates in these menus which has proved beneficial. There is also some slight evidence that polyunsaturated fats, in which seafood is often rich, may act to stimulate the pituitary-adrenal system.

Other nutrients are singularly important to adrenal function. The glands rest heavily on adequate intake of Vitamin C. Their content of the vitamin is depleted in seconds, after a heavy stress has been applied to the body. Under such circumstances, those animals which manufacture Vitamin C for themselves will up their output by a factor of seven, reaching a level equivalent, for a human being, of 14,000 mgs. of Vitamin C daily. Failures reported with Vitamin C "therapy" in rheumatic disorders have invariably been based on the use of relatively small amounts of the vitamin—100 to 200 mgs. daily. In those trials where the dose was raised to between 2,000 and 10,000 mgs. daily, very favorable results were obtained. Were this not so, saturation with Vitamin C may still be a desirable goal in the rheumatic diseases, for the vitamin is essential to the body's synthesis of collagen—the "glue" that binds our cells together, and in these diseases, the collagen is defective and structurally weak. There is also the problem of excessive permeability of the tissues, allowing fluid to collect: Vitamin C, bioflavonoids, and calcium are among a long list of nutrients required to maintain normal permeability. Even Vitamin E and Vitamin B12, as remote as their principal functions may be from their effects on the permeability of cell membranes, may be useful.

The high-protein, high-fat (with 20 percent of it derived from vegetable sources) and low-carbohydrate diet is to me the starting point for testing correction of the nutrition of the patient with a rheumatic disease. In addition to the vitamins already mentioned, there are several which may be of pointed usefulness. Paba, which is a B-Complex vitamin, has the effect of "sparing" (or working with) the cortisone type of hormone. It can be used to reduce the dose of cortisone required, while still maintaining the drug's effectiveness; or it can be used to help the patient better to respond to his own (endogenous) production of the hormone. Pantothenic acid (calcium pantothenate or equivalent) may also be helpful. It is requisite to normal function of the adrenal glands, and it helps to block adverse effects of cortisone on the stomach, an action of the hormone which may be responsible for causing peptic ulcer.

In osteoarthritis, the most successful treatments I have witnessed were those employed by Esther Tuttle, M.D., and those of the Nelson Clinic, in Beverly Hills, California. Dr. Tuttle is deceased, and I don't know if the clinic is still operating, but the principles they enunciated remain visable: This form of arthritis reflects a treatable metabolic disturbance, and isn't a wear-and-tear disease which, by its very title, must be endured. Dr. Nelson treated his patients with calcium (among other factors), which to laymen—with a disorder in which calcium deposits are part of the problem—seems at first hand to be irrational. Actually, the calcium deposits are an effort by the body to protect an area against stress. That effort will continue, with or without adequate supplies of calcium in the diet. The difference: If external calcium is not supplied, the deposits will form from calcium withdrawn from the body's reserves. This adds the toll of calcium deficiency to the problem. Nelson's philosophy viewed osteoarthritis as analogous to a fracture that refuses to unite. A well-balanced diet, supplemented with the essential vitamins and minerals, and accompanied by proper physiotherapy has proved helpful (to the point of restoring function) in many patients. Don't forget, as you reread this chapter, that we have positive evidence that arthritis occurs less frequently in well-fed people, despite the negative views of the arthritis establishment.

Years ago, Longstroth studied two groups of hospitalized patients: the first, essentially healthy, but bedded because of accidents; the second, with the same age distribution, hospitalized because of degenerative diseases, such as arthritis. The only significant difference he could find in the history of the two groups was in their diets. The accident victims, free of degenerative disease, had eaten diets higher in "protective factors"—for which our latter-day names are protein, unsaturated fats, vitamins, and minerals. Thus the hypoglycemia type of diet, an example of which is found in this book, would be a starting point to explore nutrition in arthritis; and the supplements recommended with it would be rational, too. I state this as a starting point because we are dealing with several variables, simultaneously: the type of arthritis, and the type of patients who have it. Less beef and more fish might prove the formula for some arthritics; less processed carbohydrates would probably be beneficial for a large majority; more unsaturated fat would benefit a substantial group, and harm no one. Individual differences in nutritional needs and tolerances become critically important in managing individual responses to the disease process.

Though there is always the search for the overnight cure, the fact is that the glandular imbalances or metabolic disturbances which caused arthritis were a long time in developing, and the disorder doesn't show a fast response to anything—aside from extremely potent drugs with side reactions which may be worse than the disease. Be patient with the science of nutrition; allow it a few months in which to try to help you. Work with your medical nutritionist, and be fair to him and yourself. Cheating on your diet, supplements, medications, or physiotherapy is unrewarding.

## NUTRITION VERSUS CANCER

Despite claims made for this diet or that as a "cancer cure," I have yet, in some forty years of observation, encountered a patient with a verifiable claim to a diet-induced recovery from cancer. Improvement in some, yes; cure, no. That statement applies to the Gerson diet and all other variations on the theme. Not being certain that all types of cancer are one single disease, I can't easily accept one diet system as therapeutic for all cancer cases. I am particularly interested in the fact that many of the diets for cancer lean heavily on the vegetarian side, and discourage the intake of animal protein—interested because two of my friends who were lifelong and very strict vegetarians both died with cancer.

All this doesn't subtract from the importance of nutrition in preventing cancer, and its usefulness of treating precancerous changes in tissues. Ignorance of these facts in laymen is understandable, but it is less forgivable in physicians. A few months before these lines were written, an aged physician, associated with the Mayo Clinic, vigorously denied my statement that leukoplakia—a precancerous disorder—can be cured with vitamin therapy. One would think I had been expressing a personal, and undocumented theory. Actually, niacinamide treatment for leukoplakia was reported successful, in one of the medical journals, more than twenty years ago. More recently, a medical nutritionist with whom I shared the scientific platform in a nutrition panel at a medical convention, reported successful treatment of leukoplakia with Vitamin A in large doses. Ignorance in the aged physician is deplorable enough; opinionated ignorance deprives his patients of a harmless and effective treatment.

Similarly, precancerous changes in the tissues of the throat have been reversed with Vitamin A. Tongue and mouth lesions of the type caused by persistent irritation from a broken tooth or a pipestem have been cured with large doses of Vitamin B Complex.

In preventing cancer, a number of important observations have been made, demonstrating that nutrition alone can help to raise resistance. It has been demonstrated that rats fed on a diet of hospital scraps are less likely to develop cancer if the diet is supplemented with brewer's yeast, which is a source of the Vitamin B Complex. It has been shown that the very high resistance of African primitives to bowel cancer, one of our common causes of death from cancer, can be logically traced to the high intake of fiber in the native diet—an observation which strengthens the indictment of our white flour, white rice, degerminated corn meal, white sugar, and other overprocessed cereals, grains, and flour. For in addition to depleting their content of vitamins, minerals, and other protective factors, this type of processing drastically lowers the fiber content of the American diet. A low-fiber intake tends to slow down excretion of food residues, and to induce constipation. This allows the bowel bacteria more time in which to attack certain chemicals normal to the stool; and that attack, it is known, converts these chemicals into carcinogenic (cancer-causing) factors. As the passage of the stool is abnormally delayed, and the chemical changes take place, the lower bowel is literally bathed in carcinogens—constantly, and for periods of years. Net result: bowel cancer. By way of added proof: The African native loses his immunity to bowel cancer when he deserts his native diet, and switches to ours. Which comes as no surprise: Our blacks are genetically related to the African primitive, but don't share his immunity to bowel cancer—indeed, have the same deadly rate of the disease which decimates us.

Another type of cancer which may be prevented nutritionally is breast cancer, and cancer of the uterus. Documented both by the literature and by my own research, which I have reported in several papers before medical societies, is the statement that estrogen (female hormone) can be responsible for cancers of the estrogen-dependent type, which are common in American women. The control of estrogenic activity in the body is vested in the liver, but can't be exercised unless the liver is generously supplied with Vitamin B Complex and protein. Given dietary emphasis (or the use of supplements) of this type, women respond gratifyingly. The first dividends are reduction of pre-menstrual tension, backache, cramp, and water retention with weight gain. Second, reduction of both the intensity of menstrual hemorrhaging, and its duration. Shortening of the cycle from five days to three is a common benefit from such nutrition. Third, many women respond with reduction of the size and the number of breast cysts—not only of those appearing prior to the menstrual, but those of the lingering (cystic mastitis) type. The fourth dividend is rarer, but does occur occasionally: cessation of growth or actual shrinkage of uterine fibroid tumors. Theory indicates that endometriosis should also respond, but in this disorder, I do not have sufficient observations to warrant a statement. And theory finally justifies this hope: Reduction of the activity of female hormone will help to prevent estrogen-dependent cancers of breast and uterus. And if all this does not impress you, consider the type of surgery recommended for the woman with an estrogen-dependent breast cancer: removal of the ovaries, to bring down the body's estrogen load. It makes more sense to me to reduce that load *now*— before the cancer eventuates. I might add that I take a dim view of searching for lumps, as a means of preventing breast cancer. By the time a lump is palpable, the cancer may already be five years en route.

The fact that rats raised under a lead roof have less cancer should remind us that the disorder—whether it is one disease or a hundred—has many causes. But causes operate only in a cooperative host. Which is to say that the insult is measured by the soil on which it falls. Be a well-nourished soil, and keep your resistance up.

The types of Vitamin B Complex supplements needed to control estrogen activity are those which supply generous amounts of choline and inositol, plus, of course, the other B Vitamins. A natural source of the B Complex, to supply the unknown factors, is also needed. Desiccated liver is a good choice. Lecithin may also be helpful. If your physician wishes to accelerate the process, he can prescribe mettionine, taken by mouth, and Vitamin B12, taken by injection. Paba and folic acid, which tend to increase estrogenic activity, should not be taken or if taken, should be used in very small amounts by women with estrogen-dependent disorders. The diet itself should supply up to ninety grams of protein daily, with the majority of it taken from animal sources, i.e., meat, fish, fowl, eggs, milk, and cheeses.

As we go to press with this book, the newspapers are announcing that a western university has indicted estrogen, as provided in the birth control pills, as a cause of the rise of cancer of the uterus in postmenopausal women. Prevention isn't as dramatic as surgery, irradiation, and chemotherapy—but don't you think it makes more sense?

## CONSTIPATION

When you say that you "haven't the guts to stand the situation" you are saying that the colon is a mirror of the emotions. Since it's also a mirror of the diet, it's not surprising that the colon is the frequent victim of a number of disorders, most of them extremely common in civilized man, and extremely rare in primitives. Granted that we can't shield ourselves from the stresses of civilization, but we *can* free ourselves from the limitations and the liabilities of civilized diet, and if we do, constipation will be only one of a number of digestive disorders from which we'll escape. For there is no doubt that appendicitis, like constipation, is a disease of civilization. So are diverticular disorders, diverticulitis, hiatus hernia, hemorrhoids, anal fissures, and bowel cancer. These diseases are rare to the vanishing point in, for instance, African primitives—unless they have fallen prey to the siren call of our processed and convenience foods. There appears no doubt, then, that we export our sicknesses when we export our diet. Should we not look at the primitive's food, and discover what it is that shields him from our melancholy digestive disorders?

I have already pointed out that the fiber content of the primitive diet is higher than ours, and traced the chemistry by which this one entity in the diet may protect against bowel cancer. In this chapter, we will examine that process in more detail, so you may understand what you do to yourself when you eat white bread, white rice, white sugar, and the other processed carbohydrates—degerminated and deprived of fiber—which comprise the chief source of calories in the average American diet. Lack of fiber touches off a chain of consequences in the colon, beginning with prolongation of stool-transit-time. This is simply a medical phrase for the length of time it takes for food residues, the debris left after food digestion, to traverse the colon, arrive at the bowel, and leave the body. Many laymen assume that stool transit time is abnormally long only when constipation is present, but this is a misconception. One can have a bowel movement every day, and still be the victim of abnormally slow stool transit time—because Monday's bowel movement should have taken place on the preceding Saturday. When constipation is added to the problem the situation becomes more abnormal, and more threatening. The threat arises because the bowel bacteria in a person on a low fiber diet are not of the friendly type, which they should be; and because, with a delayed stool transit time, those bacteria vent their unfriendliness by breaking down chemicals normal to the stool, and converting them into powerful carcinogenic (cancer-producing) substances. The mischief is compounded when those chemicals, thanks both to constipation and delayed stool transit, remain in prolonged contact with the bowel, thereby given the better opportunity to work their mischief.

Normal to the stool is a high content of bile. In the ordinary course of (healthy) events, the bile and its chemicals would quickly pass through the colon and the bowel, and exit with the stool. Given slow transit time and constipation, the bile is subjected to the unfriendly action of the abnormal bacteria. Two bile acids, normally harmless, are converted into extremely potent carcinogenic factors. Here is believed to be the origin of our appalling incidence of bowel cancer, which is high on the list of cancer-caused deaths—not far behind lung cancer. Conversely, bowel cancer in African primitives is a rarity. But then, so is appendicitis, and the explanation for the African's immunity to this disorder, so common in our civilization, is based on another aspect of the same phenomena: high-fiber diet keeps stool transit time down, and doesn't allow the congestion conducive to infection of the appendix; and absence of constipation prevents the formation of fecaliths, little hard pellets of stool, which can enter the appendix, and start the process of congestion and infection.

Several explanations are given for hiatus hernia, diverticular disease, diverticulitis, varicose veins, and hemorrhoids. They hover about the tremendous pressures exerted on the colon by the constipated individual who strains at stool. An alternate theory deals with the pressures exerted by the stool itself, when the colon is literally overpacked, and the stool is hard. Although the theories are far from mutually exclusive, both causes could be operative at once, they converge in an identical conclusion: Low-fiber diet makes for the troubles. Many nutritionists have found these criticisms of white bread and other overprocessed carbohydrates to be ironic, considering that many of us were labeled as food faddists in the years when those who recommended whole wheat bread were excommunicated in the scientific world. However justified their "I told you so's," the answer to the problem does not lie in eating whole grains alone, although that is an essential step toward the beginning of solving the problem. But the deficiency of fiber in the American diet cannot be overcome merely by choosing whole grain flour, breads, and cereals, for we also make the mistake of eating enormous quantities of white sugar—and the lack of fiber in that travesty of a food is too profound to be offset with a few slices of fiber-rich bread. Consider that the amount of fiber removed from sugar is so great that, as a by-product of the sugar industry, it is used to manufacture wallboard. (That's the ultimate destination of the bagasse, the industry's name for the fiber of the sugar cane.)

To compensate for the deficiency in fiber in the 120 pounds of sugar eaten yearly by the average American, one must add fiber itself to the diet. The most convenient, effective, and inexpensive way of doing that is by use of bran—unheated, unprocessed, and cheap. When this suggestion is made, medical men and dietitians of the older school will be quick to point out that many of the patients with diverticular disease aren't able to tolerate roughage. Some of them can't; most of them not only can, but may rid themselves of their symptoms by raising their fiber intake. The prejudice against roughage in disorders conventionally treated with bland, low-roughage diets is gradually disappearing, not only because clinical results with bran feeding have been so rewarding, but because the realization has grown that bran is not really roughage. If anything, because of its properties and propensity for absorbing fluid, it is "soft bulkage." Its effect is to increase the size (volume) of abnormally small, hard stools, and to soften them; and to decrease the size of abnormally large stools.

Bran may be added to many recipes—bread, cookies, muffins, pancakes, waffles. It may be sprinkled on cereals or added to berries. Bran is also available in tablet and lozenge form, for those who find these more convenient. It is generally offered in both coarse and fine grind. The coarse is more effective, but some individuals are more tolerant of the finer material. Expensive blends of bran combined with vegetable fiber are being marketed. I don't find them anymore effective, and they are much more costly.

To anticipate the question of how much bran an adult should use, note that different amounts accomplish different results for different people. We usually start with a teaspoonful of bran with each meal. Some people require two teaspoonfuls. Some may need up to three tablespoonfuls daily. Judgment is made on the basis of what is happening with the bowel movement. When it is largely free of odor (a frequent dividend), formed well and large in amount, and requires no straining in evacuation, the right level of bran intake has been established. Too much laxative effect, of course, signals the need to reduce bran intake.

While this step speeds stool transit time, helps to get rid of constipation, and encourages a more friendly type of bowel bacteria (which are less inclined to attack the stool and change its chemistry), there are other aids which can be employed. The Vitamin B Complex is extremely important to both digestive and eliminative function, and a supplement of that type is useful. So is brewer's yeast. So is yogurt, but only if taken in generous amounts, and regularly. Use a container daily, and *don't* compound your problem by buying yogurt which contains fruit or other flavors, for that is simply returning to a big dose of fiber-free sugar. A multiple vitamin-mineral supplement is also helpful, and so is the use of wheat germ. In fact, wheat germ, fortified with bran—which is a natural complement to it—makes an ideal breakfast cereal, more nutritious than the vast majority our families buy.

If you wish to know more about fiber versus our common colon and bowel diseases, and more about the use of bran in the everyday and in the reducing diet (where it's very useful) you might read my paperback, *The Carlton Fredericks High-Fiber Way to Total Health.*

If you have a digestive disorder, or a disease of the colon or bowel, your high-fiber diet should be medically supervised. If you're in good health, and would like to stay that way, now is the time to stop flirting with disaster, to stop buying cereals, breads, and sugar you wouldn't dream of feeding to your valuable, pedigreed dog. Enough said?

## DIABETES

Each of us is an omnibus loaded with our ancestors. We

are, in a certain sense, imprisoned within the boundaries of our heredity. One of the best ways to avoid diabetes is to be born into a family whose members have never had it. This does not necessarily mean that one or two diabetic ancestors doom you as inevitable prey to this disease; but if both your parents and all four of your grandparents had diabetes, the dice of hereditary influences are loaded heavily against you. If diabetes existed on both sides of your family, skipping a member here and there, blood sugar tests for you are an investment in protection and peace of mind.

The question of what constitutes proper diet and supplementing for a diabetic opens up the whole problem of the disorder's anatomy. What is this disease, which exacts its toll from one out of every forty or fifty people? Today, diabetes is considered to be primarily a condition created by insufficient production of insulin, which in turn results in a disturbance in the metabolism of sugar. This explanation invites the daily use of an injection of insulin. Thereafter, presumably, the diabetic lives to a ripe old age in good health.

This concept is so contradictory to the truth that, from one perspective, the discovery of insulin may be regarded as a tragedy; for diabetics, treated with diets low in sugar and faithfully injected with insulin, go on to develop arteriosclerosis, retinal hemorrhages and other diseases which are so common in these patients that they should be regarded as being part of the disease rather than as "complications."

There is, in fact, evidence that some of these "complications" of diabetes *precede*—by considerable periods of time—the advent of elevated blood sugar. And that is only one of the mysteries of diabetes, about which the public (and some professionals) have many misconcepts. The popular belief has it that the disorder begins with a deficiency in insulin, the hormone which burns sugar; thereby, the blood sugar (glucose) mounts too high. Oversimplification is the beginning of many errors, of which this explanation of diabetes is a good example, for many of these patients do not have a deficiency in insulin, and some actually have an oversupply. Nor is the disorder one of the pancreas, necessarily,

114

and if the pancreas is involved, it is certainly not the only organ implicated, for, if anything, the liver is more important to blood glucose regulation than any other organ. It is also a tragic error to consider diabetes as a disorder only of sugar metabolism, for the disease is total, involving every food fraction—protein, fat, carbohydrate, vitamins, and minerals.

While the juvenile diabetic always requires insulin therapy, the mature-onset disease is a totally different disorder, and more often than not, can be managed with weight reduction (if needed), dietary control, and intelligent use of vitamin-mineral supplements. The oral drugs (those which lower blood glucose) can't be used for juvenile diabetics, and are unnecessary, the majority of the time, for the mature-onset diabetic. Moreover, there is evidence that at least one type of oral drug used in diabetes may be responsible for increasing susceptibility to heart attacks, to which diabetics are unusually prone, anyway. Thus focus on proper weight, proper diet, and proper use of vitamins and minerals is more than logical in most mature-onset diabetes: It is a uniquely rational way to cope with the disorder. This is true, however, only if due attention is given to encouragement of normal liver function. (Soskin, authority on the subject, has pointed out that the animal deprived of the pancreas can, with the aid of normal liver function, control blood sugar levels, but the converse is not true. Readers interested in the experiment will find it described in detail in *Carbohydrate Metabolism*, by Soskin and Levine, University of Chicago Press.) Despite the importance of liver function to the diabetic, the traditional treatment has ignored this entity in the disease, although there is evidence that liver function in diabetics is frequently disturbed. In fact, there is autopsy evidence that in 50 percent of the diabetics examined postmortem, the pancreas was normal, but in 50 percent of the examinations, the liver was abnormal.

It is not the function of this text to provide a "diet for diabetes." Such a scientific indiscretion would be unforgivable, for there is no one diet for diabetes, and individual differences in food needs and tolerances require an individual approach. But this generalization is possible: Given a proper diet, the diabetic (again, mature-onset) will respond better if he is given high potency supplements of the Vitamin B Complex, using a concentrate high in choline and inositol, and supplements of brewer's yeast and desiccated liver. In fact, in the first edition of this book, more than thirty years ago, I included a letter from a physician, commenting on a patient with high blood glucose, who was spilling sugar in the urine, and who, for a number of reasons could not be placed on a controlled diet, but whose blood glucose was lowered nearly to the normal range, merely by use of the supplements just described, plus a multiple mineral formula.

Any competent medical nutritionist will be familiar with such a nutritional approach to this common disorder. And any competent medical nutritionist will remind you that the time to employ a controlled diet, as free of sugar as possible, and the time to employ the vitamin-mineral supplements is *now*—before diabetes appears. What nutrition cures or mitigates, it prevents or significantly delays.

## DISORDERS OF NERVES AND MUSCLES

With his medical colleagues, the author has dedicated years of research to the numerous muscle disorders which appear increasingly to plague modern man. These include the epilepsies, senile palsy (which is not senile, since it appears throughout the life span; and which is not palsy), multiple sclerosis, encephalitis, cerebral palsy, myasthenia gravis, and many others.

Using doses of concentrates made from the nutrients removed from white flour, the medical men have achieved remarkable improvements in children and adults suffering from some of these disorders. The responses in multiple sclerosis have often been virtually unbelievable. Those in cerebral palsy offer tremendous hope for the hundreds of thousands of children and adults suffering from one of the many forms of this disorder.

116

The language used in the preceding paragraphs does not give the reader the full perspective on what has been accomplished in some of these myoneuropathies by administration of concentrated wheat germ oil and others of these factors previously named. We have seen improvements in multiple sclerosis which were *not* spontaneous remissions, and which sometimes restored helpless individuals to social usefulness. We have seen improvements in children with cerebral palsy which were unattainable by any therapy which has yet been reported for that disorder. We have seen sufferers from encephalitis recover their ability to do complex (neurologically speaking) acts like buttoning buttons in a few months of nutritional therapy.

The active factor in wheat germ oil, which benefits sufferers with nerve-muscle disorders, is octocosanol, which (for the benefit of readers with technical backgrounds) is a long-chain waxy alcohol, with twenty-seven carbons. The amount of this factor in ordinary wheat germ oil is nutritionally adequate to benefit those who use the oil as a dietary supplement. It is not enough, however, to act therapeutically. Therefore, in the treatment of myoneuropathies (nerve-muscle ills) I have suggested that the physician employ the highest concentration of octocosanol, prepared from wheat germ oil, which is commercially available. This is a fifteen to one concentrate. The results, previously cited, of administration of this factor in multiple sclerosis and in cerebral palsy, invite (but have not yet instigated) research with this nutritional material in minimal brain damage, post-stroke symptoms, Parkinsonian syndrome, and in retarded neuromuscular development.

In multiple sclerosis, the diet used had been one closely resembling that employed in hypoglycemia: sugar-free, high protein, high fat, with about 20 percent of the fat unsaturated; served in frequent small meals. There are some multiple sclerosis patients who fare better if wheat is removed from the diet, and others who do not tolerate milk, and some who should be taken off both foods. Some of these patients also need the help of an external supply of a fatty acid which is normally manufactured in the body, from arachidonic acid, which in turn is supplied to the body by synthesis, within, from linoleic acid. This in turn is well supplied by germ oils, such as wheat germ oil. This fatty acid— docosahenanoic acid—is poorly supplied in the diet in the preformed form. It is believed to be the first fatty acid which is stripped from the muscle sheaths when the myelin is removed, in such disorders as multiple sclerosis. Therefore, in the diet for multiple sclerosis, constant emphasis is placed on intake of sardines and mackerel, which are among a handful of foods which do contain the desired fatty acid.

Other nutrients are, of course, emphasized in the nerve-muscle disorders—especially Vitamin B Complex, high in inositol, Vitamin B6, Vitamin B12, and choline, and Vitamin E, in the form of mixed tocopherols.

But a small percentage of patients with m.s. and other myoneuropathies will show a significant response to this adjunct nutritional treatment. But a small percentage is a considerable group when one considers the dearth of helpful therapies offered for these conditions in usual medical approaches. The nutritional treatment being adjunct, the physician may employ with it physiotherapy, medication, or other modalities experience has taught him may be helpful. Likewise, in certain of these disorders, emphasis must be placed on intake of nutrients critically important in a particular type of nerve-muscle dysfunction. In myasthenia gravis, for instance, which is a disease in which muscles become gravely weak, the medical man will want to promote production of acetylcholine, which he usually accomplishes with drugs, the effect of which can be unpredictable— ranging from beneficial to life-threatening. The nutritionist would promote acetylcholine synthesis by providing the raw materials: choline, pantothenic acid, and manganese.

These details should not be allowed to obscure the essential point: in the myoneuropathies, as in so many other disorders, nutrition offers resources which have not been adequately investigated and applied.

# FLATULENCE (GAS) AND HEARTBURN

## FOODS WHICH TEND TO PRODUCE GAS

VEGETABLES
Beans, especially dried
Broccoli
Brussels sprouts
Cabbage
Cauliflower
Corn
Cucumber
Garlic
Lentils
Onions
Peas, fresh and dried
Peppers
Potato
Radishes
Rutabaga
Sauerkraut
Swiss chard
Turnips
  FRUITS
Apples, raw
Melons
Raisins
  NUTS
*All kinds*
  SWEETS
*All sweet foods as:*
Candy
Jellies
Jams
Sugar
Preserves, etc.
  CHEESE
All highly fermented

SOUPS
Meat soups or broths
Vegetable stock from the gas-forming vegetables
   BEVERAGES
Carbonated water
Highly sweetened drinks
Coffee
   CONDIMENTS AND OTHER FOODS
All condiments other than salt
Excessively salted foods
Spices
Uncooked foods
Fried or greasy food


A final note on gas and the disturbances produced by it: There are many individuals who because of their eating habits—particularly, eating very rapidly—or talking while eating—swallow air with their food. This can be the cause of heartburn, gas, and digestive discomfort. Often, the physician must teach such individuals to press the cheeks, before swallowing food, in order to expel the air. There are also many allergic individuals in whom gas, heartburn, indigestion, and flatulence are specific symptoms of specific allergy to foods. Such symptoms are often reproduced when the neuroallergist puts a few drops of a concentrated solution of the food beneath the tongue, where absorption takes place very rapidly.

Finally, those who use supplements of bran to promote more rapid stool transit time and freedom from constipation will note an increase in flatulence. This may persist or diminish, but is not too great a price to pay for possible protection against bowel cancer.


# HEART DISEASE

Thanks to the pioneering research of Dr. Wilfred Shute, a discussion of heart disease is likely to initiate a discussion of Vitamin E, as a preventive and as a therapeutic agent for this ubiquitous killer. Thanks to the belligerent atmosphere in nutrition, and more particularly, thanks to the ancient tendency to be "down on" what we're not "up on," the subject of Vitamin E versus the heart, in sickness and in health, creates an immediate storm in the mind of any cardiologist.

There are, though, a few facts with which the public is unacquainted, and to which the heart specialist pays no attention. It has been observed that deficiency of Vitamin E creates heart irregularities in all mammalian species tested, and most of them have been. To deny any importance of Vitamin E to the health of the human heart is really to say that man, alone of the mammals, has a heart which is in no way dependent on Vitamin E.

Observations of the administration of vitamin E to patients with heart disease are the basis for other bitter arguments. One reads, for instance, of a clinical trial in which one hundred patients (cardiac) were treated with Vitamin E, without a single beneficial response in a single patient. Yet even the physicians who quote such a paper, by way of "proving" that Vitamin E has no influence on heart disease, will admit that among heart patients, there is always a group who will respond, on the basis of the power of suggestion, to a sugar tablet—if they think it is a powerful heart medicine. This placebo effect, as it's called, is so common that the double-blind experiment was devised to keep it under control. Yet I hear cited, as antivitamin evidence, experiments in which administration of Vitamin E benefited not one solitary patient. Where was the placebo effect in such reasearch? And what kind of bias, which must have been obvious to the patients, was operating?

Against such negative reports on handfuls of patients is the monumental experience of Dr. Wilfred Shute, who had prescribed Vitamin E for *thousands* of cardiacs, and observed benefits great enough to warrant his continued administration of the vitamin over a period of decades. Moreover, I have had the opportunity, rare for a nutritionist, to check these clinical observations, for I spent five years in research with a cardiologist who frequently prescribed

Vitamin E; and I watched many patients who did not respond, and a larger number who did.

My interest in Vitamin E in heart disease derives from my interest in prevention. This is to say that this chapter is not written to encourage cardiac patients to treat themselves with Vitamin E. The treatment, in fact, far from being inert and ineffective, can actually be so effective as to become dangerous. Such a situation might arise when the left side of the heart is in much more trouble than the right side—which is a frequent clinical problem. If Vitamin E is taken by such a patient, the right side of the heart, being in better condition, may respond more, and more quickly, than the left side. The net result, temporarily, would be worsening of the left-side heart failure.

The experienced cardiologist who knows how to exploit Vitamin E in heart disease will anticipate this one-sided response by giving minimal doses for the first few months, and gradually increasing them. I cite this to emphasize the point frequently made in this book: *Self-treatment for a serious disorder is inadvisable.* It also emphasizes the fact the dosage of Vitamin E, which in a healthy person might, without harm, range from low to high, must be carefully supervised in the treatment of sickness. This is particularly true in rheumatic heart disease. In angina, where the inability of the damaged heart to cope with a stress shows up as agonizing pain, I have seen Vitamin E therapy fail, but I have also seen it make the difference between a cardiac invalid and a functioning person. There is a crude, but nonetheless useful, gauge of the effectiveness of Vitamin E in some cases of angina pectoris: that is the number of nitroglycerin tablets the patient must use. When, after treatment with Vitamin E, the patient's nitroglycerin dosage drops from 180 tablets a month to 25 or even fewer, it is not the power of suggestion which is yielding the therapeutic response.

Cardiologists using Vitamin E therapy tend to use alpha-tocopherol, rather than mixed tocopherols, attributing to the alpha form all the benefits derived from Vitamin E treatment. It is true that the alpha tocopherol has the maximum effect on intra-cellular chemistry. However, it is also true that the beta, gamma, and delta tocopherols, which make up "mixed tocopherols," have the maximum effect as antioxidants, and reducing the need of the tissues for oxygen is as important in cardiac disease as it is in health. To the nutritionist, then, the preferred form of Vitamin E as a supplement is *mixed* tocopherols, with the potency expressed in terms of the alpha content, giving the best of both possible biochemical worlds.

The fact that the subject of Vitamin E dominates the discussion, to this point, should not be allowed to obscure the importance of other nutrients in heart function. Vitamin B12 has almost as much effect on the electrical activity of the heart, as does Vitamin E. The other B vitamins are intimately involved in the energy metabolism of the body, including, of course, the heart muscle. In the emphasis on Vitamin E, we must not forget that thiamin (Vitamin B1) is essential to cardiac function. So is raboflavin. So is niacinamide. So is Vitamin B6. Likewise, even the trace minerals need emphasis. Together with small doses of the vitamins, trace minerals have been used successfully to help avoid the *second* heart attack, in research by a physician associated with Johns Hopkins.

Enthusiasts who overemphasize the role of Vitamin E in prevention and treatment of heart disease place great emphasis on the rise in the incidence of heart troubles which began after the processing mills started to strip the grain of its Vitamin E value. This use of correlation to demonstrate causation is a risky philosophy, in science. (You can prove that the increase in the number of psychiatrists was accompanied by an increase in the number of neurotics, psychotics, and weirdos—but you haven't demonstrated, then, that psychiatrists drive us crazy!)

Other innovations might well be cited to explain what seems to be a sharp increase in coronary heart disease, since the early 1900's. For one thing, we shifted babies from breast to bottle—and there is animal evidence that the breast milk, when it is high in cholesterol (as a reflection of the diet of the mother) elicits a defense mechanism against cholesterol, which persists throughout life—and which is missing in animals which are not nursed. It is, therefore, impossible to sift through the evidence, and isolate a single, unmistakable cause of our troubles with heart disease. But there is no doubt that the heart, like all the other organs and tissues, requires the best possible nutrition. That calls for more than the use of Vitamin E and B Complex and trace mineral supplements. It urgently advocates eating the best possible diet, too.

The American diet, because of the stripping of the grains and other carbohydrates which make up 50 percent of the calorie suppliers in our food, is an indifferent source of Vitamin E. It supplies less than desirable in the infant's diet, and falls short by a considerable margin in the adult diet. (The same remarks might be made for the Vitamin B Complex, which departs the grain in similar proportion when carbohydrate foods are processed.)

The oils in our diet, which should be good sources of Vitamin E, may or may not be. These, too, may be victims of processing techniques which aim at palatability and appearance, rather than nutritional values. Some of the vegetable oils, too, are richer sources of less-active forms of Vitamin E. These can be identified quickly, for invariably, they are seasoned with synthetic antioxidants which they wouldn't need if they contained the natural antioxidants— the mixed tocopherols, or Vitamin E in its various forms. So it is that at least one paper has asked whether the substitution of BHT and BHA for Vitamin E may not be a cause of heart attacks. These antioxidants have been demonstrated, in any case, to have undesirable side-effects, and the presence in a vegetable oil or any other food product should be a "keep-away" red flag.

Supplements of 25 mgs. of Vitamin E daily are used for (healthy) small children; 100 mgs. may be used for older children and teenagers. The adult who has spent a lifetime as a victim of white flour and other processed carbohydrates may need 200 to 400 mgs. After the age of fifty, when the utilization of fats and fatty substances, such as Vitamin E, becomes less effective, 400 to 800 mgs. may be needed. Always, though, in the form of mixed tocopherols, rather than alpha tocopherol alone. If retaining health is not sufficient motivation for the use of the supplement (and the use of the proper form of it), let me remind you that the antioxidant effect of Vitamin E is seriously regarded as one of our more useful weapons against premature aging.


## HIGH BLOOD PRESSURE
## AND THE RICE DIET


High blood pressure has, along with stomach ulcer, been called the "wound stripe of civilization." This disease, like stomach ulcer and many more of our present-day disorders, is frequently psychogenic in origin. The logical working team dealing with hypertension should, for best results, comprise patient, M.D. and psychoanalyst. When the emotional causes are aired, hypertension abates. The physical manifestations of the disease, however, are amenable to physical treatment, and currently the treatment consists principally of drugs and the rice diet. At this point, the author displays symptoms of high blood pressure which are recognizable as emotional in origin.

The rice diet seems to have sprung from a concept that the Chinese, who are rice-eaters, are remarkably free of high blood pressure. Of 800 million Chinese, how many do you suppose have had their blood pressure taken? Moreover, did you know that millions of Chinese never eat rice? The Northern Chinese—those traditional warmakers—eat noodles.

While it must be admitted that a rice diet may be valuable in extremely aggravated cases of high blood pressure, the following facts must be pointed out:

1. The monotony of the diet brings rebellion and, ul-

timately, a loss of weight. Weight loss is known to reduce blood pressure, but reduction can be accomplished with much more palatable, interesting and nutritious diets.

2.  The rice diet is very low in salt and restriction of salt is known to reduce blood pressure. But low salt diets are available, which are much closer to nutritional adequacy.

3.  The rice diet is low in protein, but the addition of salt-free protein to that diet does not affect the blood pressure. This indicates that only in special circumstances does protein intake have any effect on blood pressure. Inasmuch as protein deficiency is undesirable, the rice diet is again subject to criticism.

4.  Allergies can cause high blood pressure, and the rice diet is admittedly one with so little variety of food and so few "allergenic" foods that it presents little risk of stirring up allergies. But it is possible to eat a non-allergic diet which is well-balanced, whereas the rice diet is not.

Similar objections can be raised to the low-salt diet. This regime is effective in lowering blood pressure only when the salt intake is reduced almost to zero. The full effect of salt restriction is not felt if there is more than half a gram of salt in the daily diet. To arrive at a salt intake of less than half a gram a day would require analysis even of the drinking water! If salt restriction is to be effective, therefore, it must be complete; there are no compromises.

Sufferers with high blood pressure are, of course, sorely disappointed when the nutritionist can't respond with a magical dose of a vitamin which will reduce the pressure, preferably overnight, to normal. Only in one type of high blood pressure has a favorable result been reported with vitamin therapy. This is the type associated with an adrenal disturbance—aldosteronism—in which treatment with Vitamin C, Vitamin E, and Vitamin B6 has been reported specifically helpful. Years ago, the observation was reported that Vitamin K reduced the blood pressure in some patients, but the observation was never retested.

There is, however, a kind of nutritional protection which should be offered to all patients with significantly high blood pressure. The physician treating such cases harbors many apprehensions concerning his patient; among these are, of course, the risk of a stroke, or an eye hemorrhage or damage to the heart. The nutrients which support heart function are, of course, doubly important to the patient with hypertension; those which strengthen the blood vessels are equally important. Among these would be Vitamin C and bioflavonoids, which may help to avoid or mitigate small strokes. Investigation of possible food allergies is important, though rarely performed. Yet allergy can raise blood pressure, and patients very often are addicted to the very foods to which they are allergic.

Nutrition has no glittering triumphs to report in the battle against hypertension. Its victories are small ones, but sometimes, significant. Take, for instance, the recent realization that the cadmium in our foods and water may contribute to hypertension. The protective factor which becomes important is zinc. Yet the processing of our wheat flour manages to remove much zinc, and preserve much cadmium. In soft-water communities, the risk of both heart disease and hypertension (which may be conducive to it) is likely to be greater; and the cadmium conveyed by the water may well be responsible. All this, of course, argues for the presence of a significant amount of zinc in mineral supplements; and, in soft-water communities, the use of such a supplement, or, in lieu of that, the use of a good, pure mineral water, of the type produced at Hot Springs, Arkansas, and at other spas.


## LIVER AND GALL BLADDER


In the discussion of diabetes earlier in this chapter, it was learned that this disease, although allotted to the pancreas, may in a substantial number of cases also represent a liver disturbance. The gallbladder, too, is frequently innocent of the blame accorded it; for there is evidence that gallbladder disturbances may reflect a primary disturbance in the liver, a condition which goes unrecognized and untreated.

The hard-working liver is the largest of the body's glands. It is charged with such a staggering number of responsibilities that no test yet devised will give any indication of the physiological well-being of this organ; for each test appears to tap only one specific function at a time, and a favorable report does not dismiss the possibility that numerous other functions may be seriously disturbed or even blocked completely.

Among the many functions of the liver is the regulation of the body chemistry of fat. This function is well known, to the general public as well as to the practitioners of medicine. One would suppose, therefore, that the liver would be immediately indicted for suspicion in "gallbladder trouble," wherein the patient is commonly unable to tolerate fats. In the current approach to gallbladder syndrome, however, this patient fact is surely overlooked. The customary procedure involves a low-fat diet. This is scarcely rational, inasmuch as fat is the only factor which stimulates the gallbladder to function. After five years on such a diet, the gallbladder shows atrophy of disuse, making surgery almost mandatory. When the surgery is performed and the gallbladder removed, the patient may be startled to find that all the original troubles have returned in full violence. Back are the belching, heartburn, flatulence, constipation, intolerance to fats and roughage, and the uncomfortable sense of fullness after eating. This, at any rate, is the history which the Mayo Clinic gives of 56 per cent of all their patients who have had their gallbladder removed!

It goes without saying, of course, that the presence of gall stones is a valid reason for removing the gallbladder, as constant irritation can be a precursor of cancer. It is not necessarily mandatory, however, that a gallbladder be removed because it empties slowly or because the patient is intolerant of fat.

When the removal of a gallbladder does not eliminate the symptoms, it would follow that the primary source of the difficulties was in another organ. Logic indicates that this would be the organ most intimately involved in the breakdown and the reassembling of fats—namely the liver.

Putting this theory to test, the author's medical colleagues have approached gallbladder syndrome with diets and vitamin supplements directed toward improving liver function and facilitating the utilization of fats. In patients whose symptoms would ultimately have probably brought them to surgery, only two actually reached the operating table; the others were relieved to the extent that surgery became unnecessary. The diet used was high in protein, low in carbohydrates, and provided with as much fat as the patient's tolerance would permit, In this diet, sugar is strictly forbidden. The intake of fat and roughage is raised as the patient's response permits. Added to this diet are supplements which include multiple vitamins, multiple minerals, the Vitamin B Complex and Vitamin E. The B Complex concentrate, however, is formulated to emphasize those factors which are intrinsic in the utilization of fats: inositol, choline and pyridoxine. Oethionine (a protein acid essential to liver function) is sometimes added to the supplements at the physicians' discretion. Also used are supplements of lecithin, a food factor which is important in the chemistry of fats.

The physician may heighten the efficacy of the treatment in many ways. He may administer the Vitamin B Complex by mouth, and accompany it with injections (intramuscularly) of the vitamins. He may combine with the injection, added amounts of Vitamin B12, which, contrary to public opinion, is as much involved in the utilization of foods, as it is in pernicious anemia. He may place emphasis on vegetable fats in the diet, since these often are better tolerated in gall bladder syndrome than are the animal fats; and for the same reason, will specify the homogenized fats, in which the smaller globules make for better utilization. He may add doses by mouth of appropriate enzyme materials, such as pancreatic enzymes. The important point is that conservative medical and nutritional treatment may substitute for irreversible surgery which, more often than not, has little or no impact on the patient's symptoms.

Somewhere in my files is a plaque, representing me, carved by a dentist using nothing more as a tool than his drill. He was supposed to have a cholescystectomy—removal of the gallbladder—more than twenty years ago. He still has his gallbladder, and he eats a normal diet—thanks to his physician's application of the information you have just read. This cited by way of letting you know that what you are reading isn't based on theory.


## MENOPAUSAL TROUBLES

There is an obvious psychological impact of the menopause, for many women (mistakenly) believe that surrendering the biological birthright of the ability to bear children is synonymous with (a) loss of femininity, and (b) loss of the sex life, and (c) the end of youth. For women who suffer such emotional reactions, skilled psychotherapy is obviously helpful, or the family physician, sans prolonged psychological treatment, may be able to persuade these patients to realize that these beliefs reflect folklore, rather than truth.

By the same token, the secure, well-balanced, and well-nourished woman, free of undue anxieties, is much less likely to bow before the storms of menopause. Yet she and her more anxious sisters may need extra help in coping with the stresses of menopause—from disturbed sleeping to the "sweats and flushes," nervousness, and feelings of inadequacy, which so often derive from the change of life.

For years, I warned my colleagues in medicine that their simplistic approach to menopausal symptoms is both inadequate and dangerous. Tranquilizers are not innocuous drugs; estrogen is distinctly dangerous. Physicians took exception to my view of estrogen as a potential carcinogen (cancer-producing) substance. Those who were willing to grant the possibility that estrogen may be carcinogenic pointed out that in menopausal women, the hormone dose was simply a supplement, designed to compensate for failure of accustomed internal synthesis of the hormone; and thereby, unlikely to be dangerous. I didn't swallow the dogma, and, in fact, wrote numerous articles and delivered several scientific papers, warning against the use of estrogen, not only in menopause, but even more dangerously, as part of the formulas of oral contraceptive pills. As this manuscript was prepared, a rash of articles confirming my apprehension concerning estrogen supplementing in menopause appeared, indicating that the risk of uterine cancer may increase by a factor of up to fourteen, in menopausal women dosed with estrogen.

This confirmation of the riskiness of medicating menopausal women with estrogen invites a fresh look at the benefits of scientific nutrition in replacing estrogen therapy, or in mitigating its dangers. Noted in an earlier chapter was the role of protein and Vitamin B Complex, high in choline and inositol, in aiding the liver to break estrogen down into less active and less threatening forms. This, of course, suggests that the physician who does prescribe estrogen can help to protect his patient, not only by frequent examinations, but by prescribing the proper high protein diet and supplements of Vitamin B Complex.

The physician who is unwilling to risk estrogen treatment is not left without resources. Vitamin E has been reported to diminish the severity of the sweats and flushes and in some cases, to eliminate them. The adverse feature of this safe treatment is the slowness with which the benefits are achieved, some women not responding for many months. Additional Vitamin B Complex and calcium (the latter in the form of the orotate) likewise are helpful in stabilizing the nervous system. Lecithin, which was described by one woman in an experiment involving its use as "dropping a blanket of peace" upon her, may benefit some patients. Paba and folic acid, which tend to increase the estrogen effect, are sometimes used to help the woman to respond better to the diminishing internal supply of estrogen.

For many menopausal women, there is little reason for overwhelming emotional and physical storms if psychotherapy is employed where it is needed; the diet is carefully balanced to meet their needs, and generous supplements of the necessary vitamins are provided.

## MOUTH MALADIES

The mouth, especially, is a sensitive reflector of your nutritional status. Less frequently heard than heretofore in doctor's offices is the command, "Put out your tongue, please," yet it is generally recognized that the tongue is a mirror of the intestine. We are familiar with the coated tongue that comes with "sour stomach," and the physician is familiar with the spectacular tongue disturbances which signal pernicious anemia, febrile diseases and other serious disorders.

Laymen tend to worry about the coated tongue, which may be a product of nothing more than regurgitation of food in sleep, or excessive smoking or mouth-breathing. The bare, naked, shiny tongue actually worries the physician and nutritionist, particularly if its color is abnormal, if newly developed cracks and fissures appear on it, or if it feels sore. Vitamin B12, frequently given by injection, but also given by mouth, is often used to treat such tongue disturbances. When these appear after doses of antibiotics, they are treated as if originating with pellagra, with a high protein diet, amply supplemented with Vitamin B Complex, both concentrated and derived from natural sources, such as desiccated liver. If the sense of taste is disturbed—absent, diminished, or distorted—large doses of zinc may be employed, up to 200 mgs. daily, or less, if the orotate form is used.

Lately, we have come to realize that the tongue we call "normal" may actually represent the almost imperceptible defect of vitamin deficiency. Further, we are aware that serious deficiencies can and do create disturbances of tongue, cheek and gum which in previous years we did not relate to the influence of nutrition.

We have learned, for example, that Vincent's Angina (trench mouth)—inadequately but traditionally treated with powerful antiseptics is sometimes two disturbances in one. The first is a vitamin deficiency; the second, the bacterial invasion which would not be tolerated by healthy, well-nourished tissue. This is why your modern dentist or doctor will treat trench mouth with 100, 200 or more milligrams of niacinamide accompanied by a Vitamin B Complex dosage, followed by a local application of antiseptic.

Research has revealed that nutritional deficiencies can produce sores at the corners of the mouth—small transverse fissures which the physician calls "cheilosis." A condition called "leukoplakia"—in which the inside cheek surfaces may suffer a fungus infection causing grey, green or white patches to appear—was for many years regarded as a pre-cancerous mouth lesion. In the light of new knowledge, leukoplakia and many kindred ailments of the tongue, gums and cheeks are prevented or successfully treated with vitamins.

The gums, also, are very quick to show vitamin deficiency, in the presence of which they may recede, swell, bleed or become painful. Additionally, the teeth may become highly sensitive to hot or cold foods, and periodontoclasia may develop. This is a loosening of the teeth without apparent cause, not always accompanied by pyorrhea. In the author's experience, many of these conditions affecting the soft tissues of the mouth are ultimately followed by nervous disturbances or digestive disorders. There is, moreover, evidence that some of the lesions of the mouth occasionally termed "pre-cancerous" are actually symptomatic of such vitamin dificiencies as we have been discussing. Certainly, therefore, these danger signals should not be overlooked.

Contrary to a popular concept, Vitamin C is not the only vitamin involved in oral health. The author has frequently heard laymen complain that they drink quantities of fruit juice and still have a painful tongue and tender, bleeding gums. The fact is that the entire Vitamin B Complex is essential to maintain the tissues of the mouth. Two single vitamins are important—Vitamin C and niacinamide. These must be used with the entire Vitamin B Complex and sometimes the B Complex dosage must be extraordinarily high. There have been cases of gum, tongue and inner cheek disturbances which were not pacified until as much as eighteen or twenty teaspoonfuls of brewer's yeast were taken along with large amounts of Vitamin C and niacinamide. Liver contains unique factors often therapeutic in such disorders.

Inextricably associated with bleeding gums, in the public's mind, is Vitamin C deficiency. This pat explanation is far from being consistently accurate. Bleeding of the gums may originate ultimately with anything from a bad bite, malocclusion, to serious system diseases. If they reflect a nutritional deficiency, this, too, may in turn be complex. Deficiency in platelets can cause hemorrhaging, for which the remedy may be an increased supply of a fat like sesame seed oil, plus rich supplies of fat-soluble nutrients, like Vitamins A, D, E, and K. If deficiency in Vitamin C is involved, the bioflavonoids may also be needed. It should be noted that most commercial supplements of Vitamin C and bioflavonoids are irrationally formulated. An orange may supply nine times as much of the bioflavonoids as it does of Vitamin C; the supplements almost invariably reverse the ratio. Deficiency in Vitamin C as a cause of bleeding gums may appear with a diet ostensibly adequate in the vitamin. The explanation may be an oversupply of sugar in the diet, which raises the requirement for the vitamin. This gives the patient the choice of raising intake of the vitamin, or, which serves him better, lowering his intake of overprocessed sugar and other similar refined carbohydrates. It is possible also to have so elevated a requirement for Vitamin C that no feasible diet could meet it.

Periodontaclasia—disorders of the gums and the supporting structures of the teeth, including the jawbone itself—is almost invariably treated as a disease confined to the mouth.

134

Since the mouth uses the circulation employed by the body, it is unlikely that oral disease does not reflect systemic disturbances. A low carbohydrate diet, amply supplemented with mulitple vitamins and minerals, including calcium and magnesium orotates, and a goodly supply of a natural source of the Vitamin B complex—from desiccated liver, brewer's yeast, or, which is better, both, is a useful adjunct to the periodontist's therapy; and has been observed to tighten loose teeth in less than a full week.

# WHEN YOU WONDER HOW YOU SURVIVE THE WONDER DRUGS

During the fascinating progress of vitamin research, it became apparent to chemists that by a very slight alteration in the formula of a vitamin they could create the antagonist to the vitamin. This "alter ego" is a chemical so close to the vitamin structure that the cells of the body accept it unhesitatingly, only to find it "indigestible." In this drama of imposture, the masquerader enters the cell and shuts out the rightful occupant—which is the vitamin.

An application of the principle lies in the treatment of disease. Suppose, hypothetically, we know a cancer urgently needs a certain vitamin for its sustenance. We now create a pseudo-vitamin and administer it to the patient in the hope that it will enter the cancer cell and dispossess the real vitamin from its rightful place, thereby starving the cancer to death. This had been tried. It was the basis of the treatment used for Babe Ruth. The death of this great American does not close the door on the possibility that such treatment may one day be found successful for cancer and many other diseases. For, we must realize, this is the precise basis on which the wonder drugs function; and, certainly, these have been successful against many serious infections.

When you take a sulfa drug you are actually taking one of these masquerading chemicals—very close to a vitamin, yet different enough so that the cell cannot utilize the drug for vitamin-action. The harmful bacteria, fooled into "eating" the sulfa drug, die of starvation. More specifically, they die because they have accepted sulfa in place of the vitamin it resembles—para-aminobenzoic acid.

While this therapeutic strategy is being enacted, what happens to you? You, along with the bacteria, have accepted the masquerader in place of the vitamin requisite to your body. The answer lies in the way you feel after you have taken sulfa drugs. You are weak, without appetite, pale and shaken. Fortunately for you, you are able to weather the storm. The bacteria cannot.

The same reaction is true of penicillin and other wonder drugs. In penicillin treatment, it is believed that the drug is converted within the body into a foam closely resembling one of the essential protein (amino) acids. Again, the bacteria are fooled. So, likewise, is your body. After prolonged treatment with penicillin you may develop allergies, prolonged blood-clotting time or general weakness. Once again, however, your body—with its reserves of essential proteins—is able to weather the storm of qualitative starvation, while the one-celled bacteria cannot.

In addition to the debilitating effects of sulfa and wonder drugs, there is another which also weakens the patient when these drugs are given by mouth. The bacteria of the intestinal tract, as innocent bystanders, are confronted with famine along with the harmful bacteria of the infection. The majority of these intestinal bacteria is friendly; they are needed inhabitants of the colon. We depend upon them for two actions: They help to synthesize vitamins which we need, and they promote absorption and utilization of foods. Accordingly, when the friendly and useful bacteria who make their home in our intestines are destroyed by sulfa, penicillin, aureomycin or chloromycetin, we have a new complication to add to the grogginess and weakness we may feel. Now our tongues are likely to turn purple. This purpling of the tongue is a typical sign of Vitamin B Complex deficiency. The deficiency is induced by a possible combination of four factors: Substitution of a drug for a vitamin needed by the cells; the possible fever of the illness which necessitated the dose; the destruction of friendly bacteria in the intestinal tract, and the heightened needs of the body for B vitamins in infection and prolonged illness.

Because of all this, the literature which accompanies certain of the wonder drugs instructs the physician to balance the dosage with generous amounts of the Vitamin B Complex, so that the patient may escape being too debilitated by the deficiencies induced by the medication. By the same token, lack of appetite following the use of wonder drugs may be anticipated and avoided by the use of supplements containing niacinamide and liver concentrate.

In the drive against "health foods," the authorities have committed many regrettable errors. Among these has been the slander directed at yogurt, which has been described by the United States Food and Drug Administration as nothing more than milk at a higher price. This was also the statement of the American Medical Association, which found itself shortly thereafter embarrassed by a report from Rockefeller Institute indicating that a great many benefits were conferred upon animals which were supplied with the friendly bacteria of yogurt. Factually, the practicing physician—whose philosophy very often does not at all coincide with that of the medical politicians in Chicago—has learned that when antibiotics disturb the friendly bacteria of the lower digestive tract, he can restore matters to normal by the use of yogurt, and connot do so with buttermilk or other types of fermented milk products. Manufacturers of antibiotics likewise recognize that yogurt has certain advantages, and often recommend that the physician who is going to administer these drugs for long periods of time not only give Vitamin B Complex, but also administer yogurt. In serious disturbances of the colon set up by antibiotics, yogurt has been labeled by medical researchers as lifesaving.

When you use yogurt—in the normal diet, or as an antidote for the undesirable effects of antibiotics on your bowel bacteria—do *not* buy the flavored or fruit-filled varieties, for these have an unbelievable amount of sugar in them. It has been shown that a single dose of sugar significantly lowers the ability of the white blood cells to cope with bacteria, a phenomenon you certainly don't want to harbor at any time, and particularly when you are fighting an infection.

There are inexpensive yogurt makers available, for home use, which are simply hot plates, which hold the milk at the proper temperature for the bacterial culture to grow. The culture itself can be purchased, or one can use commercial (nonflavored) yogurt as a starter. Full-fat or low-fat milk can be used, and the final product is much less costly than the commercial varieties. As indicated in the discussion of constipation, the regular use of yogurt is helpful, if intake is generous, in changing the bowel flora to a type less favorable to the chemical changes in the stool conducive to bowel cancer.

# CHAPTER 8

## THE FUNCTIONS OF FOOD

*An Introduction to an Understanding of Nutrition*

THERE ARE MANY DEFINITIONS OF NUTRITION. From the long point of view, since from the dust we come and to it we return, nutrition is the flow of nutrients from the soil, through man, and back to the soil. From the viewpoint of the biologist, we are a remarkable aggregation of cells, each of which needs a supply of chemical substances which we borrow from other forms of life—some fifty-five diverse compounds which range from fuels to the substances which catalyze their oxidation, from metals to complex combinations of amino acids, from fats saturated with hydrogen to those that are not.

The arithmetic of nutrition is simple: Our daily menus must provide us with the requisite supply of these some fifty-five substances. If they don't, we adapt as best we can, and when our power of adaptation is strained to the breaking point, we become ill, and, if the deficit is serious enough and prolonged enough, we die. Most of our failures, in a prosperous society, aren't lethal in degree. We fall short by margins which are less than deadly. They produce, not death, but a twilight zone of being, in which we are neither truly sick nor truly well, because our nutrient supply is neither truly optimal nor truly lethal in its inadequacies. Our nutritional needs vary so much that the twilight zone of dietary deficiency for one may be the level of adequacy for another. Unfortunately, the level of your diet is a variable determined by the vagaries of your appetite, the weight of your habits, the influence of conditioning, and even the whims shaped by the appearance and odor of food. What you *need* is another matter. There is no inner voice of wisdom that molds your cravings in food so that they target on satisfying your dietary requirements.

The level of your diet is a variable. It depends not so much on how much you eat, but what. For example, experiments with animals allow us to define diet levels on three more or less general planes and demonstrate how closely connected are diet and health. A group of animals is given the diet eaten by the average American, known to be adequate to sustain human life. This group we will call "Diet C." A second group of animals is given the same diet *plus* extra milk ("Diet B") and a third group ("Diet A") is given the same diet *plus* extra milk, fruit and vegetables.

"Diet C" produces healthy looking animals. They experience no more than the usual run of sicknesses, disorders in pregnancy and birth and degeneration or disease in vital organs. Since this is the diet of the average American, we may safely call it—temporarily—the "norm." It is not until we examine the records of the "Diet B" group, fed extra milk, that we realize how much healthier our "norm" *could* be; for the second group lived longer, had fewer infections, fewer deaths of mothers and newborn and were larger and stronger. When we come to the results of the "Diet A" group, however, we realize still more improvements. These animals lived even longer, retained their vitality much later in life, had still fewer infections and sicknesses, practically no difficulty in reproduction and were stronger and sounder in physical appearance . . . skin, fur, eyes, skeletal structure, teeth, etc. You are the master of your own fate, nutritionally speaking. No research laboratory may experiment with your diet without your permission. But are you A, B or C in diet and in health? Do you really know? Hundreds of thousands of Americans live on the experimental animals' "Diet C." They call themselves healthy while harboring frequent colds, sinus trouble, sore throats, ear infections, skin eruptions, digestive disorders, constipation, flat feet, poor posture, poor appetite, low resistance to shock, infection, fatigue, obesity, impaired vision and frequently a "touch of diabetes"!

*Calories:* Among the body's needs for food are heat and energy, which are supplied by the burning or "oxidation" of what we eat. The amount of heat or energy which foods will supply is scientifically figured for us. Many texts provide charts in which the "heat" or "energy" values of food are stated. The unit of measure used to express the amount of heat a food will supply is called a "calorie." This is comparable with an inch being designated as a unit of a measure of length. To understand the calorie, you must understand that your body manufactures heat by a process of burning. It is, to be sure, low-temperature burning, for body temperature is normally 98.6° F. Nevertheless, the burning of food in the body is identical with the process of burning coal in a furnace.

All foods contain calories, some more than others. No food should be called a "fattening" food of itself, regardless of the number of calories it supplies. It depends on what you are eating. Even a low-calorie food added to a full diet might be called fattening; and, conversely, a high-calorie food added to a diet low in calories may not be fattening at all. Since, in the caloric sense, food is fuel, the question should be—how much fuel is already in the furnace? Will one more shovelful cram it too full? Is another shovelful needed to keep the fire going?

No two individuals need exactly the same number of calories to keep the body machine functioning properly. A good rule to follow for the average person, free of glandular disturbances, is to watch body weight. When your energy output (expenditure of calories in activity) exactly balances your energy intake (the caloric value of your diet) your body weight should remain unchanged. As you grow older, however, your activities (expenditure) will decrease and you will need fewer calories in your daily food.

When one eats more food—as a soldier does in achieving a 5,000 calorie intake—the vitamin intake rises correspondingly. While it would not be good for a civilian to eat as many calories as a soldier does, it would be very good for the average man or woman to have the *vitamin intake* of the soldier. This calls for low-calorie, high-vitamin foods such as green salads, wheat germ, brewer's yeast, dry skim milk, etc., or for the use of vitamin-mineral supplements which are usually free of calories and very concentrated in vitamins and minerals.

Your requirement in calories at the age of thirty should carry throughout your adult life and begin to decrease as your activities decline in later years. Although it is better to be a little underweight than to be overweight, women especially should not allow themselves to become too thin; a few extra pounds—but only a few—will cushion the shocks of the forties. It is well to remember, however, that extra calories, which translate into extra weight, are a hazard; extra vitamins are an advantage. Vitamins have the job, among others, of helping to regulate body processes. One of their most important assignments is to help us burn foods. We eat a great many foods which burn readily in the body but which cannot be burned in a furnace under 1500°! The vitamins in our food act as little "wicks." Without them, we would need a body hot as a furnace to ignite our food intake. Life as we know it, founded on low-temperature combustion of the foods we eat, is made possible by vitamins and minerals.

Life expectancy decreases one year for each five pounds of

excess weight in the middle years. Count your calories, therefore, being sure that you have enough but not too many according to your age and occupation. Remember that an ideal diet is barely adequate in calories and very rich in vitamins and minerals. A fast way to compute your approximate calorie needs is to multiply your normal body weight by sixteen, if you are an adult. A child's normal body weight should be multiplied by twenty-five. The answer is the normal individual's total calorie requirement for a day to maintain weight without change.

*Vitamins:* In the light of their tremendous importance to health, vitality and life itself, it seems incredible that vitamins have been identified by name and composition only since the time our century passed its first decade. The name was coined by Dr. Casimir Funk in 1912 after monumental research which isolated the anti-beriberi principle from food. I was fortunate to be a consultant to Dr. Funk's staff, in the early 1940's. Dr. Funk audaciously prophesied that we should one day find similar substances which would prevent or cure scurvy, pellagra and rickets, diseases which were not then attributed to imbalanced or deficient diet. Dr. Funk's prophecy has come true, and with it a mighty weapon for man's use in the fight for better health. Lives have been saved with vitamins, personalities have been regenerated, diseases which have no conceivable origin in vitamin deficiency have been dissipated, tooth decay has been stopped.

Although we speak of vitamins being destroyed in cooking, they are not alive; they are chemicals, crystalline in semblance, which lose their potency on exposure to air or heat. They are miniscule. Our lifetime intake of vitamin factors is measurable in teaspoonfuls in seventy tons of food. Yet, without those teaspoonfuls of vitamins, you might eat the seventy tons of food and die of starvation! Here we begin to understand the meaning of the term "hidden hunger."

When a vitamin has not been isolated and made synthetically, we measure its activity in terms of *units*. A unit represents the minimum amount of food containing the particular vitamin which must be fed (in research, to an animal) in order to exert the characteristic action of the vitamin. As soon as a vitamin has been isolated from a food, we stop using "units" as a measure in deference to *weight*.

In order to become familiar with the weights used to measure vitamins, study the following table. If you learn it well, no vitamin manufacturer can fool you by stating the potency of his capsules in the smallest unit of weight, which bulks largest in numerical figures.

One gamma equals one microgram.

One microgram equals 1/1000 of a milligram.

One milligram equals 1/1000 of a gram.

One gram equals approximately 1/30 of an ounce.

Gammas (or micrograms) and milligrams are the common weight measurement terms used when synthesized vitamins are weighed. If a manufacturer tells you he has 200 gamma of B6 in his capsule, it sounds like a lot more than 1/5 of a milligram, but it is actually the same amount. Read labels carefully.

As we enter more fully into discussion of the separate vitamins, we shall explore their sources and their functions. Let it be clearly understood that there is no distinction between natural and synthesized vitamins. The vitamin found in brown rice or whole wheat is identical with the Vitamin B1 made by man and called thiamin chloride. There are, however, a great many vitamins which we have not yet learned to make synthetically; a good capsule therefore should contain some natural vitamin sources along with synthetic. For example: Vitamin B1, B2, B6, niacin, pantothenic acid and para-aminobenzoic acid are all made synthetically now, but they are part of a Vitamin B Complex which contains many other vitamins not *yet* made synthetically. Consequently, a good supplement capsule should contain liver or yeast or some similar source of the unknown or unsynthesized vitamins in addition to the synthetic ones.

## WHAT PROTEINS ARE

The term "protein" means "of first importance." Despite

this emphasis on a food factor indispensable to growth, maintenance of the adult structure, and repair of tissues and cells, the protein foods are frequently the whipping boy of vegetarians and others who impute to such foods a limitless variety of evil effects, ranging from poisoning us with the "cadaverine" of meat, to causing kidney disease. These are, of course, superstitions. Cadaverine is a normal product of the living organism, and not solely a factor produced in the putrescence of the tissues of the slain animal; and the Eskimo and Masai eat great quantities of protein, and happily ignorant of the philosophy of vegetarians, remain free of kidney disease. (To preserve accuracy, let it be noted that the loss of protein from damaged kidneys sometimes requires the replenishment of the losses by use of increased protein intake.)

A discussion of protein is, according to the Federal Trade Commission and the F.D.A., an exercise in rhetoric, for these agencies have decided that all Americans have plenty of protein in their diets. (They arrive at this conclusion by dividing the population into the protein supply, forgetting that some people are more equal than others in their ability to buy high-priced protein foods. If the same philosophy were applied to the money supply, no one would be poverty stricken.) Actually, as a nutritionist who has analyzed thousands of diets, I know that the curve of protein intake follows the classical Gaussian distribution, from woeful inadequacy all the way up to very high protein intake.

There is an observation which runs true for all living organisms: The most efficient food is that which most closely resembles the composition of the organism. The lion is quickly and adequately fed by his kill; the horse and cow, which violate the rule by eating food remote in composition from that of their tissues, must graze for hours. It is true that too high a protein intake, in the context of the Western world's diet, will cause excretion of essential minerals, a phenomenon which comes into play when the intake of protein passes some ninety grams per day. This contributes to our need for mineral supplements.

144

Protein, the building material of which living cells and tissues are made, consists of about fifty percent carbon, a little hydrogen, some oxygen and nitrogen, traces of sulfur, and, occasionally, a little phosphorus and iron. Out of these relatively few chemicals, nature constructs some twenty-two amino acids, or building blocks of protein. These amino acids are divided by nutritionists into two groups, the "essential" amino acids, and the "nonessential." These are misleading descriptions, for the body needs both groups. The division is justified on the grounds that, given the first group of amino acids from food, the body can manufacture the second group. This is misleading, for although man can get by on an external supply of the ten essential amino acids, he enjoys better growth and health if both groups are furnished to the body from its food, preformed and ready to utilize.

Protein foods are rated not only by their content of the essential amino acids, which the body must obtain from the diet, but by the proportions in which these building blocks are supplied. The closer the food comes to yielding ideal proportions of the essential amino acids, the more efficient the protein will be, measured by two indices: How much of the food is required to avoid depletion of the body's nitrogen supply, and how much of it is required to sustain growth of the young organism? Measured by these two standards, eggs and milk and such meats as liver and kidney rank very high in protein efficiency. This, it should be noted, is the list of foods forbidden or very limited in the "low cholesterol" diet, an observation which emphasizes the biological insanity of the effort to place all mankind, as if we were all biochemical carbon copies of each other, on such a distorted diet.

The proteins in our diet, however, must be divided between the "incomplete" and the "complete." These are terms used by dietitians to distinguish the protein of wheat, for example, from that of milk. The former is good but lacks certain amino acids; milk on the other hand, is so *complete* a protein that it alone will suffice as the sole protein source in the diet. Eggs are the highest quality of protein, against which the others are measured.

# WHAT PROTEINS DO—
# THE BODY'S REQUIREMENTS

Protein is essential for growth in childhood; for building new tissue (as in pregnancy and lactation), and for repair of the adult after wasting illness. It is needed also for maintenance, healing and replacement of tissue that is already built. Greater intake is not necessary to an athlete or manual laborer, for protein is not destroyed in muscle action. The hard manual laborer, however, does have the ability profitably to ingest greater amounts of protein than the sedentary worker.

The wear and tear of living breaks down a certain amount of protein in adult bodies every day, and must be replaced. The amount needed depends on the age of the individual and the condition of the body. Nutritionists agree, however, that—as with vitamins and minerals—it is best to allow a surplus of protein over your actual needs in your diet. That margin of safety is a good idea in all fractions of food, with the exception of carbohydrates and fats. Inasmuch as proteins are the most expensive of foods, however, there is always a tendency to use too little of them. When the budget is limited as a consequence, a member of your family at this moment may actually be suffering from fatigue, retarded growth or body disturbances because of "incomplete" or inadequate protein intake. Older people are particularly liable to inadequate intake of complete protein. How to surmount the obstacle of today's high cost of living and still obtain sufficient quantities of protein daily for good health will be suggested later in this chapter, and throughout this book.

Some of the hormones produced by the glands are protein substances. Antibodies which the blood carries as a barrier to disease are protein substances. Strict vegetarians and those whose protein intake is otherwise restricted run a dual risk: that of glandular disturbances and of breakdown of the immunizing mechanism of the body. The reader will now understand the physician's use of forced feeding of protein substances in long-continued infectious diseases.

Doctors suspect protein inadequacy, whose symptoms may resemble vitamin deficiency, when an individual complains of mental and physical inefficiency even though the diet is rich in protective (vitamin-mineral) foods. They also suspect it when there is a tendency to unsatisfactory reproduction, or when there are constant complaints of general ill health and fatigue. Protein deficiency can make fingernails brittle or can create a lack of resistance to infection. A rich supply of proteins means greatly enhanced growth and development throughout life and the retarding of what we knew as "old age."

To calculate an individual's protein requirement, use his body weight as a basis. For an adult, the ideal figure appears to be 1.7 grams of protein per kilo (approximately two pounds) of body weight. Thus a person weighing 150 pounds to achieve a very high protein diet will need about 120 grams of protein per day. Meat or fish averages about 20 per cent protein. If, therefore, meat or fish constitute the sole protein source in the diet, the 150-pound adult would require 600 grams of meat or fish—about one and one-quarter pounds— a day. This is mathematical computation in its simplest form, and used merely as illustration. For one should not try to obtain daily protein requirements from meat alone. This foolhardy practice would imbalance the diet; such an eater would be so filled with meat that he probably would not have the physical capacity to eat enough of other necessary foods such as the vitamin-mineral suppliers. The problem is simplified by the fact that a fairly well balanced protein intake (although by no means ideal or "optimal") for an adult needing 2,500 calories a day may be obtained by consuming eight ounces of whole wheat bread, one quart of milk and fairly liberal amounts of fruits and vegetables. There you have the two extremes, each supplying sufficient protein for survival.

We need not, however, restrict our diets to such a degree. A table of protein foods from which to choose is included at the end of this chapter. The American psychology of eating has turned us into a nation which finds it impossible to feel well fed on cottage cheese in lieu of pot roast, although many cheeses are physiologically the full equivalent of roast. Nor is it necessary to fall helplessly back on devitalized macaroni and cheese to serve a meatless menu. The good housekeeper, with some knowledge of nutrition, has a hundred devices for raising protein intake meatlessly with nutritive and gastronomical satisfaction.

## WHERE PROTEINS ARE

Our ancestors found their proteins more regularly and less expensively than we do. They fished them out of the sea, felled them on the hoof and ate some of them in edible grasses that grew all around. In our refined civilization, however, protein is the most costly element of diet. In times of national emergency, when man drops the plough for a rifle or a machine tool, meat becomes scarce and high-priced. Cereals will grow with comparatively little attention, but hogs and sheep and cattle must be watched and fed. A hundred pounds of feed may produce only ten pounds of meat, explaining the prevalence and cheapness of cereal and the scarcity and high cost of meat.

Men cannot, however, live to full potential on cereals (which are high in carbohydrates alone). Savage tribes who live almost exclusively on carbohydrates are sickly for want of vitamins and protein; African natives on such a diet are lethargic, dull-witted, without stamina and subject to disease. Indian natives who subsist on a preponderantly cereal diet suffer an incredible number of pathologies, are mentally retarded and die young. The high-fat, high-protein people—like the Eskimos—are happy and healthy, but they may become prematurely senile. The happy medium lies between the two extremes.

Milk, eggs and meat provide complete proteins, as defined in our earlier discussions; so do cheese, fish, fowl and a few other foods. Vegetables are incomplete proteins, but the addition of milk to vegetables in the diet definitely enhances the action of milk-proteins. Incomplete proteins, therefore, can and do supplement those which are complete. Whole wheat provides better protein than processed wheat (white flour) but is inferior to animal proteins. Corn, rye and barley—all unprocessed—are good proteins, but inferior to wheat. For ideal health, growth and longevity, however, you should use all the truly complete proteins, supplemented by lentils, green beans, whole grains and other incomplete protein sources.

It is on this point that vegetarians founder. If they are orthodox vegetarians, they will not eat even dairy products (which are certainly animal products) or eggs. Thus they restrict their sources of proteins to poor ones, largely incomplete, and must get along with nuts and soybeans as their only complete protein sources. In addition, because of the low amount of protein in vegetables, they must stuff themselves into obesity if they wish to maintain proper nitrogen balance.

Many orthodox and conservative vegetarians do live to a ripe, old age—and devotees of this way of life are wont to point pridefully at the illustrious among them, as for example the late great George Bernard Shaw. But good nutrition is difficult enough to achieve without fads based on unscientific premises; why avoid meat when a cow is merely walking grass? Why claim merit for vegetarianism when meat-eating animals frequently outlive the herbivorous? Since the discovery of Vitamin B12, whose sole source is animal protein, the arguments about vegetarianism should certainly end. Significantly supplied by animal proteins only, B12 is administered by doctors in treating many diseases, including anemia which is frequently suffered by vegetarians. Logic of this type, however, neither appeals to nor convinces vegetarians, for the cult represents more of a neurosis than a credo based on science. One cannot otherwise explain or justify the vegetarian who drinks milk (modified blood) and eats eggs (interrupted chickens). And what about the vegetarian who wears leather shoes and a fur coat, yet avoids eating meat on the principle that it is not right to kill in order to eat?

Among the protein foods, milk is of principal importance because its riboflavin (Vitamin B2) value will help to compensate for that which we lose when meat is scarce or expensive. In addition, milk contains the second highest quality of complete protein. The palatable combinations of milk and whole grains—for example, cereals or whole wheat bread with milk—are excellent combinations of "complete" and "incomplete" proteins. The same is true when milk is served with the legumes—beans, peas and lentils. Cheese, eggs, meat, poultry and fish are all high-quality proteins, with yellow cheeses usually superior to white cheeses as sources of both protein and calcium. Pot cheese and similar sour white cheeses, however, are to be regarded as concentrated milk, poorer in calcium than the cheddar varieties but generally as concentrated in protein values. Cream cheese might be regarded as being midway between butter and milk. Among meats, remember that the glandular types— liver, kidneys, sweetbreads—are just as rich in protein as other meats, usually less expensive, and much more concentrated in vitamin-mineral values. The savage, instinctively wise in the ways of nutrition, throws steaks and chops to his dogs and reserves the glandular meats for himself! Eskimos, too, prefer the glandular meats. It is striking that Eskimos have a lower incidence of cancer than their relatives who live near the white man's trading posts and have been seduced by the habits of civilization. In the discussion of choline in another chapter you learn why a high intake of organ meats may protect against one type of cancer.

## RULES FOR PROTEIN FOOD

Do not, in your zealousness to adhere to an adequate protein diet, serve too much of a high protein food in one meal. A medium serving of such a food in each meal is sufficient to provide enough protein. Do be sure, however, that each meal does supply at least one animal protein. Don't count milk as a protein food exclusively unless acute shortages make it necessary, for serving *too much* milk will ordinarily imbalance your diet. Remember that all your foods, with the exception of sugar and similarly overprocessed foods, contribute a little protein to your meal.

Use both animal and vegetable foods in your diet. While animal sources are best, as wide a variety of sources as possible will make you surer of completing the correct intake of amino acids.

Remember that children need disproportionately large intakes of protein. The adult is an established entity, needing only maintenance and repair of protein structures and supplies to replace those worn away in the wear and tear of living, or through illness. The child is growing, and his protein needs are fantastic. A baby will need three times as much protein per pound of body weight as an older child. That is why egg yolk is added to a baby's diet early in life. It adds high quality complete protein in good amounts (an egg is 13 percent protein) and it supplies iron, with which the newborn baby is poorly stocked and which is not present in milk in sufficient amounts. For the adult, half the proteins may be taken from animal products—meat, milk, eggs, fish, cheese; but for a child, two thirds of the proteins should come from these animal sources, with chief emphasis first on eggs and milk, second on meats, fish and fowl.

Take moderate amounts of the flesh foods. On meat or fish days, a medium-sized serving of these foods once a day is a fair rule to follow.

Use from a pint to a quart of milk daily for each person. While all forms of milk—certified raw, pasteurized, pasteurized-homogenized, and evaporated—are satisfactory foods, it should be remembered that there is evidence that certified raw milk is distinctly superior to the other forms. Condensed milk should be avoided; it is murderously high in sugar content. Evaporated milk appears to be inferior to the other forms. Puppies raised on it develop heart disease which can be prevented if Vitamin E is added to the milk. Dried skimmed milk is an excellent way to add milk-nutrients to recipes, with the advantage that where an increase in the quantity of liquid milk used would destroy many recipes, large amounts of dried non-fat milk are easily added. It must be remembered that this form of milk has been deprived of its butter-fat; therefore extra butter should be added to the diet to compensate if dried skimmed milk is the major source of milk nutrients. For limited budgets, this device yields the full benefits of ordinary pasteurized liquid milk at much lower cost. A special word about milk-haters will be found in the chapter on the Framework of Food.

Use fats sparingly when you are eating a high-protein meal. A high-fat, high-protein meal is digested slowly and with difficulty. This is one reason why the frying of protein foods is less desirable than broiling. Greasy sauces on meats are likewise antagonistic to comfortable digestion. Your butter or oleo intake at meal time will be enough fat.

## TABLE OF PROTEIN FOODS
### COMPLETE PROTEINS

## MEAT

When meat is expensive—the protein value
of one ounce of meat is replaced by:

2 tablespoonfuls of cottage cheese
(1) 1-inch cube of solid cheese
(1) 1½-inch cube of cream cheese
1 ounce of fish
1 ounce of fowl
2 shrimp
1 cup of milk soup
1½ teaspoons of soybean flour
1 egg
1 glass of milk
½ cup of custard

## INCOMPLETE PROTEINS
## (Serve Substantial Portions)

*Dried*
Marrow beans
Yellow split peas
Chick peas
Lentils
Lima beans

*Fresh*
Green peas
Green beans
Wax beans
Lima beans
Brussels sprouts
Yellow corn
Whole wheat, rye, barley
Brown rice

### SPECIAL NOTES ON SOYBEANS, POTATOES, AND RICE AS PROTEIN SOURCES

Despite the hyperbole of the claims made for soybeans by producers, marketers, and trade associations, soy products have a number of debits. Minerals well supplied by some other protein sources are sometimes poorly supplied by soy. Copper, an overload of which can contribute to the troubles of the depressed and the schizophrenic, is too generously supplied by soy products. Vitamin B12, which used to be called the "animal protein factor," obviously isn't supplied by soy, explaining the unsatisfactory growth and reproduction derived from diets in which soy is the sole protein source. Excesses of soy in the diet, particularly in the case of babies from families with a tendency to thyroid underactivity, may contribute to goiters. Soy is a valuable protein source, particularly for one of vegetable origin, but it isn't the miracle food the advertisers make it.

Our American rice—deriving from a genetically different grain from that used in the Orient, isn't as good a source of high-quality protein as the Eastern world's; yet rice protein, for a cereal protein, can be astonishingly efficient. The over-processing of our white rice doesn't help.

Potato protein, while diluted with too much carbohydrate, is also of surprisingly high efficiency. What with its Vitamin C value, the potato is sometimes described as the "poor man's orange." When eaten in sufficient quantities to make its Vitamin C contribution helpful, the potato also contributes a significant amount of useful protein. The secret of saving money on protein is diversification of sources. This invokes the complementary effects of such foods, allowing the amino acids missing or inadequately supplied by one protein food, to be made up by another. For this effect to be useful, the foods must be served at the same meal. Thus the nonfat milk in the oatmeal raises the efficiency of the oatmeal protein, but the milk at lunch doesn't help the oatmeal protein at breakfast. Even mixing cereal proteins heightens their efficiency—a secret of nutrition well understood even by primitive groups, for they will, if possible, try to serve mixtures of cereals simultaneously.

# CHAPTER NINE

## CARBOHYDRATES: CAUTION!

IN A CENTURY AND A HALF, WE HAVE RAISED OUR SUGAR intake by about one hundred pounds, per person, per year. Consumption of sugar and sugar-containing foods, both natural and processed, has risen to the point where sugar now contributes about 20 percent of the calories in many diets. Not only is this bad food ubiquitous and pervasive, but the influence of the huge income of the industry is likewise to be found everywhere—from the elementary school text-

where sweets are misdescribed as important sources of energy (though man has no physiological need for sugar) to the large universities where generous grants and gifts spark eulogies of sugar from venal professors.

Misleading is the well-entrenched belief that carbohydrate is carbohydrate—that starches are eventually converted into sugar, making it academic whether you choose to eat rice, potato, or a candy bar. Also misleading is the statement that sugar gives us energy, for millions of people with hypoglycemia have discovered that sugar can create fatigue (and a half-hundred neurotic symptoms), and millions of diabetics have learned to avoid sugar in order to retain the privilege of living. While it is quite true that starch is converted into glucose, which is the body's favorite form of sugar, and sugar is also converted into glucose, there is a missing link in the statement. Sugar *is* converted into glucose, but that's only half the truth: 50 percent of sugar is converted into fructose, or fruit sugar (levulose): and that's where the mischief begins, for fructose in large quantities can have extremely adverse effects. They have been described by Dr. John Yudkin, with whom I have had the pleasures of conducting workshops in carbohydrate metabolism, as: raising the fasting blood levels of insulin, cortisone, uric acid, cholesterol, and triglycerides; increasing the adhesiveness of blood platelets; increasing excessively the stomach production of hydrochloric acid and pepsin; increasing the size of the liver and the adrenal glands (indicating that sugar acts as a stress on the body); and shrinking the pancreas. These observations, made in experiments on both animal and human subjects, indict sugar as contributing to gout, heart attacks, strokes, hardening of the arteries, and gastric ulcers, among other illnesses.

In psychiatric patients, ranging from the neurotic to the psychotic, and in many children with hyperactivity, behavioral problems, learning difficulties, and autism, sugar has been found to be both physiologically and mentally extremely disturbing. In dental patients, sugar has been demonstrated conclusively to be a prime cause of tooth

155

decay, and a prime contributer to the periodontal diseases which threaten loss of teeth in over 80 percent of Americans over the age of thirty-five. It has been shown that fluoridation would be totally unnecessary (if, indeed, it is in any way desirable) if the public could be persuaded to stop catering to the sweet tooth, both in children and adults. With all these debits, sugar adds another: the need for B vitamins increases as sugar intake rises; and yet the supply of vitamins falls, for sugar contains nothing but calories, and displaces the vitamin-containing foods. Nor does all that complete the indictment: chromium is needed to avoid or mitigate diabetes, and not only does sugar contribute to the onset of the disorder, and not only has sugar lost the chromium orginally contained in its source—beets or sugar cane—but eating sugar causes excretion of chromium.

In research reported to the International Academy Metabology, of which I am a member, I reported that reduction of sugar intake contributed markedly to mitigation of premenstrual tension, backache, cramp, water retention and weight gain, nervousness, hysteria, and other disturbances associated with the menstrual cycle. In that paper, I traced the metabolic route by which sugar may contribute to increased susceptibility to endometriosis, the painful menstrual, cystic mastitis, uterine fibroids, and breast and, perhaps, uterine cancer.

Finally, the addition of generous amounts of sugar to an otherwise balanced diet has been demonstrated to cause symptoms indistinguishable from those of severe neurosis. Which leads to a simple conclusion: Don't stay as sweet as you are. And that admonition applies to all forms of sugar—white, yellow, brown, or raw. This doesn't mean switching to similar abuse of the artificial sweeteners, which may, in the light of Dr. Jacqueline Verret's research at the FDA (ignored by FDA), be equally dangerous. It means re-educating your palate so that you don't crave excessive sweetening in your foods.

Overprocessed cereals, whether cooked or dry, and overprocessed grains—rye, barley, buckwheat, wheat, rice, and corn—are equally undesirable. Eat whole grains, and compensate for the unavoidable sugar in your diet by use of extra bran and wheat germ, added to your recipes.

As you munch on white bread, consider the inconsistencies of what you are doing: Bread without bran creates constipation, for which you buy back the bran removed from the bread. The cotton texture of white bread largely eliminates the need for chewing, which is a step toward periodontal diseases for which you will buy water-massage machines to give your gums the exercise your bread should supply—and didn't.

One of our problems in persuading people to reduce their intake of overprocessed sugar and other carbohydrates is the widespread unwillingness to recognize exactly how much of such foods you eat. For those who think, for instance, that the sugar bowl is the prime source of the sweet, see the table listing some sources of sugar you never think about.

## APPROXIMATE REFINED CARBOHYDRATE CONTENT OF POPULAR FOODS
### EXPRESSED IN AMOUNTS EQUIVALENT TO TEASPOONFULS OF SUGAR

100 gms = 20 teaspoonfuls = 3½ oz. = 400 Calories

| FOOD | AMOUNT | SERVING | SUGAR EQUIVALENT |
|---|---|---|---|
| *Candy* | | | |
| Hershey Bar | 60 gm. | (10¢ size) | 7 tsp. sugar |
| Chocolate cream | 13 gm. | (35¢ to lb.) | 2 tsp. sugar |
| Chocolate fudge | 30 gm. | 1½ inches sq. (15 to 1 lb.) | 4 tsp. sugar |
| Chewing-gum | | 1¢ stick | 1/3 tsp. sugar |
| Life saver | | 1 usual size | 1/3 tsp. sugar |
| *Cake* | | | |
| Chocolate cake | 100 gm. | 2 layer icing (1/12 cake) | 15 tsp. sugar |
| Angel cake | 45 gm. | 1 pc. (1/12 large cake) | 6 tsp. sugar |
| Sponge cake | 50 gm. | 1/10 of average cake | 6 tsp. sugar |
| Cream puff (iced) | 80 gm. | 1 average custard filled | 5 tsp. sugar |
| Doughnut plain | 40 gm. | 3 inches in diameter | 4 tsp. sugar |
| *Cookies* | | | |
| Macaroons | 25 gm. | 1 large or 2 small | 3 tsp. sugar |
| Gingersnaps | 6 gm. | 1 medium | 1 tsp. sugar |
| Brownies | 20 gm. | 2x2x¾ inches | 3 tsp. sugar |
| *Custards* | | | |
| Custard, baked | | ½ cup | 4 tsp. sugar |
| Gelatin | | ½ cup | 4 tsp. sugar |
| Junket | | ⅛ quart | 3 tsp. sugar |
| *Ice Cream* | | | |
| Ice cream | | ⅛ quart | 5 to 6 tsp. sugar |
| Water ice | | ⅛ quart | 6 to 8 tsp. sugar |
| *Pie* | | | |
| Apple pie | | 1/6 of med. pie | 12 tsp. sugar |
| Cherry pie | | 1/6 of med. pie | 14 tsp. sugar |
| Custard, coconut pie | | 1/6 of med. pie | 10 tsp. sugar |
| Pumpkin pie | | 1/6 of med. pie | 10 tsp. sugar |

## Sauce

| | | | |
|---|---|---|---|
| Chocolate sauce | 30 gm. | 1 tsp. thick hp. | 4½ tsp. sugar |
| Marshmallow | 7.6 gm. | 1 aver. (60 to 1 lb.) | 1½ tsp. sugar |

## Spreads

| | | | |
|---|---|---|---|
| Jam | 20 gm. | 1 tablespoon level or 1 heaping tsp. | 3 tsp. sugar |
| Jelly | 20 gm. | 1 tbsp. level or 1 hp. tsp. | 2½ tsp. sugar |
| Marmalade | 20 gm. | 1 tbsp. level or 1 hp. tsp. | 3 tsp. sugar |
| Honey | 20 gm. | 1 tbsp. level or 1 hp. tsp. | 3 tsp. sugar |

## Milk Drinks

| | | | |
|---|---|---|---|
| Chocolate (all milk) | | 1 cup, 5 oz. milk | 6 tsp. sugar |
| Cocoa (all milk) | | 1 cup, 5 oz. milk | 4 tsp. sugar |
| Cocomalt (all milk) | | 1 glass, 8 oz. milk | 4 tsp. sugar |

## Soft Drinks

| | | | |
|---|---|---|---|
| Coca Cola | 180 gm. | 1 bottle, 6 oz. | 4-1/3 tsp. sugar |
| Gingerale | 180 gm. | 6 oz. glass | 4-1/3 tsp. sugar |

## Cooked Fruits

| | | | |
|---|---|---|---|
| Peaches, canned in syrup | 10 gm. | 2 halves, 1 tbsp. juice | 3½ tsp. sugar |
| Rhubarb, stewed | 100 gm. | ½ cup sweetened | 8 tsp. sugar |
| Apple sauce (no sugar) | 100 gm. | ½ cup scant | 2 tsp. sugar |
| Prunes, stewed, sweetened | 100 gm. | 4 to 5 med., 2 tbsp. juice | 8 tsp. sugar |

## Dried Fruits

| | | | |
|---|---|---|---|
| Apricots, dried | 30 gm. | 4 to 6 halves | 4 tsp. sugar |
| Prunes, dried | 30 gm. | 3 to 4 med. | 4 tsp. sugar |
| Dates, dried | 30 gm. | 3 to 4 stoned | 4½ tsp. sugar |
| Figs, dried | 30 gm. | 1½ to 2 small | 4 tsp. sugar |
| Raisins | 30 gm. | ¼ cup | 4 tsp. sugar |

## Fruits and Fruit Juices

| | | | |
|---|---|---|---|
| Fruit cocktail | 120 gm. | ½ cup, scant | 5 tsp. sugar |
| Orange juice | 100 gm. | ½ cup, scant | 2 tsp. sugar |
| Grapefruit juice, unsweetened | 100 gm. | ½ cup, scant | 2-1/5 tsp. sugar |
| Grapejuice, commercial | 100 gm. | ½ cup, scant | 3-2/3 tsp. sugar |
| Pineapple juice, unsweetened | 100 gm. | ½ cup, scant | 2-3/5 tsp. sugar |

# HOW MUCH SUGAR AND STARCH IS NEEDED?

It is as impossible to set a standard for carbohydrate intake as it would be to answer the question: How much money does a person need? The requirement for carbohydrates varies from individual to individual; so does the *tolerance*. There are those who feel best when on a low-carbohydrate diet, supplying from sixty to one hundred grams of carbohydrates daily. There are those who conquer their weight problem and feel best with less; and there are those who need more. One sees these individual differences sharply delineated in patients with low blood sugar. They all profit by—and *must* have—a diet as low in sugar as possible. Many of them function best when the carbohydrates, in the form of complex starches, are held to about sixty grams daily. Some of them acutely need more, and the extra amount which makes the difference between feeling truly well and feeling ill and tired may be as little as that supplied by a half of a baked potato, twice daily. All this casts a light on man's dietetic history, over the millenia. He evolved in an environment in which concentrated starches and sugars were virtually nonexistent, and didn't achieve staple sources of high starch foods until he invented agriculture, which wasn't so very long ago. Sugar, in the concentrated form, came later, and consumption of it was limited, for it was scarce and expensive. Some of us adapted to the high carbohydrate diet. Some even adapted to generous intake of sugar. Many of us adapted to neither. Which means that only practical experience, coupled, sometimes, with the tests and advice of a competent medical nutritionist, can tell us at what carbohydrate intake we function best. But this generalization can be made:

Physiologically, it is best to eat carbohydrates that furnish body-building elements—vitamins, mineral protein—as well as calories. This means, eat whole grain cereals, breads, cornmeal, barley, buckwheat, and rye, and brown rice in preference to white. It also means minimizing the use of white sugar and its products—candy, syrup, sugary drinks, jelly, jam and other similar stomach-filling but body-starving concoctions. A famous physician who practices the science of nutrition has seriously proposed that a law be passed forbidding the sale of sweet foods and drinks within a quarter of a mile of any school!

## RULES FOR EATING CARBOHYDRATES

Do not serve more than two foods rich in sugar or starches at the same meal. When you serve bread and potatoes, your starch license has expired for that meal. Dinner that includes peas, bread, potatoes, sugar, cake and after-coffee mints should also include a Vitamin B Complex capsule, a dose of bicarbonate of soda and the address of the nearest specialist in degenerative diseases!

Aviod eating insufficiently baked hot breads. If you must eat them, chew them thoroughly. The rumor that hot breads are indigestible appears to be superstition, and so is the mistaken belief that day-old bread is somehow more nutritious and digestible than fresh. No food gains nutritional value by standing.

Do not eat any carbohydrate foods which are soggy in texture because of improper frying.

To the housewife: If your family is accustomed to processed carbohydrates, don't try a head-on attack on an established food habit by suddenly switching to whole wheat bread, brown rice, and other whole grains. And never tell the family that such new dishes are "good for them," for this is a phrase inviting any red-blooded male (and his imitative children) to protest that he will not eat anything which threatens him with good health. Begin a subversive and surreptitious and outflanking attack on established habits with impoverished carbohydrate foods by (a) doing more home baking, and (b) using unbleached flour, and (c) adding a teaspoonful of bran to each cup of flour. Switch to brown rice, next. Then try some undegerminated corn meal, and finally, some whole wheat baked recipes.

# CHAPTER 10

## FATS FOR YOUR FURNACE

NO DIET, NOT EVEN ONE DESIGNED TO REDUCE overweight, should be completely devoid of fats. The human body needs fat to provide fuel, to help utilize the fat-soluble vitamins, to protect nerves and support internal organs. Fat also serves as a reserve supply for emergencies. If you skip a meal, either through necessity or deliberation, you do your body an injustice for it never skips its needs. A reserve supply of fat comes in very handy at this time, for, in the absence of nourishment, your body feeds on itself.

A diet that is too low in fats produces great irritability, as you must know if you have ever attempted a starvation diet. The reason for this is that the nerve sheaths lose their protective cushions—hence, "raw" nerves, exposed to the impact of irritations. Faddists in diet who resort to fasting in order to lose weight rapidly run into other difficulties as well. When the body is driven to feeding on its own fat, the fat burns with what is called a "smoky flame" and results in a dangerous condition of acidosis. By this is meant true acidosis, which can sometimes be fatal, not the word employed by lay advertisers who claim that it will respond to this or that mild medication.

Fats also supply a flavor to make foods taste better, and eating should be fun. They give a satisfying quality to meals because they slow up digestion, making meals "stick to the ribs." Too much fat, however, retards digestion excessively. This is why too many fat-rich foods in one meal make you feel lethargic. Fats are the natural carriers of some vitamins, too. Some fats—wheat germ oil or corn oil, for instance—contain fatty acids which may aid in the digestion of other fatty substances.

Do not be indiscriminately harsh on all fried foods, for some may be eaten in moderation without causing distress. Frying has actually been found *less* destructive to certain

162

vitamins than broiling (see "The Ten Commandments of Cooking") but fried foods are somewhat more difficult to digest and should, therefore, be omitted for children or for adults who are tired or ill.

In the process of frying, fat is heated to a temperature which is sometimes high enough to break it down, producing decomposition elements which are highly irritating. There have been reports that overheating fats, or fats carried to the smoking point too often, can cause cancer in animals. Therefore, it is important to select fats which have not been cooked to the decomposition point.

## DECOMPOSITION POINTS OF FATS

| | |
|---|---|
| Olive oil | 175° C. |
| Butter | 208° C. |
| Leaf lard | 214-221° C. |
| Hydrogenated fats | 219-232° C. |
| Cottonseed and corn oils | 222-232° C. |

These figures do not mean that you must discard butter for frying. Simply adjust your frying temperature to suit the characteristics of the particular fat you are using, but have it as hot as possible—without decomposition—before putting the food in. This way, you sear the food and prevent the loss of juices and the absorption of fat. After the food is seared, reduce the heat. Starchy foods fare better in frying than do proteins. The frying of proteins nearly always lowers their digestibility.

Be careful to avoid using rancid fats, for they interfere with the utilization of Vitamin E. Always refrigerate fats, salad oils and fatty foods, but remember that even refrigeration will not protect these foods against rancidity forever. This is why you may keep beef in a food freezer for a year or longer, while frozen pork, which is fattier, can be stored for only a few months.

The body has a requirement for two different types of fats—the unsaturated fatty acids and the saturated. It is believed that adults have the capacity to synthesize some of the required fats, but that children do not. For this reason, the theory holds, children up to the age of twelve are more subject to infections. Inasmuch as certain of the unsaturated fatty acids must be available if the body is to manufacture the saturated ones it requires, at least 10 percent of the total fat intake should come from corn oil, wheat germ oil or other vegetable oils which are rich in unsaturated fatty acids. Neither butter nor margarine nor the hydrogenated vegetable shortenings will supply the requisite unsaturated fatty acids. How important unsaturated fatty acids may be is realized when one sees the eczemas which newborn babies develop as a result of a deficiency in this type of fat in the mothers' prenatal diets. The responses of these children to a few teaspoonfuls of lard, corn or wheat germ oil daily is sometimes dramatic.

In choosing and using fats, therefore, remember the rule of "not too much, not too little."

One should also remember that the intake of polyunsaturated fat is directly related to the requirement for Vitamin E. While vegetable fats of this nature ordinarily contain Vitamin E, the amounts vary from oil to oil, as does the type of Vitamin E supplied. Vitamin E in the active form is not well supplied by all vegetable oils. When the authorities informed the public that deficiency in Vitamin E is impossible because of the wide occurrence of the vitamin in foods, they choose to ignore that fact that the forms of Vitamin E occurring in many foods are often relatively inactive in the body, or at least very much less active than the alpha, beta, gamma, and delta tocopherols. Which explains a previous admonition for those who supplement their diets with Vitamin E: Always take it in the form of mixed tocopherols, with the potency expressed in terms of alpha tocopherol. The preferred type of alpha tocopherol is the d-alpha. "D-L" is an unnatural form, which means that it is the synthetic vitamin; and in the case of Vitamin E, we have the only vitamin which in synthetic form has been demonstrated to be less effective than the natural.

## SPECIAL NOTES ON SPECIAL OILS:

Coconut oil is the most undesirable of all the vegetable oils.

Sesame oil has a unique effectiveness in helping to increase the number of blood platelets, which in certain hemorragic disorders, may be depressed.

Olive oil, for those concerned about the effects of animal fat on cholesterol levels, is likely to behave more like an animal than a vegetable fat.

Wheat germ oil, properly extracted, has unique properties, some of which were discussed in the section on nerve-muscle disorders, but wheat germ oil also shows unusual helpfulness, when given with zinc and Vitamin B6, for the benign enlarged prostate gland.

Finally, the term "cold-pressed" on health food store oils is somewhat misleading. The laws of physics dictate that pressure will cause heat. In addition, the processes of deodorizing and clarifying oils involve much treatment with bleaches, charcoal filtering, applications of cold, use of alkali, and virtually all oils are treated with one, and usually more than one, of such processes. The chief virtue of health food store oils is the absence of BHT, BHA and other preservatives. Virtually the only supermarket oil devoid of these undesirable chemicals is cottonseed oil. This has been criticized on the grounds of excessive use of pesticides on cotton, as a nonfood crop, but such critics forget that there is a legal ceiling on pesticide residues, whatever the product.

Elsewhere in this book, you will find explicit suggestions for the use of Vitamin E supplements. Remember that higher intake of polyunsaturated fat *demands* such supplements. The requisite ratio between intake of these fats and intake of Vitamin E has been established: It requires .6 mgs. of alpha tocopherol to allow the body properly to metabolize 1 gram of polyunsaturated fat. When you don't know the Vitamin E content of a fat or oil, your

Vitamin E supplement becomes an important protection against a type of fat oxidation, which can be the first step toward premature senility.

# CHAPTER 11

## BULKAGE

THE WORD USUALLY EMPLOYED TO DESCRIBE THE FOODS under discussion here is "roughage." This, however, seems too harsh and impolite a word to use for the residue carrying foods that are helpful to normal elimination, and nutritionists prefer the gentler, more complimentary term of "bulkage."

The bulkage foods are fruits, vegetables and whole grains, and they have in common types and amounts of indigestible residue which serve to encourage natural elimination. Moreover, they provide vitamins and minerals which may not be offered by the low-residue foods.

"Wake up sluggish intestines!" the ads say, offering a pill. Well, there is a certain amount of justification here. Our modern food technology refines and processes the food we eat to a perilous degree. It offers us white bread which has been deprived of bran. We eat the white bread, develop constipation and then for relief buy separately the bran which has been removed from white bread. Civilization also gives us pretty, polished rice purged of its uncouth brown coating. Since the discovery of vitamins, however, those polishings are carefully saved and sold back to us in drug stores as one of the important ingredients of supplementary capsules. Seems silly, doesn't it?

Overprocessing removes the natural vitamins and minerals from food and also removes the indigestible residue. The intestines, which have not been consulted about all this refinement, still work on the old principle that they have a job to do. Left without work, they go on strike—frequently a lie-down one. Low-residue foods (such as white sugar or flour) "burn" so completely that they leave no "ashes" on which the lower intestine may work; they are also low in vitamins and minerals needed to stimulate the proper functioning of the intestine.

Here are the reasons why fruits, vegetables and whole grains—the bulkage foods— are important in the daily diet:

1. They contain valuable vitamins and minerals.
2. They have a stimulating effect on appetite, flow of gastric juices and digestion.
3. A uniquely high Vitamin C intake is made possible with fruits and vegetables, many of which can be eaten raw. Since Vitamin C is easily destroyed, this is an important consideration.
4. These foods—along with milk—promote intestinal hygiene. They favor conditions in the intestines which rout undigested food residues, which consequently do not remain in your interior as a happy hunting ground for putrefying bacteria.

The acids and minerals in fruits have a specific effect in stimulating the muscular contractions of the intestines. In addition, these foods are "basic"—or alkaline—in their reactions. This is important, for poor dietary habits usually lead to a predominance of acid-forming foods, an undesirable condition.

At whatever price, therefore, fruits and vegetables are not luxuries. In some of the author's diets, fruits are used more than vegetables. Botanically, there is nothing magical about fruits; they are similar to tubers and roots in nutritional properties. They do not, however, impose a tax on the digestive organs because they contain little or no fat. Their digestible parts are *very* digestible, and their undigestible parts constitute desirable bulkage. And, of course, they are extremely palatable. All of this does not mean that the faddist is right when he "fasts" on orange juice or "cleanses" his system with five days of grape juice and little or nothing else. Starvation is an unwise extreme, and so is an imbalanced diet. Fruits hold no magic. They are merely ingredients in a balanced diet.

Nearly everyone can eat raw fruit and, except for green salads, raw food is not easy to introduce into the modern diet. For this reason we specify a goodly amount of fruit, for raw food in reasonable amounts is a fine source of certain vitamins. Vegetables are susceptible to abuse in cooking, for many homemakers have a tendency to overcook, thus destroying vitamins.

## DIETARY RULES FOR FRUITS AND VEGETABLES

1. Eat fruit at least twice daily. Do not count dried fruits such as prunes, dried apricots, dried apples, currants or raisins. These do not supply Vitamin C. Eat them, if you will, for minerals and for other vitamins; but when you serve prunes for breakfast, remember that you still have not served your daily requirement of Vitamin C. Sun drying is essentially a process of slow cooking. Vacuum dried fruit is, therefore, preferable. Do not worry about the sulfur dioxide about which you may have heard caustic criticism. The body rejects sulfur from inorganic sources. It is true that sulfur dioxide destroys some of the thiamin (Vitamin B1) in dried fruits, but these foods are not good sources of Vitamin B1 anyway.
2. Use eight ounces of fresh or frozen fruit juices daily, ten of canned. The extra two ounces of juice compensates for Vitamin C losses in canning. Do not buy sweetened juices—your diet is saturated with sugar as it is.

Take fruit juices AFTER breakfast if they have been disturbing you. On an empty stomach they are sources of indigestion for many people. If they continue to disturb you, here are two things to try: First, reduce your quota of toast and cereal at breakfast, and take your juice after the meal. Or—and this is better—take your juice an hour or so after breakfast. Hot water *plus* fruit juice is a good pre-breakfast habit. Be sure to use equal parts of water and juice. Do not use lemon juice—it attacks teeth—unless you use a straw.

Unsweetened frozen orange juice of tree-ripened fruit is distinctly more palatable than either canned juice or fresh fruit which is not tree-ripened. The Vitamin C value of frozen fruit is at least as high as the others, and often higher.

When you purchase whole oranges, select those with a natural deep yellow *juice*. (The color of the skin is not important.) There is nothing very wrong with "color-added" oranges, but paleness of the juice indicates that it is low in carotene, which is Vitamin A in vegetable form. Be guided by your purse. Color-added oranges are still a good source of Vitamin C.

Whenever possible, eat the whole fruit rather than just its juice. Most of the bioflavanoid value is adjacent to the skin of the citrus fruits. The pulp, left behind in squeezing, contains 75 percent of the minerals inherent in the fruit. Besides, your teeth need the exercise of chewing more than your arm needs the exercise of squeezing. Remember, too, the skin of fruits (except oranges, grapefruit and lemons) are good for a normal person with a healthy stomach. They yield bulkage as well as a very high vitamin-mineral content.

3. Eat vegetables twice daily. Among cooked vegetables include a green leafy one, if possible. Pick your vegetables for color. The yellow, green and red ones are always richer in vitamins and minerals than the white. Avoid bleached vegetables, such as bleached escarole, celery or endive; their whiteness is a sign that their vitamin content has been lowered. Here is another example of civilization's irony. The housewife pays a premium price for white celery, but green celery—usually lower in cost—is much richer in vitamin value.

4. Eat potatoes or any other starchy vegetables only once a day. Do not peel potatoes! Why work so hard, when the result of your labor is that you are discarding the part of the potato that is most concentrated in minerals? Baked

or steamed potatoes are preferable; boiled and served with the skin on, next. Potatoes with the skin on can be concealed in stews and hash, so that no one need know he is eating healthfully, if inelegantly. The cooking water from scrubbed unpeeled potatoes is an excellent soup base. Do not accept potatoes with a touch of green on them. This may mean that they have been grown too close to the surface of the ground, in which case they sometimes develop solinase—a poison.

5. Eat salad at least once a day, and make it a heaping plateful. Better yet, eat two smaller servings daily. Be a pioneer—select salads from the long list of greens listed at the end of this chapter. There is more to a salad than a piece of lettuce, a few slices of tomatoes and a dab of dressing. There are salad greens—escarole is one—which have ten times as much vitamin value as lettuce, yet cost less.

Please remember that the nutritionist has been forced to reverse himself on the question of using the peels and rinds of vegetables where possible. The insecticide residues present enough risk so that this is no longer good advice. It is quite true that vegetables and fruits may internally pick up some of the toxic insecticide residues from the soil—but there is no possible way to obtain food from outer space, and therefore we can only minimize our difficulties by sacrificing the peels of foods, however vitamin-mineral rich they may be. Washing vegetables does not remove an appreciable amount of insecticide residue. Cooking may degrade a certain amount of that residue.

## RECOMMENDED GREENS
## FOR SALAD OR COOKING

In the following list of highly nutritious greens you may run across some which are strangers to your table. Befriend them. They will reward you with gratis gifts of vitamins and minerals. They will, moreover, add the piquance of variety to your meals.

Use the young tender shoots for salad, and cook the older ones for about four minutes. You can serve these with a mixture of thoroughly rendered bacon chopped with onions and browned with a little flour. This is both palatable and nutritious. For eye appeal as well as good nutrition, fill the center of backed squash with this mixture. When such an attractive vegetable dish is served with liver in any form it is virtually a vitamin eye-prescription, rich in the vitamins and minerals which affect twilight and night vision!

For salad, toss together as many of the tender young leaves as you can garnish with carrot, tomato, scallion, onion, cucumber, green pepper or pimentoes. To persuade the jaded palate, serve salads with French, Russian, garlic or cheese dressings. If your husband insults this course as "rabbit food," remind him that rabbits don't have bay windows. Permit children to eat salads with their fingers. The novelty obscures their prejudice against a strange food.

Choose greens from this grouping:

Tender Beet greens, Turnip greens, Mustard greens, Collards, Chicory, Kale, Escarole, Swiss Chard, Loose leaf green lettuce, Broccoli, Cabbage, Lettuce (outer leaves), Chinese Cabbage, Watercress, Parsley, Carrot and Celery tops.

## WEEDS ARE GOOD NUTRITION

The weeds you curse in the garden can be a blessing on the dining table. Such weeds as dandelion greens are treasured foods to New Englanders and other informed people. Unknown to millions of Americans are many other similarly delicious weeds. Consult the research of Dr. George Washington Carver for guidance.

# CHAPTER 12

## ALL ABOUT VITAMINS

### *A Condensation of the Latest Vitamin Information*

THIS SECTION COMPRISES A SURVEY AND DISCUSSION OF those all-important microscopic substances, the vitamins. You will learn what they are, where they exist and how vital they are to the healthy functioning of your body.

In order to realize the importance of buying foods rich in these vitamins, it is essential that you understand what happens when an animal or human being is deficient in them; it is also edifying to know for what medical purposes they are given to patients by physicians. It is hoped that the knowledge you gain here will help you remember the urgent necessity for intelligent food shopping and preparation, for vitamins must be shielded from alkalies, light, air and excessive heat if they are to be profitable to your well-being.

## VITAMIN A

### GUARDIAN OF YOUR EYES, TEETH, BONES, SKIN, SOFT TISSUES

Although green growing things are the original source of all the Vitamin A in the world, this essential vitamin does not exist *per se* in any vegetable. This may seem to be a contradiction until we learn that the source substance in edible green leaves, fruits and vegetables is *carotene*, the mother substance from which your liver manufactures the true Vitamin A. It therefore follows that when we eat domestic animal liver, fish roe, eggs and other dairy foods—all of which are high in true Vitamin A—we are actually eating *carotene* which has very kindly been assimilated and transformed into the true vitamin by the creatures of earth and sea.

Vitamin A deficiency reveals itself in many ways. It dries the skin. It delays the formation of the visual purple in the eyes, thereby causing difficulty in adjusting vision to changes in the intensity of light—as, for example, going from a light room into darkness, or vice versa. The soft tissues of the body need the vitamin—those of the nose, mouth, throat, digestive tract and the male and female genital organs. Other signs of Vitamin A deficiency are soft enamel and many cavities in the teeth; inflammation or pimples at points where hair comes through the skin, especially on the upper back, thighs and legs; susceptibility to colds, sinus trouble, ear infections, tonsilitis, bronchitis and similar respiratory infections. A deficiency may predispose an individual to kidney stones and may be a contributory cause of certain allergies.

You will begin to understand why physicians use large doses of Vitamin A to help break a cold, to treat certain skin disorders and disturbances of the eyesight, to help guard against return of kidney stones and in treating some disturbances of the soft tissues.

In nutrition, as in all else, we are highly individualistic. Not all of us convert our *carotene* (from vegetables) into Vitamin A in adequate percentages. Some persons change only 25 percent of their carotene into the true vitamin; diabetics change it inefficiently and must be fed sufficient quantities of the true vitamin, from animal sources, or they may remain deficient even though their diet is high in vegetables and fruit.

Some diseases which interfere with utilization of carotene also block utilization of true Vitamin A. In liver disease, gall bladder disturbances and other ailments which include disturbance of fat metabolism, both carotene and Vitamin A utilization may be impaired. In such cases, true Vitamin A in concentrated form, *accompanied by bile salts and lecithin*, may be better utilized, and the diet must be kept as high in fats as tolerance permits.

It is not only the ailing, however, who are poor carotene

metabolizers. The milk from a perfectly healthy Jersey cow is yellowish because carotene is yellow and the Jersey cow does not efficiently convert carotene into Vitamin A, which is colorless. The Holstein's milk, on the other hand, is white because this breed does change carotene into Vitamin A with full efficiency. A child who displays decayed teeth on the same diet which his tooth-healthy brother is eating may be the "Jersey Cow" type of child—a poor carotene converter.

"To see or not to see" was never part of Hamlet's famous soliloquy, but it might well be included in your own philosophical regard for Vitamin A and its colleague, Vitamin B2 (riboflavin). Ask yourself these questions:

1. When you come from darkness to a brightly lighted room or a sunlit street, do you blink, squint or find your eyes watering or burning?

2. When you read, knit or play cards under bright artificial light do you develop a headache, eyestrain, facial twitching or eyelid tic even when your sight is supposedly perfect or your eyeglasses presumably correct?

3. When you drive at night do approaching bright headlights blind you?

4. When you enter a dark movie house from a brightly lighted lobby do you have to wait awhile until your eyes adjust sufficiently for you to spot an empty seat?

If you answered yes to these questions, you may not have enough Vitamins A and B2 in your diet. Let us examine what happens when you use your eyes.

As a light ray strikes your eyes it is believed to pass through a visual screen of Vitamin B2 (riboflavin), which turns the light into a green wave-length whose restful quality eases the strain of a bright light. After passing through the visual screen of Vitamin B2, the light ray strikes the visual purple rods of the eyes. In these rods is a purple dye, sensitive to light and comprised of a loose chemical union of carotene, Vitamin A and protein. When the light ray strikes the rods, the sensitive dye is bleached out and the loose combination of vitamins breaks up. Now the carotene and the Vitamin A—naked and defenseless, since they are no longer protected by the protein—are partly destroyed by the light ray. As this happens, the eye's visual ability is impaired. Without knowing what caused it, you may have experienced the temporary "blindness" that occurs when you stare at a bright light too long. What happens is that you destroy part of the Vitamin B2 in your eyes, then part of the Vitamin A, and you "see" blackness. Coming to the rescue, your body marshals reserves of these two vitamins, rebuilds the purple color in the rods and restores your vision. If, however, you do not have enough Vitamin A and B2 in your blood, trouble with vision is inevitable.

When extra Vitamin A is given to industrial workers who labor under bright lights, they become much more efficient in their work and complain less of eyestrain and headaches. These workers also find that their colds are less frequent and far less severe. It must be pointed out, however, that Vitamin A alone is often not enough to correct conditions of eyestrain and chronic colds. Other vitamins and certain minerals are also involved, which is why multiple supplements are preferable to single vitamins or arbitrary combinations. In order to utilize Vitamin A properly, the body needs bile salts. (This is true of any fat-soluble vitamin—A, D, E, K.) If the diet is deficient in fat or the body deficient in bile salt production, the efficacy of vitamin capsules is decreased. Individuals who do not seem to gain heightened resistance to colds through the use of multiple supplements sometimes do so when the vitamins are administered in unconcentrated cod-liver oil. The answer to this puzzle is found in the oil's *fat* content which is not present in the fish-liver *concentrate* ordinarily used in a capsule.

If you are someone who continually has colds, despite a faithful routine of multiple capsules, and other physical causes have been excluded, try the fish-liver *oil* as a preventive. Remember, however, to continue your use of the multiple capsules, for the oil supplies only two vitamins—A and D. These alone constitute a poor insurance policy for a diet which may be low in twelve vitamins, plus assorted minerals. The rule is—use a complete supplement, not a partial one; take all the vitamins, not a few; be sure to get all the necessary minerals, not just two or three. They all work better together. If you do not utilize Vitamin A properly, use a multiple vitamin supplement, unconcentrated cod-liver oil and a small amount of lecithin.

Some Vitamin A is destroyed in cooking and there are some losses in canning. Freezing of foods, however, sacrifices only a slight amount. Losses in dried foods may be quite high. A fresh apricot contains 50 percent more Vitamin A than its dehydrated counterpart. By the same token, milk during the winter season—when cows eat dried food—is lower in Vitamin A value than summer milk. Yet you need a uniform supply of the vitamin all year 'round and a dip in that supply certainly should not occur in the winter when colds and respiratory infections are most prevalent. It is not coincidence that winter, when vitamin supplies are likely to be lower, is the time of greatest health threats. Here is further evidence of the advantages offered by certified raw milk, which is discussed more fully in Part III, chapter 1. Certified cows are fed such a fine diet that the vitamin value of the milk remains uniformly high throughout the entire year.

A word about your requirements: Although the government believes that 5,000 units of Vitamin A daily is sufficient for an active man or woman, 6,000 for a pregnant woman and 8,000 for a nursing mother, research has convinced many authorities that these amounts do not represent a sufficient margin of safety, even for the "average" person. For those who are not "average," such minimal intake may actually result in deficiency. Dr. H. C. Sherman of Columbia University has reported that increased intake of the vitamin—four times the maintenance intake—adds considerably to the life-span of animals, literally extending their prime of life. We therefore agree that 15,000 to 25,000 units of Vitamin A daily are likely to raise individual resistance to respiratory infections and tooth decay. The higher amount also provides protection to eyes and soft tissues.

Try to obtain generous amounts of Vitamin A in your diet from both animal and vegetable sources. You may raise your intake to ideal amounts without increasing calories by using multiple supplements. Consult the chart on foods and their vitamin contents at the end of this section. Regular consumption of recommended foods should yield at least 10,000 units of Vitamin A daily. When you "feel a cold coming on," large doses of additional Vitamin A may be used to throw it off. Don't wait until the cold breaks in all its miserable fury; reach for extra Vitamin A at the first sniffle.

The preceding sentence was first written more than thirty years ago. Research and observations in the intervening years have brought into being an added body of knowledge concerning the action of Vitamin A in colds. Earlier in this text, it was noted that there are individuals whose colds respond to Vitamin C—and not to Vitamin A; and others in whom the situation reverses. The long perspective has taught me that these are two different populations: the Vitamin A responders, and the Vitamin C responders. (Do keep in mind that there are nonresponders, and that there are colds that respond to nothing but a dozen handkerchiefs and the proverbial hot toddy or raspberry tea.)

If a Vitamin A responder takes high doses of Vitamin C to break his cold, he moves the cold from his head to his chest, and winds up with a bronchitis, which will last until the Vitamin C dosage is markedly reduced or eliminated.

If a Vitamin C responder takes the large doses of Vitamin A to break a cold, nothing happens.

If a pessimist, not knowing which type he is, takes both large doses of Vitamin A and of Vitamin C, he may reduce his cold to a lower level of activity, but it will persist at that low level.

It becomes obvious that those who don't know to which vitamin they will respond, if at all, should begin with Vitamin A as an initial trial. I note ruefully that I can't persuade my friend, Dr. Linus Pauling, that high doses of Vitamin C will create a bronchitis in a Vitamin A responder, but I *know* whereof I write.

The orthodox medical establishment, of course, denies that vitamins do *anything* for a cold. They don't seem to know that Dr. C. Ward Crampton, more than two decades ago, published a study in the *New York State Journal of Medicine,* reporting successful use of 250,000 units of Vitamin A daily, for five days, in aborting colds. They seem to forget that Vitamin C in high dosage was demonstrated in 1941 to have an antihistamine effect—and they don't remember that every physician prescribes antihistamines to benefit cold sufferers. In fact, all the cold tablets and capsules on the market *are* antihistamines.

Mention of 250,000 units of Vitamin A daily, for five days, will immediately stir questions about the toxicity of Vitamin A. This issue is synthetic, contrived by the FDA as an effective component of their unending drive against the use of vitamins, a drive which well suits the commercial purposes of the processed foods industry, whose products look much better if the importance of vitamins is minimized. In the cases of Vitamin A toxicity cited by the FDA to "prove" the vitamin is toxic, vast overdoses were given for periods of many months or many years. In the same scale of overdoses, I have demonstrated, equal toxicity will be displayed by the caffeine in coffee, and death (not just toxicity, but lethal effect) would be derived from ordinary table salt. No one is suggesting routine, everyday use of hundreds of thousands of units of Vitamin A, but no one should be suggesting potential harm from everyday use of quantities of Vitamin A, which some people actually *need.* FDA limits Vitamin A potency to 10,000 units per capsule—which doesn't stop anyone from taking fifty a day, and thereby accomplishes nothing in protecting the public. But has anyone reminded my older readers that the cod-liver oil they took as babies contained as much as 33,000 units of Vitamin A per teaspoonful? And not having a vigilant FDA around, you didn't have the sense to fall dead?

Though this text has always emphasized the importance of the interrelationships between vitamins and minerals, one observation on a specific interaction between Vitamin A and a mineral now requires special emphasis. That is the interdependence of Vitamin A and zinc. Some people who should (and don't) respond to Vitamin A supplements will sometimes do so, if given moderate supplementation with zinc, a metal which, unfortunately, like so many others, is depleted in food processing, and not restored in any of the enrichment techniques.

In otosclerosis, an ear condition frequently interfering with hearing—especially in women—Vitamin A therapy, in high doses, has been reported helpful. The vitamin has also been used in dysmenorrhea (the painful menstrual) in high doses, its helpfulness probably deriving from a stimulating effect on the pituitary gland. The realization has grown that long before Vitamin A deficiency causes night blindness, it will diminish the sensitivity of the eyes to light, by up to 90 percent, thereby interfering with the acuity of vision. In icthyosis, a skin condition resembling fish scales, large doses of Vitamin A have been found helpful, particularly when the vitamin is administered in the emulsified or water-dispersible form. The vitamin is now available in synthetic form, which appears to be as effective as the natural, and this may be a boon to those who are allergic to fish or, at least, to fish-liver oils.

I have long had an uneasy feeling that some of the "trivial" components of fish-liver oils, such as cod-liver oil, may be important to small children, if not to adults. That translates into a dissatisfaction with the Vitamin A-D concentrates, which are used in infants' and children's multiple supplements and vitamin-drop preparations. I think babies, at least, lost added benefits when we discarded the use of old-fashioned cod-liver oil for infants.

## VITAMIN B

### "GROUP INSURANCE" FOR YOUR
### NERVES, BRAIN, AND ENERGY!

Vitamin B was the first of all the vitamins to be discovered and, at the beginning, was believed to be a single substance. A quarter of a century of intensive research later, the original substance was divided into two parts, one of which was Vitamin B1 as it remains today. The second part, named Vitamin B2, was soon discovered to be divisible also, and the scientists began to realize that they had in their hands a very complex situation indeed. Eagerly probing the secrets of this amazing Vitamin B complex, the chemists soon extracted and synthesized an orange powder which we call Vitamin B2. The English call this same vitamin B2, and it is also known in chemical circles as "riboflavin." This information is included here in the event you find yourself on a radio or television quiz program and are asked what are the differences among Vitamin B2 and riboflavin. Just remember to answer—there is no difference.

Having gone so far, the scientists ventured further and soon triumphantly brought to recognition Vitamin B6 which was finally synthesized as pyridoxin, a vitamin of many marvels. Synthesis—a molecular and atomic duplication of the natural form—brought the price per gram down to pennies; without man's ingenuity in exactly copying nature, the process of extracting pyridoxin in its pristine state from foods would be as tedious and costly as radium extraction.

Next in the romantic saga of the B Complex came niacin (nicotinic acid) which was found effective in treating pellagra. Ironically, nicotinic acid was first manufactured around the time of the Civil War, before vitamins were known. A reaction product of nicotine, the therapeutically precious factor of niacin remained a laboratory curiosity while thousands of people died of pellagra.

Still more treasures were to come from the remarkable B Complex, and our lives are now enriched by the factors choline, biotin, para-aminobenzoic acid, pantothenic acid, and many others. Some of these have been synthesized and some have not. To put the unsynthesized ones into a capsule, therefore, it is necessary to use natural sources such as yeast, liver, rice polishings, wheat germ or milk whey. This brings us inevitably to a discussion of natural and synthetic vitamins and their use in supplemental diet.

First, of course, a natural vitamin must be isolated so that it can be examined and fully identified chemically. This accomplished, the vitamin can be exactly duplicated atom by atom, molecule by molecule, in a chemical laboratory. The synthetic vitamins are identical with the natural in the cases of Vitamins B1, B2, B6, and other B vitamins. Synthetic Vitamin A has been made, and the natural vitamin can be concentrated and put into capsules. Natural capsules are apt to have a fishy aftertaste, but the synthetic capsules do not.

Before we take up separately each of the busy B's, the author wishes to issue a cautionary note: Take individual B vitamins only with the whole B Complex, and use supplements which give you not only the synthesized B Vitamins but also contain one of the natural sources (to provide those B vitamins which are not yet made synthetically).

Each of the B Vitamins has a separate and distinct function in the body. Although some of these functions overlap, one vitamin cannot replace another. These vitamins are always found together in the same foods, but in varying proportions. Since they are always found together, you cannot be deficient in only *one* of them. Therefore—even though symptoms may, on the surface, indicate a Vitamin B1 deficiency alone—it is not wise to take only that vitamin. Full results will be obtained only by using the entire Vitamin B Complex to provide supplies of all the vitamins of the B group, which you may need, and the absence of which probably counteracts the effect of the B1 you are getting.

To the nutritionist, many of the symptoms of that period of life we call "middle age" are sometimes based on Vitamin B Complex deficiency. Certain of our customary food habits contribute unnecessarily and destructively to these deficiencies. We perpetuate deficiency, for example, when we eat processed carbohydrates from which Vitamin B factors are removed. In our chapter on the functions of food, we learned that vitamins act as "wicks" for the burning of carbohydrates in the body. We now learn that these wicks are

181

the Vitamin B Complex and that all of them must be present, for the absence of one interferes with the work of the others. If, therefore, the food you eat has been deprived of any of the B vitamins, you are asking your body to burn sugar, rice flour and similar foods without wicks. It is an unfair demand, for your body cannot and will not do so. The result is that you fill the furnace (your body) with fuel (carbohydrates) which will not burn fully. Your furnace then will be filled with the smoke of partial burning. That is its technical description. In daily living, this "smokiness" translates into nervousness, indigestion, constipation or any of a thousand common disorders.

It follows, therefore, since every mouthful of carbohydrate requires a certain amount of Vitamin B1 and Vitamin B Complex to help burn it, that eating too much starch or sugar can create a deficiency. Our intake of sugar alone creates a 90 mg. deficit of thiamin yearly. Every calorie you consume must be released (burned) before you can utilize it. Calories from carbohydrates—and that means sugar and starch—cannot be released without the vitamins of the B Complex. Unprocessed carbohydrates—whole wheat, brown rice, whole buckwheat, whole corn, whole barley—contain the needed vitamins. Their overprocessed counterparts—white rice, white flour and white sugar—will not. Although "enriched" flour contains three important vitamins of the B Complex group, we consider it less than sensible to remove fifteen and replace three. This, however, is what we accept from the baking industry.

Remembering always that the entire B Complex is necessary in the diet, let us examine the various components of this group in close-up.

*Vitamin B1*

Known also as *thiamin chloride,* this vitamin is specifically necessary for growth, normal heart function, circulation, blood building, appetite, digestion and functioning of the nervous system.

Persons deficient in Vitamin B1 develop neurasthenia (nervous breakdown), apathy, lethargy, oversensitivity to pain or noise, uncertainty of memory, loss of morale, digestive disturbance, faulty metabolism of starches and sugars, constipation, nausea, lack of appetite and excessively rapid beating of the heart which is sometimes followed by excessively slow beating. With these disturbances may also come abnormally low activity of the thyroid gland and practically no resistance to fatigue.

At one-third of a milligram of Vitamin B1 daily, a deficiency disease will inevitably develop. This is beriberi, a native word translated as "I can not," an excellent description of the lack of will-to-do, which inadequate intake of this vitamin will cause. The higher the intake of sugar and starch, such as white sugar and other overprocessed carbohydrates, the quicker and more intense the symptoms of deficiency. At one-third of a milligram of Vitamin B1 daily, deficiency disease is unlikely in those individuals whose requirements for the vitamin are not elevated—which, in some people, they are, by a considerable margin. At two-thirds of a milligram of Vitamin B1 daily, we strike a twilight zone: There's enough of the vitamin to ward off beriberi, but not enough to let the body, the brain, and the nervous system function properly. Now the symptoms that develop simulate perfectly those of severe neurosis.

Large doses, up to 500 mgs. of thiamin daily, are used in the treatment of shingles, tic doloreaux—which is trigeminal neuralgia—Bell's palsy, and other neurological disorders. Such doses are also used by orthomolecular psychiatrists for depressed patients.

The authorities insist that less than two mgs. of Vitamin B1 daily will fully satisfy the needs of 99 percent of the population. The statement is too sweeping. I know of a chemist whose migraine headaches recur when he drops his intake of thiamin below ten mgs. daily, and he is not alone in his elevated need for the vitamin. Those who eat large amounts of sugar, which most of the public does—raise their need for thiamin. I'd rather play safe, with an intake of two to ten mgs. daily. The subjective reactions of the person are a more reliable guide to his needs than the computerized, abstract calculations of "average needs" ground out, in Washington.

## Vitamin B2

Vitamin B2 (or G—riboflavin) is needed for the soft tissues of the body, where it helps the cells to exchange oxygen. It is, therefore, used with Vitamin B1 to help the "burning" of starches and sugars. It is important to the eyes, where oxygen transfers are vital; and because riboflavin is sensitive to light, the vitamin also functions specifically to aid vision. Large doses are used for tremor.

Disturbances of digestion, faulty blood building, burning of the eyes and lids, cracking of the corners of the lips, impaired lactation in nursing mothers, skin disorders and cataract are among the deficiency symptoms produced by lack of riboflavin. Large doses of this vitamin have been reported to reduce the "sweet tooth" of children and adults, to raise resistance to athlete's foot and similar fungus infections and to bring relief to sufferers of neurodermatitis, atopic eczema and allergy. Riboflavin is found in liver; somewhat less richly in lean meat, in milk and in yeast. At least five milligrams of riboflavin daily, in *addition* to normal intake of food, is the author's personal habit.

## Vitamin B6

The other name for this vitamin is pyridoxin, and it is important to the skin, to the utilization of fats and protein, the building of blood and the function of the nerves and muscles. This is one of the most promising of all the vitamins and it is almost certain that continuing research will discover more marvels than are now known. It has already been seen to accomplish near miracles—restoring function to paralyzed legs (where nerves were involved in the pathology); shrinking enlarged hearts, and relieving distressed intestinal tracts after a lifetime of misery for dyspepsia sufferers. Doctors have reported that pellagra patients do not recover their full strength until given Vitamin B6. Surgeons administer the vitamin before operations to avoid post-operative nausea from either and many obstetricians find that the nausea of pregnancy can sometimes be interrupted with Vitamin B6.

Because of the effects of this vitamin on muscle tone and nerve function, it is frequently used in the treatment of multiple sclerosis, muscular dystrophy and numerous other nerve and muscle disorders which increasingly trouble our generation. It is also helpful for its effects on the centers of the autonomous nervous system which control rhythm and fine movements. Hence, Vitamin B6, Vitamin E and other food factors are used in the treatment of cerebral palsy, Parkinson's disease (senile palsy), epilepsy and similar disorders where there is faulty transmission of nerve impulses to the muscular system. It has been found helpful in the treatment of adolescent acne, as well.

Vitamin B6 has the effect of conserving protein and is therefore administered when there are losses of protein, as in kidney disease. While oral use of the vitamin is possible and occasionally helpful, many of its uses are best introduced by injection, which necessitates the help of a physician. Vitamin B6 is incorporated in some of the multiple vitamin capsules available on the market, and it is sensible to supplement diet with a minimum of two milligrams daily. Again, this supplementary intake might not be necessary if our more popular foods were not robbed of it in the course of processing.

According to an article in the *New York State Journal of Medicine,* large doses of Vitamin B6—as much as a thousand mgs. daily, in divided doses—have been found to reduce or eliminate intolerance to sunshine in people with extreme solar sensitivity. This twenty-year-old report has been confirmed in an unexpected way: There is a type of schizophrenia in which such sensitivity to sunshine is almost routinely exhibited. In these patients, who are often paranoid, sometimes have amnesia, often have convulsions, large doses of Vitamin B6, zinc, and small amounts of manganese have been found to bring all these symptoms—including the schizophrenic psychosis, under complete control. In such patients, up to a thousand mgs. of Vitamin B6 daily—and more, when they're under stress—may be needed, rather than the two mgs. recommended for normal people. Other exceptions are found in disorders like hypertrophic arthritis, which Dr. John Ellis labels as a product of deficiency in Vitamin B6 and potassium, and which he has cured with doses of the nutrients. If you base your pyridoxin intake on Dr. Ellis's recommendations, you are more likely to supplement your diet with twenty-five mgs. of the vitamin daily, than a mere two. Subjective feelings of well-being are again a more reliable guide than any laboratory test, for tests show us what's *there*, but not how much is needed.

## Vitamin B12

This vitamin, originally called the "animal protein factor," is manufactured in two forms: cyanocobalamin and hydroxycobalamin. The cyano form is the type commonly used in medical practice and in vitamin supplements. Its use has been criticized on two grounds: Some patients may be sensitive (neurologically) to the cyano form, and this form must be converted to the hydroxy compound before the body utilizes it. Thus, if your physician speaks of giving you Vitamin B12-b, he is thereby avoiding the use of the cyano compound of the vitamin. This vitamin, being associated with animal protein, can't be adequately supplied by a vegetarian diet, although it is conveyed in such foods as milk, eggs, and cheese, which some vegetarians consume. Pure vegetarianism, thereby, encounters the risk of deficiency in the vitamin. Amazingly small doses, as little as a half milligram, of Vitamin B12 have produced benefits in pernicious anemia, stimulated retarded growth in children, helped recovery in disorders of the nervous system, aided in the treatment of asthma, and served as a tonic factor for adults—greatly increasing energy reserves, in some people.

Psychosis has been helpfully treated with the vitamin. A

type of schizophrenia has benefited, and in some patients, a feeling has been created of more adequacy in facing their problems. An oral supplement of twenty-five to one hundred mgs. daily has been useful for many individuals. Where utilization of the orally administered vitamin is unsatisfactory, the physician may give a source of hydrochloric acid with it, and doses of dried stomach tissue. Such tissue supplies a "conveyor" factor for the vitamin, without which it may not properly be utilized.

Important note: Deficiency in Vitamin B12—*without causing pernicious anemia*—can cause degeneration of brain and nervous system, which can result in paranoid behavior. Such delusions of persecution are often present in "senile" aged persons, some of whom may actually be suffering from a deficiency in Vitamin B12, rather than from the tool of aging. It has been estimated that 1 percent of the "senile" paranoid aged could be rehabilitated with injections (not oral doses) of Vitamin B12, if given in sufficient amounts, five mgs. per injection, three times weekly.

## Niacin, Niacinamide

Known also as nicotinic acid, nicotinamide, nicotinic acid amide, niacin is needed, like the other B vitamins, for normal liver function; for the functioning of the nervous system and the brain; by the soft tissues—from mouth to reproductive organs; by the skin; and for burning of starches and sugars.

Niacin deficiency upsets the higher centers of the brain, causes nerve disorders ranging from simple neurasthenia to outright insanity. In the presence of a deficiency, the brain disturbances include loss of a sense of humor, uncertainty of memory, negative behavior, and delusions. The tongue may appear purple or bright red, bare and shiny. The gums become swollen and angry and rise on the teeth. The skin breaks out.

Although we speak of niacin and niacinamide as being synonymous, the average vitamin supplement contains niacinamide rather than niacin. This is because the amide does not dilate the blood vessels and stimulate circulation as noticeably as does niacin. The manufacturers of vitamins protect you against feeling excessively warm after taking their capsules.

In medical treatment, however, physicians use niacin to stimulate circulation in conditions ranging from simple cold feet to disturbances of hearing and even migraine headache. They also use niacinamide to treat nervous disorders, skin diseases, disturbances of the mouth and gums (such as trench mouth), liver disorders and chronic digestive upsets. The American Medical Association has remarked that "the health of the mouth in many supposedly normal individuals is improved by dosages of niacinamide."

Those who have read the anti-vitamin-supplement propaganda of the A.M.A. might here pause to reflect on the contradiction in the statement that niacinamide supplements may improve the condition of a supposedly normal mouth. Please note that this means (a) we don't know what constitutes normalcy, and (b) can make no statements concerning the amounts of vitamins which will create or support normalcy—except that the dosages of niacinamide suggested by the *J.A.M.A.* to improve the condition of a "normal" mouth are far beyond the amount of the vitamin that some journal insists will be enough for everyone.

When niacin creates a flush, the action doesn't come from the vitamin itself, but from its effect in inducing the mast cells to release histamine. It is the histamine itself which causes the feeling of warmth. Since, as demonstrated by the use of antihistamine drugs in treatment of symptoms of allergy, histamine is one of the causes of such symptoms, the depletion of histamine by niacin means that the individual's capacity for severe allergic reactions is thereby reduced. While the histamine release is taking place, the mast cell is also being induced to release heparin. The anticlotting factor is used to help protect against heart attacks based on clots; it also has the effect of reducing blood fats, including cholesterol. This explains the use of niacin in reducing blood cholesterol levels. Niacinamide doesn't have this effect. On the other hand, the amide has an action which ordinary niacin doesn't: that of slowing up the mitosis, the multiplication of cancer cells; an action it shares with Vitamin C. For this reason, large doses of niacinamide and Vitamin C are used experimentally in treatment of certain types of cancer.

Finally, it should be remembered that a pinch of niacinamide stands between us and insanity, for delirium is one of the symptoms of pellagra, the deficiency disease in which niacinamide deficiency is the prime deficit in the diet. A milder deficiency of niacinamide still plays havoc with the brain, loss of a sense of humor being one of its more subtle effects. The impact of such deficiency on brain function creates many disturbances which, when severe, curiously resemble some of those which occur in schizophrenia. This was the inspiration that led Dr. Abram Hoffer and his colleagues to try niacin and niacinamide treatment for schizophrenics. Part of the purposes of that treatment, however, are unrelated to correction of deficiency, involving a chemistry too complex for discussion within the scope of this text. Interested readers will find such added information in my recent book, *PsychoNutrition*. Do not fall prey to the mistaken belief that psychoses can be rectified with a dose of a single vitamin, such as niacin. This one vitamin is helpful in significant degree only in very early, very mild schizophrenia. (The tests "disproving" the value of niacin in schizophrenia were conducted on schizophrenics whose illness was neither early nor mild, as demonstrated by the fact that all the patients were hospitalized. This is an example of the techniques used to discourage the interest of the public and the professions in nutritional therapies.)

The authorities have decided that adults need 13.5 mgs. of niacin daily. (Imagine how hurt a person might feel if he were socially rejected because he needs, say, 13.9 mgs. daily!) Actually, some individuals function best when their intake is fifty mgs. or more daily, and in improving the condition of a supposedly "normal mouth," that is the figure set by the *J.A.M.A.* And some of our college and high school dropouts might suffer less from fuzzy and disorganized thinking if their niacinamide intake were raised to one hundred mgs. or more daily. Even larger doses have been used to help children with "metabolic dysperception," resulting in total cures of conditions easily mistaken for learning disabilities or outright psychosis.

## Paba (Para-Aminobenzoic Acid)

Strangest of the vitamins in many ways, paba has also had the strangest treatment by the authorities, who first labeled it a vitamin, then decided it is neither a vitamin nor a drug, which reduced it to being a chemical, but oddly, a chemical which (a) is part of an essential vitamin's molecule—folic acid; and normal to man's food, since virtually every source of Vitamin B Complex is a source of paba.

I have employed paba to stimulate fertility in both sexes, which it often does. That implied action on the pituitary gland is confirmed when we see paba cause recoloring (or retardation of depigmentation) of graying hair. The vitamin interacts with salicylates, permitting physicians to prescribe less of the drugs, and still obtain the desired therapeutic actions. It interacts with insulin, and together with the Vitamin B Complex, may help thereby to permit lowering of insulin dosage in diabetes. It interacts with estrogen, or inhibits destruction of the hormone by the liver, an effect which can be a boon to women with too low a production of this hormone; but undesirable for those with estrogen overactivity. It interacts with the cortisone type of hormones, again permitting lowering of dose of drugs which often have undesirable side-effects. Paba, perhaps because of its interaction with hormones, is helpful in several types of arthritis, and in bursitis and myositis—which is fascinating, when you realize that the medical profession is taught, and the Arthritis Foundation assures the public, that no vitamin helps arthritis. (You'll find the potassium salt of paba advertised in medical journals as helpful in arthritis and allied disorders.)

Finally, paba slows down the aging process, perhaps by

pituitary stimulation. It is the active principle in the so-called ASLAN rejuvenation therapy, for the prime factor in procain injections and in—you guessed it—paba; one hundred mgs. of paba daily has been a helpful supplement for many people.

## Inositol

Originally considered a "muscle sugar," and thereby called "myo-inositol" (*myo* means muscle), this vitamin—which isn't recognized as one by the authorities—deserves more attention than it has received. It has been used to reduce blood glucose levels in diabetes. Together with choline, I have found—in research for more than twenty years—that it aids liver degradation of estrogenic (female) hormone, and thereby is not only beneficial in premenstrual tension, the painful menstrual, and cystic mastitis, but contributes to stabilizing estrogen activity at a level which may offer heightened protection against breast and uterine (endometrial) cancer.

The inaptness of the term "muscle sugar" for inositol is demonstrated by the fact that this factor is highly concentrated in brain tissue. I have used it helpfully in mental retardation. Because of its relationship to liver function and fat metabolism, inositol is helpful not only in diabetes, but in arteriosclerosis, gallbladder syndrome, fat intolerance, fatty infiltration of the liver, and numerous other disorders. I have observed its helpfulness in multiple sclerosis and muscular dystrophy, when given with Vitamin E and wheat germ oil, and I believe that it may one day be demonstrated to be helpful in heart disease. Like paba and like most other B Complex vitamins, inositol is processed out of the carbohydrates which form the bulk of the American diet.

Up to 250 mgs. of inositol daily is a supplementary intake which has benefited many individuals. Most food supplements contain only token amounts of this vitamin, and one must search for a Vitamin B Complex concentrate containing enough paba, inositol, and choline to be useful. Such supplements, however, do exist. Those who consume whole

grains, grain germ, bran, and brewer's yeast obtain significant amounts of these vitamins from such sources. Requirements for calcium may be elevated, if inositol intake is high.
This presents no problem to those whose use of milk, cheese,
or calcium supplements is adequate.

## Choline

Generously provided by organ meats and eggs, choline is
essential to normal metabolism of fats. It is needed by the
kidneys, for lactation and for liver function. It is required by
the thymus gland and is important to the kidneys and spleen.
Choline deficiency impairs liver and kidney function,
causing hemorrhaging of the kidneys; it produces intolerance to fats and fatty degeneration of the liver, and may
result in a blocking of the transmission of nerve impulses to
the muscles. For these reasons, physicians are prescribing
choline in large amounts in the treatment of diabetes,
gallbladder trouble, intolerance to fats and numerous other
disorders. Choline is also used in the treatment of muscular
dystrophy, glaucoma, and arteriosclerosis. It is more effective when accompanied by inositol and other vitamins which
affect fat utilization.
Choline is used by the body in the synthesis of acetylcholine, which is a transmitter of electrical impulses in the
nervous system, making it vital in nerve-muscle function. To
convert choline into acetylcholine, pantothenic acid (another
vitamin) and manganese are necessary. Thus these factors,
choline, pantothenic acid, and manganese, have been
employed in my research in myasthenia gravis and in
glaucoma, two disorders in which acetylcholine synthesis is
important. This chemistry has implications for normal brain
function, as well.
It should be noted that the foods richest in choline are
those which are forbidden (or the intake significantly reduced) in the low cholesterol diet, an observation strengthening the indictment of this experimental type of diet as carrying penalties which may offset its purported benefits.

Quantities of choline in commercial vitamin supplements tend to be unsatisfactorily low, as compared with the amount of this factor supplied in a high quality diet. At least 500 mgs. of choline should be provided in the daily supplement.

## Calcium Pantothenate

Available commercially, this vitamin is a growth essential, important to the skin and needed by the adrenal gland. It also affects the functioning of the entire digestive tract. Although symptoms of deficiency in this vitamin are not clearly known, it is known that animals lacking the factor develop gray hair, toughening of the skin, skin disease, constipation, granulation of the eyelids, destruction of adrenal tissue and digestive disorders. Pantothenic acid deficiency also prevents the animal from building antibodies in its blood, thus decreasing resistance to infection.

Physicians use calcium pantothenate as they use other Vitamin B Complex factors—in the treatment of digestive disturbances (especially in cases where the stomach empties too slowly) and occasionally as an adjunct in the treatment of anemias. Since the vitamin favorably affects the adrenal gland, it is used in the treatment of rheumatoid arthritis and other conditions showing depressed adrenal function. This includes allergies.

This factor is, like so many others, processed out of many popular foods. It will be found in protective amounts in good multiple supplement capsules.

## Folic Acid

Essential to normal size and amounts of red blood cells in the blood, folic acid is also necessary to liver function, where part of blood manufacture takes place. Folic acid is also interrelated with gland function; chicks deficient in this vitamin respond to female-hormone treatment only one-fortieth as much as chicks well supplied with it. Folic acid deficiency contributes to digestive disturbances and liver dysfunction and may also contribute to pernicious anemia and lowered hydrochloric acid production. Physicians are therefore using folic acid in the treatment of anemias and intolerance to fats.

Vegetables subjected to room temperatures lose a considerable portion of their folic acid values.

*Biotin*

This vitamin is an enormously potent stimulant to the growth of cells and is therefore, undoubtedly, important to general growth. Deficiency is known to produce a type of anemia, complicated with a skin disease. Biotin is among the host of vitamins removed from processed foods. Daily supplements supply us with added biotin, for it is intrinsically a part of any source of concentrated Vitamin B Complex. We can obtain added quantities of it by the use of brewer's yeast and wheat germ.

# VITAMIN C

## ESPECIALLY IF YOU'RE RESTLESS— OR PREGNANT!

This interesting and temperamental vitamin was recognized by function, if not by name, among primitive peoples throughout the world. Explorers from civilization, coming to bring the savage enlightenment, often found themselves in the humiliating position of having had their lives saved by the loin-cloth set. The explorers frequently developed scurvy. Found near death by a primitive band, they were restored to health when given the adrenal glands of animals or a brew of pine needle tea—both concoctions rich in Vitamin C. The natives did not know our alphabet system; they merely knew that these particular foods made sick men well.

British seamen of the windjammer days were prone to

scurvy because their diets included no fresh fruits or vegetables. When the coincidence was discovered, they took to sucking limes and lemons and accomplished two things; they became less susceptible to scurvy—and they earned for themselves the name, "Limies."

Vitamin C is an excellent example of the "Factor of Demand," one of the elements in life which determine our need for vitamins and for other food elements. If you work very hard, "normal" nutrition—normal, that is, for the average person—becomes inadequate for you. During the middle ages, soldiers developed the hemorrhages of scurvy in their legs; the blacksmith suffered with scurvy of the right arm. These, respectively, were the points of stress. The sailor fell prey to a total scurvy, because he was active with all his muscles.

Thus it is that a pregnant woman may develop varicose veins. Not only is she carrying extra weight and walking for exercise (both of these constitute hard work) but her unborn child imposes a greatly increased demand for Vitamin C. Unless the expectant mother's intake is appreciably higher than "normal," her supply becomes exhausted and, in protest, her legs develop varicosities. The subject of varicose veins is discussed at greater length in another chapter. Vitamin B Complex and protein are also important because of their indirect affect on controlling female (estrogenic) hormone activity.

Of all the vitamins, C is the easiest to obtain in assured amounts from natural foods, for citrus juice or whole fruit is always rich in it. One of the most important functions of the vitamin is in its material aid to the body in the manufacture of "collagen," the "glue" which holds the cells of the body together. An early sign of Vitamin C deficiency is bleeding gums, another is a tendency of the small blood vessels in other parts of the body to break on slight strain. This breaking produces *petechia*. One of the clinical tests for Vitamin C deficiency is binding the arm and counting the number of petechial hemorrhages exhibited. If too many appear, the patient is sent home with a high citrus fruit diet.

The so-called "country rheumatism" which used to manifest itself among farm people after a long, hard winter is believed today to be a hemorrhagic joint condition produced by a lack of Vitamin C.

The above are very direct and discernible signs. There are others less pronounced. The United States Department of Agriculture states that there are probably thousands of people in this country suffering from an *unrecognized* Vitamin C deficiency. Restlessness and irritability in infants and children; "spring fever" in adults, or a run-down feeling at any time of the year may mark the deficiency. Without one outward symptom of trouble, a person may be in a state of deficiency more dangerous than scurvy itself, says the Department, which warns that such a condition—undetected and unchallenged—can damage teeth and bones and weaken the blood system to the point where it can no longer resist or fight infections.

The precise role of Vitamin C in building resistance to shock and infection is not yet clearly understood, nor is its function in helping the body to create immunity. We do know that an animal extravagantly nourished with the vitamin will throw off the effects of a dose of poison which quickly kills an animal less well nourished with the vitamin. This, even though the succumbing animal is not deficient in the true sense of the word. It dies by poison although not a single sign of scurvy itself is displayed. Hepatitis has successfully been treated with massive doses of Vitamin C.

Loss of appetite marks a C deficiency, and so do a disinclination to activity, a congestion and sponginess of the gums and an anemia which does not respond to liver or iron feedings. Infants low in Vitamin C have poor muscle function, lack of appetite, anemia, cessation in weight gain or actual loss of weight, susceptibility to infection, intestinal disturbances and a tendency toward frequent crying.

Because of increased requirements, deficiency may occur frequently in pregnancy, tuberculosis, osteomyelitis, overactive thyroid states, rheumatic fever, pneumonia and other diseases in which high fever depletes the body store of the vitamin. For, although obtainable with comparative ease, the vitamin is poorly stored by the body. Ulcers, both peptic and varicose, require high Vitamin C intake to guard against delayed healing; yet the peptic ulcer diet is often deficient in this vitamin. Dental decay may arise through Vitamin C deficiency, among other vitamin-mineral factors involved. It should be noted, however, that *large intake of citrus juice may expose the teeth to the ravages of citric acid.* It is therefore wise for individuals—especially those with weak enamel or decalcified teeth—to wash the mouth with water after drinking citrus juice. This also applies after drinking milk or cranberry juice.

In many persons, utilization of Vitamin C is very poor. Cases have been known in which a full pint of orange juice daily did not bring a response in patients known to be deficient. This means that a high intake of Vitamin C is necessary on two counts: because saturation of the body with C is believed to be the ideal state, and because such a precautionary intake *overcomes* the danger of poor utilization.

Allergies to fruits—particularly those rich in Vitamin C—are frequent. Those who are in this position, as well as those who have limited budgets, must turn to other sources for this vitamin. In using the Vitamin C chart, therefore, you need not despair if citrus fruits are beyond your capacity or your purse. Depend on cabbage, preferably served as cole slaw, green and red peppers and the recommended fresh green leaves. Tomato juice, although only half as rich in Vitamin C as citrus juice, is still a good source and may be used by those allergic to citrus fruits. Drink twice as much.

An investment in high Vitamin C intake is a profitable one; a deficiency carries penalties which are irreversible. We are learning that a few months of slight deficiency may alter vital tissues irreparably. Who is to say, in the light of our present limited knowledge, how such changes may alter our physical destinies? Among other requirements, Vitamin C is specifically needed by the adrenal gland. When a shock of any kind stimulates this gland into producing its hormones, the reserves of Vitamin C present there would be exhausted in as little as five seconds. If the blood does not generously and promptly resupply the vitamin, both you and your adrenal gland will suffer. Vitamin C helps the body to conserve iodine. It is a vitamin which appears to have the property, in large doses, of stimulating latent tuberculosis into revealing itself. A very large intake of the vitamin may, therefore, be undesirable in those cases of bronchial asthma which portend latent tuberculosis. This is for your physician to decide, but it should be remembered that Vitamin A offsets this action. Because Vitamin C has a diuretic effect, it is useful in congestive heart disease and other conditions which prompt the physician to promote fluid excretion. Concentrated Vitamin C is sometimes very effective in relieving the symptoms of food and inhalant allergies. Requirements for Vitamin C are, like all other subjects in nutrition, over-subjected to the pressures of a $120-billion-dollar yearly market, a focal point for argument.

Dr. Linus Pauling has ascertained that the animals which can synthesize Vitamin C make roughly the same amount in proportion to body weight. Applying this proportion to man, we should expect that human beings would synthesize 2,280 mgs. of the vitamin daily. Moreover, if we increased our manufacture of the vitamin when we are under stress, as other animals can and do, we'd raise our output of Vitamin C to about 14,000 mgs. daily. Dr. Pauling suggests, therefore, we have set our human Vitamin C requirement entirely too low, offering the hypothesis that our range of requirements probably goes from 250 mgs. daily to about 2,500. Despite the rancorous debates his theories (and facts) have aroused, any objective student of the problem will be forced to agree that mankind would reap some very worthwhile benefits by ingesting far more Vitamin C than the amount needed to avoid scurvy. For, as Dr. Pauling has pointed out, vitamins should do more than to keep us from a premortal stage of sickness.

The moral in terms of supplementary Vitamin C is obvious. Find your optimal intake. There will be one which lessens allergic reactions, since Vitamin C in high dosage *is* an antihistamine (and moreover, one without side reactions such as the drugs yield); there will be one which maximizes resistance to fatigue and infection, and expedites healing when you're injured. Don't let the voices of reaction permit you to forget some of the dividends medically reported for high Vitamin C intake—ranging from avoidance of surgery for "slipped disks" to reduction of frequency, severity, and duration of colds.

In terms of dietary supplies: Don't buy punch which is 10 percent fruit juice, and often taxed as a soft drink; buy fruit and fruit juice. And remember that C doesn't stand for cooking. The vitamin doesn't like heat, and hates alkalies.

## Bioflavonoids, Rutin

There are many flavonoid compounds in nature, only a few of which are active in the body, and thereby merit the name "bioflavonoids." These active forms aid Vitamin C in its functions in the body. Vitamin C is important to the larger blood vessels, where the bioflavonoids increase the strength and reduce excessive permeability of the walls of the very small blood vessels. For this reason, both vitamins are used in disorders involving fragility of the blood vessels, or excessive permeability, such as may appear in allergy.

The bioflavonoids are thereby useful in diabetes, in helping to avoid or mitigate eye hemorrhages, and in such disorders as edema (swelling due to fluid collection) of the tissues, such as we see in the ankles of some people after they stand for a few hours, where no physical disease can be found as a cause for the problem. Vitamin C helps to protect against allergy; the bioflavonoids help to reduce the severity of extremely potent allergic reactions, such as anaphylaxis. In a single report, the bioflavonoids were found helpful in reducing the number and severity of hemorrhagic attacks in people with hemophilia (the disease in which blood clotting is impaired).

There are several types of bioflavonoids, among which are rutin, less useful because it is less soluble; hesperidin and hesperidin chalcone, and the bioflavonoids extracted from citrus fruits, principally lemons. The latter is probably the most active form. Many supplements supply inadequate amounts of these factors, for to be effective, the bioflavonoid dose should probably be at or near the level of the Vitamin C dose; 500 mgs. of the bioflavonoids would be a good level for supplementary purposes, but much more may be needed in therapeutic uses. Generous intake of unstrained citrus juice supplies much more of the bioflavonoids than the strained juice, and eating the whole fruit is still better.

# VITAMINS D, E and K

*Vitamin D*

Modern man knows much more about the Vitamin D requirements of pigs and cows than he does about his own. Livestock must be bred and fed in such way as to make them healthy or the profits of farmers, producers, packers, distributors and retailers suffer. Human beings have no market price—at least, they haven't since the presidency of Abraham Lincoln. And so we employ our best scientific skills to insure the health of our cattle, but often give ourselves a bum steer when it comes to our own nutrition.

Today, after decades of research with Vitamin D, there remains confusion about the precise quantitative need for this vitamin in adult human beings. There is no argument for cows, horses or pigs; their requirements are definitely charted. The people concerned studied these needs carefully and came up with a positive answer. They drafted elaborate maps of the distribution of sunlight in various seasons in various parts of the United States, so that the breeder of swine or other livestock may know how much supplementary Vitamin D to give his porkers and prancers. No such maps for the human population exist.

Millions of two-legged Americans, not having the advantages reserved for their four-legged domestic animals, do not get enough Vitamin D. The chief reason for this is that they do not, will not or cannot expose themselves to sufficient contact with sunshine. Sunlight impels the factories in every green leaf to function; and here are concentrated the Vitamins A and D of the plant. Sunshine falling on the skin converts ergosterol in and within the skin to a new substance, which we know as healthful, helpful Vitamin D. Incidentally, the ancient religions founded on worship of the sun and its light based their beliefs on forces vital to man. They were not very wrong, speaking practically and not theosophically.

Human beings need Vitamin D in several ways. It affects our glands; it is concerned in reproduction; it mobilizes and helps distribute calcium (and, indirectly, phosphorus); it increases the rate at which the skin "breathes"—or takes up oxygen; and it is charged with the direct responsibility of keeping us free of the softbone disease, rickets. In its function, Vitamin D is helped by other vitamins—A, B Complex and C—which assist either by their effects upon calcium metabolism or by their cooperative actions with Vitamin D itself.

The soot and smoke of our great cities retard passage of the sun rays which create Vitamin C. These are certain specific rays. Not all sunlight has this effect; that which has passed through a glass window, for instance, will not create Vitamin D. Clothing retards the formation of Vitamin D, of course, which speaks a good word for nudists and plunging necklines. Certain colors of clothing retard Vitamin D formation more than others; pink is amenable to the passage of the rays.

The lack of exposure to sunlight, almost inevitable in civilization, is believed partially to be responsible for the great incidence of osteomalacia and osteoporosis—diseased or brittle bones—in adults over fifty. (Calcium or phosphorous deficiency contribute also.) Winter sunshine in the northeast is weak; the air is like a filter; the clothing is a barrier, and many of us do not seek exposure to sunshine in winter or summer. Weekend treks around a golf course are not enough; the vitamin is needed every day.

Consider this experiment with two groups of expectant

mothers. One group lived in Chicago, the other in Oklahoma. They were fed identical diets. The Oklahoma babies were a pound heavier at birth and their dentition and muscle development were several months earlier in reaching the norm. What spelled the difference? Oklahoma sunshine is strong and, consequently, that group of expectant mothers had a plentiful supply of natural Vitamin D.

Some years ago, it was discovered that real or artificial sunshine falling on ergosterol would create Vitamin D. Enterprising food processors, egged on no doubt by their publicity and advertising mentors, promptly began to "irradiate" their products. You can buy "irradiated" milk, candy, frankfurters and soda pop. While "irradiated" milk certainly won't hurt you, it seems a waste of money to spend extra pennies for a quart of milk which contains only 400 units of Vitamin D. (What this nutritionist thinks of candy and soda pop, whether irradiated with D or not, will be found in frequent references throughout this book.) Those 400 units of Vitamin D offer little safety margin as protection against rickets for an average group of infants. Moreover, 400 units fall below the amount we set as optimal for adults who want strong bones throughout life. In addition, the "irradiated" foods contain a form of Vitamin D which is often less effective than the "natural" Vitamin D in fish-liver oils. We also disapprove of the irradiated Vitamin D concentrates offered as yeast cakes or drops for babies. In high dosage, such irradiated products may be toxic; in low dosage, they are less effective than the concentrated fish-liver oils of tuna, herring, cod or percomorph.

Actually, no foods will offer a safe supply of Vitamin D. Daily intake of 1,000 units will be safe and adequate for adults. An *infant's* intake of Vitamin D should be set by the pediatrician. This amount may be derived from:

1. A few hours of summer sunshine on the body daily.
2. Alphabet capsules or syrups containing natural fish-liver oil concentrates.
3. A sun lamp of the carbon arc type, or one of the quartz tube type. (These give the full quota of "bands" of sun-

light which create Vitamin D; other types may give fewer "bands.")

Vitamin D is not used only to *prevent* rickets. The preventive dosage—1,000 units daily—may rise to as high as 50,000 units or more daily to *cure* active rickets. The vitamin is sometimes helpful in acne, together with B6, and superimposed on supplementing with alphabet vitamins. It is most important to dentition. Breast-fed babies need just as much Vitamin D as formula-fed; premature babies need twice as much, and expectant nursing mothers need as much as 2,000 units daily.

High dosage of synthetic Vitamin D is sometimes very helpful in arthritis. In this use, the vitamin is employed in such high dosage that it is acting as a chemical rather than as a vitamin. The amount may run from 50,000 to 200,000 units daily, or even higher. It should be administered only under a physician's direction, because this vitamin—especially in such large quantities—*is sometimes toxic.* Individuals with heart trouble complicating the arthritis should be particularly careful in this use of Vitamin D, for the nausea which it may cause would be dangerous to a cardiac patient.

Other uses for Vitamin D include the treatment of tetany, myopia (near-sightedness) and disturbances in the parathyroid glands. Remember that Vitamin D (and, for that matter, all other vitamins) cannot perform its work without minerals—primarily calcium and phosphorous, secondarily magnesium and iron.

Here is a note for those who have house pets: If you wash a dog or cat too frequently you will remove from the fur the natural oil from which (on exposure to sunlight) comes the natural Vitamin D needed by your pet. In such cases, supplement the animal's diet with Vitamin D from fish-liver oil or with one of the multiple vitamin mineral syrups now available specifically for these pets. It's nice to keep a house pet clean, but it's equally important to keep him healthy.

A red flag of warning against Vitamin D deficiency should be raised at two stages of the lifespan. Mothers of preschool children tend to monitor vitamin mineral intake carefully, but as the child matures, less attention is paid to this important protection. The result of the neglect was demonstrated dramatically in a study of sick children, at or just past puberty, in whom many cases of unsuspected rickets, for lack of Vitamin D, were diagnosed. Another group in the population whose Vitamin D needs are not fulfilled are the elderly—particularly when they are institutionalized or housebound, and can't obtain adequate exposure to sunshine. (Even for those not confined, there is little sunshine available in areas with harsh winters.) The result of the deficiency in Vitamin D is, of course, an intensification of the decalcification of the skeleton which is so common in elderly people that we blame it on age alone, so that we automatically expect senior citizens to sustain a fracture, even with a mild fall. A multiple vitamin mineral supplement and a B Complex concentrate may soften the rigors of aging for the elderly, and even reverse some of the changes. Even old-fashioned cod-liver oil alone, if cost is a factor, may help to preserve the well-being and prolong the life of an aged person.

Regard the newspaper stories of Vitamin D toxicity as overstated, and part of the antivitamin propaganda. Even very high doses of the vitamin, medically supervised, can be safe, and, in some disorders, markedly beneficial. In any case, no one has ever suffered toxicity from the amount of Vitamin D provided by everyday supplements.

*Vitamin E*

Contrary to popular concept, Vitamin E is not the middle letter in the word "sex." Like all nutrients, it is involved in reproduction. Like some nutrients, it has a specific role in the functioning of the male sex glands, for they tend to atrophy when the diet doesn't adequately supply this vitamin. But Vitamin E isn't an aphrodisiac, and will not endow the male with historic virility, or guarantee the infertile female a baby. Actually, the most important role of this vitamin in the body, if one must select such, is a function rarely mentioned. Vitamin E is an antioxidant, and thereby helps to protect the cells against oxidation (which one might translate as rancidity) of the unsaturated fats which make up so large a part of the cell membrane and the fat content of the cell. This can be retranslated into an antiaging effect of the vitamin. That particular action is derived primarily from the beta-gamma and delta-tocopherols, the forms of Vitamin E to which the public (and many of the professionals) pay least attention. Everyone seems preoccupied with alpha-tocopherol, which is the most active form of the vitamin in influence on intracellular chemistry, but the least active as an antioxidant. This adds up to a simple recommendation: When you supplement your diet with Vitamin E, use the entire E Complex, meaning the alpha, beta, gamma, and delta forms combined. The potency will be stated in terms of so many milligrams of alpha tocopherol, leaving you in the dark as to the content of beta, gamma, and delta forms, and it is to be hoped that manufacturers will, one day—arbitrary rulings of the F.D.A. swept aside—let us know just how much of each form of Vitamin E a supplement supplies.

All this boils down to a negative recommendation: Unless your physician has prescribed alpha tocopherol alone, always buy mixed tocopherols when you want Vitamin E. Which leads to the question: Why do physicians frequently prescribe the alpha form, and omit the rest of the E Complex? This stems from the research of my good friend, Dr. Wilfred Shute, whose decades of study of Vitamin E in heart disease have been devoted entirely to the use of alpha tocopherol alone. But you who use a Vitamin E supplement which is self-selected are not, hopefully, trying to treat heart disease.

The "d-alpha tocopherol" which you find on vitamin labels, incidentally, signifies that the vitamin is of natural origin. "Dl alpha tocopherol" has to be synthetic. "D" stands for the "right-handed" form of the vitamin, which Nature prefers. "L" stands for the left-handed form, which Nature avoids. When you have both forms, as represented in "dl," you are dealing with a man-made product. Contrary to the public's thinking, the spelling of "tocopherol" gives no information concerning its being natural or synthetic.

While Dr. Shute medically prefers the alpha form of tocopherol in the treatment of heart disease, there is much to be said for the theoretical superiority of *mixed* tocopherols when the vitamin is being used preventively, for antioxidant effect translates as reducing the need of the tissues for oxygen, an action which must benefit the healthy heart. It should also be remembered that wheat germ oil contains factors other than Vitamin E, which benefit the heart. (See discussion of "octocosanol," on page 117.) Among those benefits: increase in the cardiac reserve.

I have seen benefit from Vitamin E in the treatment of menopausal symptoms and in the epilepsies, cerebral palsy, Parkinson's disease, in Mongoloids, chorea, hydrocephalus, and many neuromuscular disorders. When physicians refuse, as many do, to believe that a single factor could be beneficial in so many unrelated disorders, they are at least guilty of inconsistency. Have you ever seen the list of diseases—unrelated to adrenal disorders—in which cortisone and similar hormones are helpfully prescribed? The point is better made than the lay reader will realize, for there is evidence that Vitamin E is essential to pituitary function, and it is this gland which influences adrenal activity. It is for this reason, possibly, that Vitamin E has been helpful in several types of arthritis.

Those who make a career of criticizing the public's waste of money, as they put it, on vitamin supplements, seem particularly exercised concerning Vitamin E supplementation. Isn't it strange they never find time to complain about the removal of Vitamin E from the carbohydrate foods which supply 50 percent of the calories in the average American diet? Your wheat, barley, rice, corn, and other cereals and flours have all been degerminated, which means their Vitamin E values are totally or significantly reduced. In white wheat flour, the loss is well over 90 percent, and what escapes processing is further depleted by bleaching of the flour. It seems that vitamin removal is socially approved; only restitution irks the nutrition establishment.

Children deserve a supplement of Vitamin E, starting in the first month of life, for studies of the Vitamin E intake of infants show it to be below the bare minimum stipulated by the authorities, and that minimum is already too low. Twenty-five mgs. of Vitamin E, in the form of mixed tocopherols with the potency stated in terms of d-alpha tocopherol, will benefit infants and young children. The teenager will profit by one hundred mgs. This amount will hold until the aging process brings with it declining efficiency in "managing" fatty substances, at about the age fifty, when the amount may profitably be raised to two hundred. At sixty, it ought to be doubled.

Remember these two notes: The more polyunsaturated fat your doctor recommends, the more Vitamin E you need to protect it against rancidity in the body. And second, the addition of more Vitamin E to the nutrient medium for human cells raised them from a postulated genetic limit of 50 generations, to more than 120. Interestingly, the establishment scientists who made this discovery announced that one can't extrapolate from simple cells to the complex human organism, but confessed that they are now taking supplements of Vitamin E.

## Vitamin K

In some specific instances, Vitamin K is administered on direct order of physicians, but daily requirements have not yet been determined.

Vitamin K is essential for the production of prothrombin, a substance which aids the blood in clotting. It is, therefore, important to liver function, the liver being involved in the manufacture of blood. It is also essential to the proper utilization of Vitamin E.

Vitamin K is fat-soluble, requiring a good fat intake and bile salts to metabolize it. Consequently, diseases like obstructive jaundice interfere with utilization of the vitamin. When obstructive jaundice was operated upon in the past, the Vitamin K deficiency inherent in the disease would cause prolonged bleeding and, in too many cases, death in the operating room. In liver diseases, obstructive jaundice and other similar conditions, therefore, the doctor orders Vitamin K especially if an operation is scheduled. An injection of the vitamin is sometimes given in labor; it may be given to a newborn baby. The Vitamin K activity in the blood of a brand-new infant is rather unsatisfactory until the first week passes. This means that if a baby less than a week old is cut or injured, bleeding is prolonged. In this connection, it is interesting to recall that the Hebrew religion taboos operations upon a child until it has lived through its first week.

New evidence indicates that supplements of Vitamin K will help to protect the liver and blood of those who work with lead or other heavy metals, or those who must regularly take cinchophen or salicylates (such as aspirin).

Vitamin K has been used successfully in the treatment of coronary thrombosis, which seems paradoxical when it is remembered that this is a blood-clotting vitamin and that coronary heart disease results from the formation of a clot. It has been shown, however, that in some cases of this cardiac disorder, the hemorrhage is within the wall of the artery. Vitamin K would help to stop the hemorrhage and thereby rectify the trouble at its source. Thus, in two groups of patients with acute attacks of coronary thrombosis, the mortality in the group given high doses of Vitamin K was 38 percent; in the group given high doses of the vitamin, it was less than 4 percent. Many green leaves, some fats and egg yolk supply Vitamin K.

## THE NEED TO PROTECT VITAMIN-MINERAL INTAKE

It has been said, in fact, I myself unthinkingly repeated it, that none of us would need to be concerned about vitamin-mineral intake if we all had our own gardens, cows, chickens, and a dash of common sense in selecting foods. That statement is categorically untrue, and it is time that our modern knowledge of nutrition retired it from circulation.

Behind that statement is an assumption: All vitamin-mineral needs of human beings can always be satisfied by proper selection of properly fertilized fruits and vegetables, and by proper diversification of the sources of other foods in the diet. That assumption is fallacious. There are people whose vitamin needs are so high that *no* diet could supply them. There are individuals whose mineral needs are so elevated that it wouldn't be feasible to supply those requirements from food. There are sick people whose utilization of foods is disturbed, and who can't achieve nutritional adequacy without their taking steps which go beyond correct criteria of food selection. And if you wish to protest that these are a minority, you'll lose the argument, anyway. Consider, for instance, that the iron requirement of women—eighteen mgs. daily—can be achieved only by meeting two inescapable stipulations: 1) The food must be carefully selected for maximum iron values. 2) Since such carefully selected food will yield no more than six mgs. of iron per thousand calories, the woman *must* eat at least 3,000 calories per day. Given a choice between obesity and anemia, since very few women can possibly eat 3,000 calories daily without excessive weight gain, which do you think women will choose? And how many men, leading a sedentary life as so many men do, will eat enough food to meet *their* vitamin-mineral requirements?

The authorities claim that 99 percent of the population will achieve vitamin-mineral adequacy by eating a diet supply the very modest levels stipulated in the Recommended Dietary Allowances. Dr. Roger Williams has taken the pains to perform exhaustive statistical studies of that statement, and finds that only thirty-three people in every thousand will have their nutritional needs perfectly satisfied by the Recommended Dietary Allowances. For some of the others, the R.D.A. will be generous; and for the rest, the R.D.A. will condemn them to a lifetime of inferior health based on inadequate intake of vitamins and minerals.

Even for those with modest vitamin-mineral needs, achieving a "well-balanced diet" isn't easy. One doesn't arrive at that well-balanced diet by buying foods on the basis of seasonal availability, impulse buying, religious influences, taboos based on allergy and other disorders, habit, and the conditioning of advertising, much of which is devoted to selling poor nutrition. (Makers of really good foods don't often advertise on television—it is the snack food, the overprocessed cereal, the devitalized flour on which millions of advertising dollars are spent.)

And if buying habits were not critical, the inimical influences on the nutritional values of foods would be, and are. Your meat comes from cattle stuffed with grain and dosed with hormones, the objective being fast growth, with no consideration of nutritional values. Your fruits and vegetables are fertilized for maximal growth, not for nutritional value. (The F.D.A. likes to say that poor soil and poor fertilizer reduce quantity, not quality of food. If you read Andre Voison's *Soil, Grass, and Cancer,* you will discover just an inkling of the vast amount of evidence which negates this F.D.A. doctrine. The doctrine was severely criticized by an F.D.A. expert. They pigeon-holed the report, and silenced the critic. I *know.* I had to go to a legislator to pry the report out of F.D.A. files—and it took a dozen telegrams to force them to disgorge it.)

In shipment, food doesn't gain vitamin value. It loses. In storage, the losses increase. In processing, vitamin-mineral values are so depleted that pigs, according to Dr. Henry Schroeder, of Dartmouth College, are superbly fed on what is removed from the white flour we eat. In cooking, losses multiply. Without markedly elevated nutritional requirements, it isn't easy for a person to select a diet adequate in vitamins and minerals—*and remember that deficiency in these factors interferes with the utilization of everything else a diet must supply.*

We don't even feed an optimal diet to our infants. Our baby foods are contaminated, which is the only word to use, with excessive salt and excessive sugar—added, if you please, to please the mother's palate, because the baby couldn't care less. We deprive our babies of fiber in foods, as we introduce them to overprocessed cereals, grains, breads, and cookies, and thereby start them on the road to bowel cancer, appendicitis, and other digestive disorders—which primitives on high-fiber diets escape until we seduce them into our supermarkets.

Since we spend some ninety billions of dollars yearly on what we misterm "health care," which is actually *sickness* care, it is obvious that millions of us are ill with the sicknesses we export to primitives when they import our foods. That explains the statement by the U.S. Department of Agriculture, which has said that 90 percent of our diseases could be mitigated or wiped out by improvement in our diet. (This, while the F.D.A. is assuring us that we don't need to be concerned about vitamins, minerals, protein, or any other dietary factor.) As sickness strikes, utilization of nutrients may become disturbed. The following lists some of the common conditions where ill health demands a rise in vitamin-mineral intake.

### CONDITIONS UNDER WHICH VITAMIN-MINERAL INTAKE MUST BE RAISED
(Assembled from medical reports)

*I. Interference with Food Intake*

Gastro-intestinal diseases as:
Acute gastro-enteritis
Gallbladder disease
Peptic ulcer
Diarrheal diseases
Food allergy
Mental disorders as:
Neurasthenia
Psychoneurosis
Operations and anesthesia
Loss of teeth
Infectious diseases associated with lack of appetite

Heart failure (nausea, vomiting)
Pulmonary disease (vomiting due to cough)
Toxemia of pregnancy (nausea and vomiting)
Visceral pain (as in renal colic, and angina that produces nausea and vomiting)
Neurologic disorders which interfere with self feeding
Migraine

II. *Interference with Absorption*

Diarrheal diseases as:
  Ulcerative and mucous colitis
  Intestinal parasites
  Intestinal tuberculosis
  Sprue
Gastro-intestinal fistulas
Diseases of liver and gallbladder
Lack of hydrochloric acid

III. *Interference with Utilization*

Liver disease
Diabetes mellitus
Chronic alcoholism

IV. *Increased Requirement*

Abnormal activity, as associated with prolonged strenuous physical exertion, with lack of sufficient sleep or rest
Fever
Hyperthyroidism or other instances of high glandular activity
Pregnancy and lactation

V. *Increased Excretion*

Biliary or gastro-intestinal fistula

212

Perspiration
Loss of protein in nephritis and nephrosis
Long-continued excessive fluid intake as in urinary
    tract infections

VI.   *Therapeutic Measures*

Therapeutic diets, as in:
    Sippy regimen
    Gallbladder disease
    Antiobesity diets
Antacids
Mineral oil
Diuretics

Omitted from the preceding chart is a common factor which markedly raises vitamin needs. This is the use of the birth-control pill, which causes systemic deficiency in Vitamin B Complex factors, and local tissue deficiency, at the cervix, in at least one of the B vitamins. Moreover, the deficiency intensifies the risk of a cancer-causing effect of the estrogen in the contraceptive pills based on that hormone.

The Harvard nutrition department recently suggested that the public ought to eat more sugar. It is a fascinating proposal, not only because it originates with a department which in public has acknowledged its debt of gratitude to the sugar industry, for its support of the department, but because increasing sugar intake amplifies the need for vitamins—which sugar doesn't supply, and the use of which the Harvard professor considers to be a token of food faddism. But then, the same "authority" doesn't disapprove of everything. He views food additives as an unmitigated boon, regards criticism of pesticide residues on foods as "crackpot," and has nothing but kind words for overprocessed foods. Those of us with a more objective view see additives and pesticides as an aspect of our internal pollution, and overprocessing of food as a diminishing of the vitamin-mineral supply we need to detoxify ourselves.

For all these reasons, and others too technical for this text, I have for many years urged upon the public the intelligent use of a multiple vitamin, multiple mineral, and Vitamin B Complex (natural source) supplement, with additional amounts of individual vitamins added to this basic regime, as required to meet the needs dictated by individual differences. Since I now write for, broadcast to, and author books for the third generation to receive this advice, it is obvious that my readers and listeners must have earned dividends. I wish them to you, too.

# CHAPTER 13

## FOODS AND THEIR VITAMIN CONTENT

THE FOLLOWING CHARTS LIST THE MORE HIGHLY nutritious foods which are richest in vitamins and minerals. In using these charts, remember that the foods under Group I are usually higher in vitamin-mineral values than those under Group II. Consequently, you might serve and eat larger portions of Group II foods thatn of those in Group I. All of the foods in both groups are nutritious, however, and the list is intended as a useful guide for shipping. If one food is more expensive than the other and they are listed in the same group under the specific vitamin, let price and taste be your criteria.

The omission of a food does not mean that it has no value. It means only that it is not a *rich* source of vitamins and minerals. Such unlisted foods do have distinct usefulness. For example, whole gelatin desserts have no vitamin content at all of themselves, yet the use of gelatin—aside from its value as a source of some protein acids—permits you to serve fruits and vegetables in appetizing forms, thereby raising the vitamin-mineral content of your diet.

When you prepare food for the table, please observe the cooking instructions which are given to you under the title of

"The Ten Commandments of Cooking." This is a serious injunction. If you ignore these cooking methods, it will be of little or no avail to rely on the food charts because you will destroy a substantial part of the vitamin value and possibly lose some of the mineral value through faulty cooking.

Intelligent use of these charts will happily result in lowering your food bills while improving your nutrition.

# VITAMIN A *(Carotene—Pro-Vitamin A)*

Light helps destroy Vitamin A, and air devitalizes it.
Shield your foods!

*Functions*—needed for growth, eyes, skin, nose, throat,
ears, lungs, reproduction, energy, resistance against
infection.

## VEGETABLES
### Group I

Beet Tops
Broccoli
Cabbage Leaves (as
  greens)
Carrots
Chard Leaves (chicory)
Collard
Dandelion Greens
Endive (green)
Escarole
Green Soybeans

Green String Beans
Green Peas
Kale
Lettuce (loose green leaf)
Mustard Greens
Red Peppers
Red Tomatoes and Juice
Sweet Potatoes
Turnip Tops
Watercress
Yellow Squash

### Group II

Artichokes
Brussels Sprouts
Cabbage (green head)
Celery (green)
Chinese Cabbage

Lettuce (green head)
Okra
Peppers (green)
Tomatoes (green)
Yellow Corn

## ANIMAL PRODUCTS
### Group I

Butter
Cheese
Cream
Eggs
Fish-liver Oils
Fish Roe
Liver, any kind

### Group II

Beef Fat
Ice Cream
Kidney
Oysters
Poultry Fat
Red Salmon
Whole milk

*(Fish-liver Oils are very rich in true Vitamin A)*

## GRAINS AND SEEDS

Soybeans                                    Yellow Cornmeal

### FRUITS

*Group I*                    *Group II*

Apricots                     Bananas
Avocados                     Canteloupe
Mangoes                      Cherries
Papayas                      Oranges (yellow juiced)
Prunes                       Pineapple
Yellow Peaches

## Vitamin B  *(Thiamin)*

*Functions*—needed for growth, starch and sugar utilization, appetite, nerves, intestinal action, energy.

## GRAINS AND SEEDS
### Group I

Beans                        Wheat Germ
Bran                         Whole Barley
Brown Rice                   Whole Cereals (Breakfast)
Buckwheat                    Whole Corn
Cow Peas                     Whole-Grain Cereals
Oats                         Whole Grain Hominy
Raw Peanut Butter            Whole Rye
Raw Peanuts (Va. Reds)       Whole Wheat
Rice Polishings              Whole Yellow Cornmeal
Soy Bean Flour

### Group II

Almonds                      Pecans
Brazil Nuts                  Roasted Peanuts and Roasted
Chestnuts                    Peanut Butter (Va. Reds)
Hazelnuts                    Walnuts

*(Milling methods that remove the grain germ also remove B Vitamins.)*

# ANIMAL PRODUCTS

| Group I | Group II |
|---|---|
| Chicken | Bacon (rare) |
| Heart | Beef |
| Kidney | Brains |
| Liver | Eggs |
| Oysters | Milk |
| Pork (lean) | |

## VEGETABLES

### Group I

| | |
|---|---|
| Artichokes | Green Peas |
| Beet Greens | Green String Beans |
| Broccoli | Kale |
| Brussels Sprouts | Spinach |
| Cabbage | Sweet Potatoes |
| Carrots | Sweet Yellow Corn |
| Collards | Turnip Greens |
| Fresh Soybeans | White Potatoes |
| Green Lima Beans | Yeast |

### Group II

| | |
|---|---|
| Asparagus | Mustard Greens |
| Dandelion Greens | Okra |
| Eggplant | Tomatoes |
| Kohlrabi | Turnip |
| Lettuce | Watercress |

*(Vitamin B dissolves in water. Save and serve your cooking water in soup or gravy.)*

# FRUITS

## Group I

Avocados          Oranges
Bananas           Pears
Canteloupe        Pineapple
Citrus Fruits     Raisins
Dates             Red Raspberries
Figs              Watermelon
Grapes

*(Excessive cooking, high temperatures and air are all destructive of vitamins.)*

## VITAMIN B2 (G)
### *(Riboflavin)*

*Fuctions*—Needed for lifespan, skin, eyes, digestion, energy.

## ANIMAL PRODUCTS

Visceral meats, such as liver, are very rich in Vitamin B2 (G) as well as other vitamins.

| *Group I* | *Group II* |
|---|---|
| Cheese | Bacon |
| Eggs | Ham |
| Heart | Mutton |
| Kidney | Pork |
| Liver | Veal |
| Milk (whole, skim, evaporated) | |

# FRUITS

## Group I

Avocados                    Peaches
Grapefruit                  Prunes
Mangoes                     Pears

## Group II

Apples                      Guavas
Bananas                     Melons
Figs                        Raisins

# VEGETABLES

Light destroys Vitamin G. Cook carefully to preserve this vitamin in these delicious vegetables.

## Group I

Beet Greens                 Green Lettuce
Broccoli                    Green Peas
Collards                    Kale
Dandelion Greens            Mustard Greens
Endive                      Other Green Leaves
Escarole

# GRAINS AND SEEDS

Yeast and grains are perfect complements—as found in whole grain bread.

## Group I

Peanuts                     Soybeans
Pecans                      Wheat Germ
Rice Polishings
   Many foods rich in Vitamin B1
Nuts                        Whole Grains

## VITAMIN B6 *(Pyridoxine)*

*Functions*—Needed for skin, utilization of fats, blood, nerves, muscles.

| | |
|---|---|
| Cabbage | Meat |
| Egg Yolk | Milk |
| Fish | Rice polishings |
| Kidney | Wheat Germ |
| Liver | Whole grains |
| Legumes | Yeast |

## VITAMIN B12

*Functions*—Needed for nerves; preventive for pernicious anemia.

| | |
|---|---|
| Milk | Liver |

## NIACIN
### *(Nicotinic acid, Niacinamide)*
### *Vitamin P-P*

*Functions*—Needed for liver, nervous system, brain, soft tissues, skin, circulation and for burning of starch and sugars.

| | |
|---|---|
| Bran | Meat (lean) |
| Eggs | Peanuts |
| Fish | Wheat germ |
| Heart | Whey |
| Kidney | Dried Yeast |
| Liver | |

## INOSITOL

*Functions*—Needed for hair, muscles, liver, brain, heart.

| | |
|---|---|
| Beef brain | Nuts |
| Beef heart | Vegetables |
| Fruits | Whole grains |
| Meat | Yeast |
| Milk | |

# CHOLINE

*Functions*—Needed for kidneys, liver, spleen, thymus gland, lactation.

| | |
|---|---|
| Brain | Pancreas |
| Egg Yolk | Root Vegetables |
| Fish | Soy Beans |
| Fruits | Sweetbreads |
| Heart | Tongue |
| Kidney | Whole Grains |
| Meat | Wheat germ |
| Milk | Yeast |

# PANTOTHENIC ACID
## *(Calcium Pantothenate)*

*Functions*—Needed for growth, skin, digestion, adrenal glands.

| | |
|---|---|
| Beef (lean) | Peanuts |
| Broccoli | Peas |
| Cabbage | Potatoes |
| Corn | Rice bran |
| Dried Yeast | Rolled oats |
| Egg Yolk | Salmon |
| Liver | Wheat germ |
| Milk | Whey |
| Molasses | |

# FOLIC ACID
## *(Pteroylglutamic acid)*

*Functions*—Needed for red blood cells, liver, glands.

| | |
|---|---|
| Eggs | Oysters |
| Fowl | Vegetables |
| Fruits | Wheat germ |
| Meat | Whole grains |

# VITAMIN K

*Functions*—Needed for liver, blood clotting.

| | |
|---|---|
| Cabbage | Liver |
| Carrot greens | Rice bran |
| Cauliflower | Spinach |
| Egg yolk | Soy bean oil |
| Hempseed | Tomatoes |
| Kale | |

## VITAMIN C *(Ascorbic Acid)*
*Freshness is important in Vitamin C foods.*
*Functions*—Needed for healing, teeth, gums, bones, joints, eyes, energy.

## FRUITS
This vitamin is very sensitive to heat. Whenever possible, eat your fruits uncooked.

*Group I*

| | |
|---|---|
| All Fresh Fruit Juices | Canned Citrus Fruits |
| Grapefruit | and Juices |
| Guava (fresh) | Oranges |
| Lemons | Strawberries |
| Limes | Tangerines |
| Mangoes | |

*Group II*

| | |
|---|---|
| Bananas | Loganberries |
| Blueberries | Melons |
| Canned Pineapple | Peaches |
| and Juice | Persimmons |
| Cherries | Raspberries |
| Cranberries | |

## ANIMAL PRODUCTS

Brains (rare)          Liver (rare)
Clams (raw)          Oysters (raw)

## VEGETABLES

Vitamin C dissolves in water. Quick-cook these vegetables and save and serve the cooking water.

| Group I | Group II |
|---|---|
| Asparagus | Beets |
| Cabbage | Broccoli |
| Carrots | Brussels Sprouts |
| Collards | Cauliflower |
| Dandelion Greens | Cucumbers |
| Endive | Horseradish |
| Escarole | Lettuce |
| Kale | Onions |
| Kohlrabi | Parsnips |
| Leeks | Red Radishes |
| Mustard Greens | Rutabagas |
| Peppers | Sprouted Grains and Seeds |
| Tomatoes (whole and juice) | Spinach |
| Turnip Greens | Sauerkraut (fresh) |
| Watercress | Watercress |

## BIOFLAVONOIDS

*Functions*—Needed to aid Vitamin C.

Asparagus          Liver
Grapefruit          Oranges
Grapes

## VITAMIN D *(Calciferol)*

*Functions*—Needed for digestion, bones, teeth, energy.

Note: No food is naturally an adequate source of Vitamin D, although it is present in concentrated liver derivatives. Nature intended that man obtain this vitamin through the action of sunlight on the skin. Properly designed sun lamps may be used where natural sunshine is not available.

### Group I
Fish-liver oils (tablets, capsules)

### Group II

Beef liver
Butter
Cheese
Chicken liver
Cream

Eggs
Fortified or irradiated milk
Fortified or irradiated
   cereals
Salmon

## VITAMIN E

Whole grains             Undefatted wheat germ
Salad (Vegetable) Oils not destructively processed.

MINERALS—The mineral content of foods will be found in the following chapter devoted to minerals, their sources, functions and requirements.

# CHAPTER 14

## REQUIRED MINERALS—FUNCTIONS AND SOURCES

*Calcium*

NEEDED FOR BONES, TEETH, AND NORMAL NEUROMUS-
cular responsiveness. Regulates heart rhythm. Convulsions
may be caused by serious deficiency in blood levels; un-
wholesome personality, by lesser deficiencies. Inadequate
amounts of ionized calcium in blood may contribute to
breath-holding spasms in children. Metabolism affected by
parathyroid glands, and by Vitamins A and D. Excessive
amount of phosphorus can contribute to calcium deficiency.
BEST SOURCES: dairy products, such as milk, cheese, and
yogurt. Milk is a particularly good vehicle, since lactose
(milk sugar) is so helpful to calcium utilization that this
sugar has been used to replace Vitamin D in the treatment of
rickets. Vegetables are poor sources.

Bone meal, dolomite, and oyster shell calcium are often
used as supplemental sources. Calcium orotate is probably
the best utilized supplemental source of calcium.
ADULT REQUIREMENTS: estimated to be between one and
two grams daily. Growing children, about one and one-half
grams. Expectant mothers, two grams. A quart of milk or
about four ounces of yellow cheese will yield one gram of
calcium. When the diet is high protein, but not high in dairy
products, it will be high in phosphorus. If a calcium
supplement is used with such a diet, likely, since low dairy
intake means low calcium, it should be one free of
phosphorus, in order not to perpetuate the phosphorus-
calcium imbalance. Failure to recognize this problem in the
pregnancy diet can contribute to leg cramps, common in
expectant mothers.

*Phosphorus*

Needed for bones and teeth; important in brain function,

nerve and muscle activity, enzyme processes, vitamin utilization. Its most important indirect function is its relationship to calcium metabolism.

BEST SOURCES: protein foods, such as meat, poultry, eggs, yellow cheeses.

REQUIREMENTS: slightly higher than those for calcium.

## Iron

Vitally important to the formation of hemoglobin, therefore important to transport of oxygen and metabolism of food materials in the cells. Without iron, you would need three hundred quarts of blood to absorb oxygen; with it, you need only six quarts. Copper or a trace of certain rare minerals are needed for the best utilization of iron in blood building. The metabolism of Vitamin A depends on hemin iron, and so a good supply of the mineral is indirectly important to teeth and bones. Not all anemias come from iron deficiency, although it is responsible for many.

*Important note for women:* It is very difficult for a woman to offset her iron loss in the menstruals and meet her physiological needs for the metal, and still within the limitations of a calorie intake which will not cause weight gain. A multiple-mineral supplement neatly solves the problem.

BEST SOURCES: pork and other types of liver, molasses, apricots, eggs, oysters, organ meats, dark and blackstrap molasses.

REQUIREMENTS: eighteen mgs. daily for women. About fifteen for men; about five for children under four.

## Sulfur

This mineral is a constituent of protein and vegetable matter, well supplied in the amino acids in which eggs and other animal protein foods are rich. Such sources of sulfur are the only reliable ones from which man can obtain a supply of the mineral in a form readily utilized. Ignore the extravagant claims made for inorganic sulfur supplements.

BEST SOURCES: wheat germ, lentils, cheese, lean beef, peanuts, clams, eggs.

REQUIREMENTS: estimated to be in excess of one gram daily.

*Sodium Chloride*

This is common table salt. Our problem is oversupply, rather than deficiency. Keep in mind that so many foods are (unsuspectedly) rich in salt, and the water in many cities so good a source of it, that achieving a low-salt diet, sometimes prescribed medically, becomes very difficult. Our national salt intake is uncomfortably close to the level of intake, which for animals brings life-shortening hypertension. Keep in mind that blood levels of sodium in many individuals who never eat salty foods or use a salt cellar, may be right in the middle of the normal range. On the other hand, the low-salt diet, sometimes prescribed for hypertension, needs better management than it often receives. Merely discarding the salt cellar and salty foods is not enough, for it reduces the sodium intake to about two grams daily, and to be effective in hypertension, the intake must drop to about 25 percent of that amount. This often requires the use of specially processed milk, avoiding city water where high in sodium, and other special precautions.

RICH SOURCES; caviar, rye krisp, salt butter, clams, cream cheese, American cheese, rye bread, Boston brown bread, oysters, graham crackers, whole wheat and white bread, molasses, condensed milk (filled with sugar, too), dates, turnips, greens, escarole, banana, and many varieties of fish.

*Potassium*

A mineral particularly important in periods of rapid growth, potassium is so widely distributed in foods that deficiency in it should theoretically occur only with a badly imbalanced diet. Theory, as so often happens, fades before fact, for deficiency in potassium and Vitamin B6 has been found frequent in hypertrophic arthritis, and administration of the two nutrients has proved helpful to many patients. Those taking prescribed diuretics may encounter potassium deficiency, as a byproduct of increased excretion of fluid. Food sources of potassium are safer than supplements of the mineral, for some patients have reacted to concentrated potassium by developing intestinal ulceration. Like calcium, potassium helps to normalize neuromuscular responsiveness.

BEST SOURCES: beans, bananas, pecans, olives, molasses, raisins, almonds, peas, figs, dates, etc.

## Iodine

Vital to the production of thyroid hormones; sometimes useful when thyroid is overactive or in the presence of goiter. This mineral also affects hair coloring and texture. To answer a frequent question, iodine deficiencies spring from diets which are low in this mineral, or because the soil from which the food came did not contain iodine. It is therefore wise to use iodized salt unless you are taking a mineral supplement which includes iodine.

## Fluorine

A toxic substance which is being added to the drinking water of helpless citizens to overcome tooth decay caused by a diet filled with foods manufactured by companies which recommend fluoridation. Such foods help to cause loss of the supporting structures of the teeth, with the result that the tooth decay prevented by fluorides will not be present when the teeth are lost by virtue of the type of diet which fluorides encourage the public to continue to eat.

## Zinc

Other than its direct and indirect roles in the body's utilization of sugars and starches, zinc's most dramatic effects are on the senses of taste and smell. Deficiencies in zinc can either diminish or banish these senses; and in some instances, will pervert them, so that normally pleasant odors and tastes appear vile. Zinc deficiency, if pronounced, sharply interferes with growth. Therapy with zinc (and manganese) with Vitamin B6 has been found helpful in a sharply defined type of schizophrenia. For no particularly good reason, zinc has been long labeled as a "trace" mineral, meaning one required in small amounts. This makes no sense, since the requirement is higher than that for iron, which is not considered a trace mineral. Zinc deficiency was long labeled as virtually impossible on any normal diet. Like so many sweeping declarations of this type, this statement has been found fallacious. Zinc deficiency does occur, in this and other countries. The overprocessing of carbohydrates depletes their zinc content. This is regrettable, for this metal is the biological antagonist for cadmium; the latter is implicated as a cause of hypertension. Zinc can be an antagonist of calcium, and is sometimes administered in large doses when there is too great a body burden of calcium. It is also used in benign hypertrophy (enlargement) of the prostate, and is sometimes administered in diabetes.

REQUIREMENTS: at least twenty mgs. daily for adults; thirty for pregnant women; about seven mgs. for children over four; about five mgs. for younger children.

## Magnesium

This mineral is the balance wheel for calcium metabolism. It is interrelated with Vitamin C metabolism to a degree which renders the vitamin useless without it. Magnesium also exerts a quieting action on neuromuscular irritability, promotes elimination and is important to bones and teeth.

BEST SOURCES: beans, bran, Brussels sprouts, chard, clams, corn, nuts, oatmeal, peas, prunes, raisins, spinach, whole grains, honey.

REQUIREMENTS: 270 mgs. daily.

## Manganese

Essential for proper functioning of the mammary glands. Together with calcium and many vitamins, this mineral is important in lactation. It is interrelated with Vitamin B1 metabolism and is necessary to reproduction, glandular function, tissue respiration, and the utilization of Vitamin E. It is interesting to note that animals deficient in this mineral are lacking in maternal instinct.

BEST SOURCES: bananas, beans, bran, celery, liver, oatmeal, onions, peas, filberts, chestnuts, walnuts, whole grains.
REQUIREMENT: 1 mg. daily.

*Aluminum*

This mineral is included in our discussion only to throw the light of reason on the claim that aluminum may cause cancer. Mayo Clinic's Dr. Russell Wilder says: "Many physicians are giving hydrated alumina as an antacid in the treatment of ulcer of the stomach and the duodenum. This treatment has been popular for many years, and so far as I know has never aroused any suspicion of provoking cancer in the stomach. The amount of aluminum given by this means exceeds by many hundred times what would be obtainable from the cooking of foods in aluminum vessels." The literature notes that aluminum is a component of two essential enzymes in the body.


# CHAPTER 15

## FOODS AND MEALS FOR BEST NUTRITION

**THE NUTRITIONAL VALUE OF MILK**

A good rule to follow is two or more glasses of milk daily for adults, three to four glasses for growing children. Milk intake need not be confined to drinking it as a liquid. Milk used in cooking or in desserts, or with cereals, is equally beneficial. Except for infants, the primary value of milk in the diet is as a source of protein and calcium. Cooking losses in milk are of negligible concern to adults or growing children, as we do not depend on it for vitamins, with the exception of riboflavin. But the changes in protein value and the vitamin loss in the boiling of formulas for babies is a serious matter, and may be compensated for only partially by an infant multiple vitamin-mineral supplement.

For those who do not readily drink milk, it may be concealed in junket, custard, soup, pudding, desserts, sauces and baked products, or it may also be consumed in cheese—preferably the yellow types such as American or Cheddar. Six ounces of yellow cheese provides the nutritive equivalent of one quart of milk. If you are allergic to milk, try adding a little lemon juice to it before drinking, or boil and chill it.

It is milk's contribution of calcium which is of great value in the diet. A negative calcium balance leads to brittle bones in old age.

## THE MILK CONTROVERSY

### *Pasteurization vs. Certification*

Despite common legend, pasteurization of milk was first practiced in order to avoid or lessen souring, with little thought to the prevention of milk-borne disease. As knowledge of bacteriology grew, pasteurization became an important weapon against tuberculosis, undulant fever and other infections which were commonly carried by raw milk produced under unsanitary conditions. On the credit side of pasteurization is safety. On the debit side, however, there are losses of nutritive value too important to be ignored.

The authorities admit that pasteurization lowers the Vitamin C content of milk, but deny the evidence which shows that the process definitely robs milk of other vital factors. This is an incomprehensible denial, for scientific literature contradicts it.

The loss of Vitamin C in pasteurization deprives babies of a staggering amount of this essential vitamin. In addition, pasteurization causes a smaller loss of thiamin (Vitamin B1) and riboflavin (Vitamin B2). There is also an appreciable loss of calcium—more than 2½ million pounds a year. The authorities who persist in denying this loss apparently do not read the diary journals which are filled with advertisements for detergents effective in removing precipitated calcium from the pasteurization tanks.

Milk as it comes from the cow contains an anti-stiffness factor which is curiously akin to adrenal hormone in its effect in preventing arthritis among animals. This anti-stiffness factor is destroyed in pasteurization. Also destroyed in pasteurization are anti-anemia and anti-ulcer factors. Moreover, raw milk contains a natural germicide which interferes with the multiplication of bacteria in the milk. This germicide is likewise destroyed, thereby bringing about the ironic fact that raw milk produced under hygienic conditions will "keep" better than pasteurized milk when both are exposed at room temperature.

Raw milk contains more than a dozen enzymes which lose their activity when exposed to heat. Hence, pasteurized milk lacks these factors which aid in the utilization within the body of many nutrients which milk contains. Among these enzymes is phosphatase, which assists in the utilization of phosphorus and calcium. Far from recognizing the value of this enzyme, milk inspectors test for the presence of phosphatase when determining whether milk has been "properly" pasteurized. If the processor has left in the milk any of this enzyme which aids in the utilization of milk calcium, he is subject to a fine or more severe legal penalties!

Rats, by virtue of efficient calcium utilization, can free themselves of rickets with small amounts of Vitamin D. This vitamin in proportionately higher amounts often will not protect babies fed on pasteurized milk against rickets. It can be concluded that the fortification of pasteurized milk with synthesized Vitamin D, in the absence of the enzyme phosphatase, does not represent full protection against rickets. The medical journals, indeed, frequently report "refractory" rickets which does not respond to doses of vitamin-D-enriched pasteurized milk. Breast milk contains the enzyme—giving nursed babies more resistance to rickets.

Cats maintained on a diet comprised of two-thirds pasteurized milk and one-third raw liver will not maintain good health. In the third generation, they encounter sterility, resorption of the embryo, arthritis, eczema, allergies, degeneration of the vital organs, gum disorders and crippling nerve and muscle diseases of the type which crowd human hospitals and puzzle medical men. Cats maintained on the same amount of liver with two-thirds of the diet comprised of raw milk remain in good health for generation after generation. When evaporated or condensed milk are used as the mainstay of the animals' diet, the degeneration is even more severe.

These remarks are not an endorsement of raw milk per se, for it remains today what it was when pasteurization was instituted to wipe out the epidemics of disease resulting from infected milk. There is, however, one type of raw milk on the market which is safe. This is *certified raw milk*. It is produced under extremely strict state and federal regulations, under a voluntary code of the milk industry which is even stricter than the governmental regulations and under the close supervision of the medical milk commissions. Physicians have been so intensively indoctrinated with the concept that pasteurized milk is nutritionally adequate and raw milk violently dangerous that they are prone to extend their prejudice blindly to certified raw milk. The professional man, as well as the public, should be reminded that certified raw milk is accepted for advertising by the publications affiliated with the American Medical Association and that this milk is described in medical journals as being superior in nutritional value and completely safe.

A statement in the *New York Journal of Medicine* reveals that "no communicable disease has been traced to this (certified raw) milk since the year 1897." It is proved that certified raw milk is safe and also that it contains many important nutritional factors which are lost in pasteurization. There are still other advantages in certified raw milk. Ordinarily, pasteurized milk is a fluid of indefinite composition, since the diet of cows is good in the season of pasturage and indifferent during the months of dry feed. So it is that pasteurized milk sinks to its lowest Vitamin A value—half that of summer milk—in the season when respiratory infections are most prevalent and Vitamin A most needed. Certified raw milk, however, is consistent the year round because the cows' diet is arranged consistently. Pasteurized milk may be laxative in the spring and constipating in the fall, in accordance with the changes in cows' diet; but certified raw milk does not exhibit these tendencies because of diet precautions. The wheat germ, bran, middlings, blackstrap molasses and other nutrients fed to cows whose yield is certified are weighed and apportioned scientifically. The bacteria count of the milk is taken not categorically but quantitatively, each type of bacteria being counted individually. The result is that certified raw milk actually has a lower bacteria count than pasteurized milk and is a better food.

## SPECIAL NOTE FOR MILK-HATERS

Man's needs for calcium are so high that civilized man's eating habits cannot satisfy these needs unless milk and cheese are consumed in substantial amounts. Peoples who do not consume dairy products obtained their calcium from sources which we are too finicky to use. The savage, for example, eats an animal in its entirety, including the bones and marrow, which are rich sources of calcium. The Chinese, who count themselves as fabulously wealthy when they own cows, treasure pickled pig's feet as a delicacy in general and as a necessity for expectant mothers. In this way, they obtain calcium which has dissolved into the vinegar. Our knife-and-fork niceties do not sanction the consumption of animals from nose to tail, avoid blood and visceral meats and seldom encounter pickled pigs' feet. We need milk. Of course, calcium is contained in other foods. But to replace a quart of milk or four ounces of American cheese with equal calcium value, we would have to eat three pounds of spinach, two dozen eggs or thirty medium-sized oranges. Let's drink milk, eat cheese, or use a calcium supplement, unless your doctor, because you're malutilizing the mineral, has lowered your calcium intake.

# VEGETABLES

Two or more servings of vegetables every day, in addition to your other foods, will put you on the right nutritional track. Select vegetables from the green and yellow types for maximum nutrient value, and remember that leafy vegetables are usually more complete foods than the root types. Both should be used, however. For example, you might serve whole, sliced or diced beets—and steamed beet tops. One vegetable may be omitted from the daily diet if you serve a substantial portion of a green leafy salad once a day. Work up your own recipes, using these inexpensive green leaves as a base. By the addition of fruit, cheese, tongue, chicken or cold seafood, such salads are made attractively palatable even to those diehards who term all salads "rabbit food." Flavored brewer's yeast also adds zest to mixed salads. Despite their higher carbohydrate content, potatoes are also excellent food although they should not be counted as one of your vegetables. They are at their nutritional best when baked or boiled—and eaten—with the skins on. When boiling, scrub potatoes well so that the cooking water may be used in soups or gravies.

# FRUITS

Serve two or more daily, one of which should be a citrus fruit. Raw fruits are best. As a matter of fact, dried fruits cannot be considered as good sources of Vitamin C. Remember that if you are substituting tomatoes for fruit as your Vitamin C source, you must serve approximately twice as much as you would of citrus fruit. Refer to the discussion on Vitamin C for detailed information.

# EGGS

These are really superb in food value, packed full of animal protein and containing almost a complete alphabet of vitamins. When meat is scarce or expensive, let eggs be a protein mainstay of your diet. Don't play a "numbers game" with eggs unless your doctor has so decided for you.

## PROTEIN

With each meal, serve meat, cheese, fish, fowl, or other animal protein. On a meatless day, if you decide on a cheese dish you can safely reduce your milk intake for that day. This will save food pennies and also give you your supply of protein and calcium. Study the discussion on protein in another chapter so that a "legume" meatless day will supply enough dairy products, fish, fowl, or egg dishes to offset the incompleteness of the bean protein. Frequent servings of fish, liver and other low-cost high-protein foods will help balance your budget and your diet.

## CEREALS

Insist on whole grains when you buy cereals and bread, and serve whole grain foods at least three times a day. This can be managed by serving a whole grain cereal for breakfast and, for lunch and dinner, whole wheat, whole rye or whole corn bread.

## FATS

Serve moderate portions of butter and fortified margarine twice daily. Remember that all edible fats are a good fat source—corn oil, peanut oil, soy oil, cottonseed oil, etc.

## DESSERTS

Gooey desserts may be a pictorial delight, but they are a nutritional negative. They can be, and frequently are, downright harmful. Forsake the creamy pastries and sugarladen tidbits in favor of simple desserts, and be ingenious about using them to bring milk, cream and butter to the diet. For example, a Brown Betty made with white sugar, apples and corn flakes is a graveyard of lost vitamins and minerals, but a delicious Brown Betty built on a recipe using apples, butter, whole wheat bread crumbs and molasses or honey or maple syrup (which is surprisingly rich in calcium)—while it has still lost Vitamin C—is a dessert of better nutritional value.

## WORKING WITH THE DAILY FOOD FRAMEWORK

The preceding general outline of a framework for your diet is the first step toward understanding of your daily requirements. It is important to remember that your body's requirements *are* daily ones, for nature has decreed that the human body must be replenished every day. You cannot go without food one day, eat twice as much the following day and expect a mathematical average to protect you for both. There is no turning back in nutrition.

Moreover, no meal can be analyzed and called "adequate" when considered alone. Meals are relative to each other within the waking hours of your day. The "right" breakfast and dinner combined with a "wrong" luncheon result in a "wrong" food *day*. When planning your menu for a single day, check it carefully with the Food Framework to be sure that you have included all of the required foods. This framework has purposely been made flexible so that your meals need not fall into a dull routine. Vary your food plan and your seasonings. Serve dishes as attractively as possible.

The next step in learning to live and eat on a nutritionally well balanced keel is—*please plan breakfasts and dinners by the week, not by the day.* Luncheons can be fitted in afterwards, when the lists of breakfasts and dinners have been checked to see what foods demanded by the Food Framework are missing! This scheme makes it easier for you to control each day's menus—and besides, you will save money when you budget your shopping in terms of an entire week. When you shop, consider the costs in terms of availability and season. The fruit or vegetable that is out of season is usually expensive and is often devitalized by forced growing or storage. Remember, too, that the vitamin content of vegetables declines rapidly after picking; it is false economy, nutritionally speaking, to accept a wilted head of cabbage because it is a penny or two cheaper. Remember also that the larger sizes in many fruits and vegetables do not deserve a premium price. Forced into larger growth, or merely left too long on vine or tree, their flavors may be inferior. As a rule, buy average sizes. You'll save money and yet obtain the best in flavor and nutrients.

Plan your week's dinner by filling in the meat or meat substitute courses first. Remember to include liver and other glandular meats liberally—they are nutritious and usually lower in cost. Don't forget fish, fowl, cheese, beans and dairy products for your main courses. Study the side variety of complementary or complete proteins before making your selections.

When your main courses are filled in for your weekly dinners, plan your green salads next. Raw vegetables, mixed greens, cole slaw, occasionally spiked with fruit, tongue, chicken or fish and with Russian, roquefort, garlic or French dressing offer a basis for a different salad each night. Chop the greens fine for better taste and fewer disparaging remarks from husbands who do not take kindly to salads, no matter how nutritionally beneficial they are. A good idea is to serve the salad early in the meal, rather than at the end. It will encourage nibbling on good food while appetites are keen.

Next choose the vegetables for the week. Remember the rules about vegetables, including potatoes, as stated in the general Food Framework. If at one meal you serve baked potato and your salad is comprised of many leafy green vegetables, your second vegetable should be a leafy type, nonetheless. If your salad portions are large, the baked potato can be the only other vegetable portion.

From this point on, the dinner menu will be determined in

relation to what was served for breakfast and luncheon. Here is where you balance each day's intake. If breakfast was deficient in Vitamin C, your dinner salad may include citrus fruit slices. If breakfast and luncheon were short of Vitamin B foods, dinner can be more abundant in whole wheat or whole rye foods—bread pudding or muffins for dessert, for example. Be careful to remember, however, if potato is served along with whole grain breads, muffins or desserts, avoid another starchy vegetable. Half of your day's citrus juice or raw citrus fruit may be taken with dinner. Vitamin C may be utilized better in your body if you do not saturate your system with the vitamin in one gulp—as you might by drinking a water tumbler full of the juice at breakfast. Despite common practice, fruit or tomato juice served as a first course is not the best stimulant for appetites. A warm snack, or a little wine, is the best stimulant. Fruit or tomato juice may, however, be served during the meal as a beverage.

Always watch carefully the milk intake for each day. If your family is not drinking the required amount, fill in with custards, puddings, creamed soup or cheese dishes.

Your weekly breakfasts will be primarily dictated by your family's preferences, and balance out dinners in the consumption of carbohydrates, proteins and Vitamin C. There is no law which says that breakfast must be a light meal. The New Englander does well with pork chops or other meat at breakfast. He works it off if his work is active, whereas a New Yorker might not. As a nation, however, with the exception of our acceptance of eggs as a breakfast dish, we seem to prefer a carbohydrate breakfast. Waffles, French toast and cereals at our first meal of the day are largely carbohydrate and consequently quickly digested and turned into energy, but may lead to midmorning "SLUMP" based on low blood sugar for want of protein.

# CHAPTER 16

## THE TEN COMMANDMENTS OF COOKING

*Plus Some Other Thoughts for Food and Vice Versa*

**HAVING LEARNED WHAT FOODS ARE NUTRITIONALLY** desirable, and why, you are now ready to select for your family a variety of edibles that are rich in natural vitamins and minerals, high in protein and bulkage, correct in carbohydrate and fat content. So far so good. Having brought them into your kitchen for preparation, you are about to distribute the largesse of their healthful benefits to your family. STOP! Almost as much malnutritional mayhem is committed in our beautifully appointed American kitchens as in transportation, storage, and over-processing. In order to avoid the crime of unintentional nutricide, punishable by that run-down feeling, do please obey these *Ten Commandments of Cooking:*

### 1. AVOID WHITE FOOD

Do not discard edible outer green leaves of vegetables such as cabbage, broccoli and lettuce. Implore your vegetable man not to strip off these leaves, which have been kissed by sunlight and are filled with vitamins and minerals.

Avoid bleached celery and bleached endive.

Prefer brown sugar to white, brown unpolished rice to white, brown whole wheat to white flour, brown whole rye to grey. Choose yellow turnips in preference to white, buy sweet potatoes more frequently. Color in food is usually the sign of its vitamin value. Whiteness is the indication of lower vitamin-mineral values, generally speaking. This does not, of course, apply to milk.

### 2. AVOID STALE FOOD

Keep your food in the coolest available place, preferably a

good ice box or refrigerator. Do not stock up on perishable food—unless, of course, you have a freezer. Calculate your menus to avoid long storage of leftovers; try, if possible, to avoid leftovers entirely. (This is not only good nutrition, but will also make you popular with your family.) Buy the freshest food your market offers and your budget permits.

## 3. EAT RAW FOOD

Select and serve raw once or twice a day fruits and vegetables of which a portion can be left uncooked.

## 4. CHOOSE COOKING METHODS CAREFULLY

Select cooking methods least conducive to vitamin-mineral losses. In order of preference, we should list pressure-cooking, waterless cooking, rapid boiling, steaming without pressure, broiling, deep-fat frying, baking, simmering or slow boiling and shallow-fat frying. Try to avoid frying entirely—use broiling instead. Always remember that every cooking method has its fault and may destroy vitamin value to a certain extent.

## 5. UNDERCOOK RATHER THAN OVERCOOK

With the exception of such foods as pork, dried beans and peas, it is advisable to sacrifice some tenderness to save vitamin content. A degree of cooking and tenderness may be achieved in two ways: First, by cooking a short time at a high temperature; secondly, by cooking a longer time at a low temperature. The first method is much less destructive to vitamins.

## 6. COOK FOR THE MEAL YOU ARE GOING TO EAT

Serve food promptly after cooking. Do not prepare food for the next day. Abbreviate the time period which will elapse between the purchase of food, its preparation and its consumption. Time, heat and exposure to air are all destructive to vitamins. If there must be leftovers, use them as promptly as possible, without cooking them if they are palatable when cold.

## 7. KEEP AIR AWAY FROM YOUR FOOD

Air destroys some vitamins; it belongs in your lungs, not in your food. Cook in closed vessels. Avoid whipping air into your food and refrain from putting hot food through strainers.

## 8. DO NOT USE SODA WHEN COOKING VEGETABLES

The use of soda to make green vegetables look greener after cooking is a perfect method of destroying vitamins. You will not need soda to keep the green color in vegetables, if you cook them quickly enough. (A very small amount of soda may be used with green peas and beans only.)

## 9. DO NOT DISCARD COOKING WATER

Retain all cooking juices and water. Do not pour them down the drain and do not let them burn down to the bottom of the cooking utensil. Sometimes there may be more vitamin and mineral values in these waters than are left in the vegetables themselves after they have been cooked.

## 10. FOUR QUICK RULES

1. Cook in covered pots.
2. Use as little water as possible.
3. Raise the temperature quickly.
4. Avoid violent boiling.

*One Special Note:* If you never know exactly when the family will come home for dinner, precook it until it is nearly done and then pop it immediately into the refrigerator. When your hungry men finally arrive, put the meal back on the stove and raise the temperature very rapidly until cooking is completed. There is no validity to the superstition that hot or warm foods must not be chilled quickly. It's better for them. You may raise your refrigerator bill, but you'll save vitamins—and that's what refrigerators are for.

## GET TO KNOW THESE MEATS

Because the housewife concentrates her buying on about a dozen cuts of meat—and because animals will not obligingly limit their anatomy to filet mignon—the result is that the law of supply and demand makes some cuts very expensive, some much less so. This has nothing to do with the nutritional value of the meat. Actually, chuck steak has more protein than porterhouse for the obvious reason that the more expensive cut represents protein marbled with fat, which makes it tender. To tenderize the inexpensive cuts of meat, marinate them with wine or vinegar or treat them with papaya tenderizers.

## BEEF

| | |
|---|---|
| Arm Pot Roast | Rib Steak |
| Flank Steak | Arm Steak |
| Blade Steak | Rolled Neck |
| Short Ribs | Chuck Rib |
| Pin Bone Sirloin | Knuckle Pot Roast |
| Bottom Round | Ground Chuck |
| Heel of Round | Rolled Brisket |
| Swiss Steak | Rolled Plate |
| Ground Round | Boneless Shank Meat |
| Rump Pot Roast | Boneless 6-7 Ribs |
| Rump Steak | Salisbury Steak |
| Stew | Flank Stew |
| Brisket | Shank Bone |
| Skirt Steak | Neck |
| Corned Brisket | Plate |
| Corned Plate | Standing Ribs |
| Rolled Boston Cut | |

## MUTTON

Steaks
Loin Chops
Rib Chops
Rolled Shoulder
Rolled Rack
Leg
Sirloin Roast

Ground for Loaf
Neck
Shoulder Chops
Shoulder
Breast
Stew
Shanks

## LAMB

Blade Chops
Arm Chops
Leg
Rolled Shoulder
Shanks
Breast
Boneless Breast
Breast with Pocket

Riblets
Neck
Boneless Neck
Neck and Shoulder
Patties
Shoulder Stew
Ground for Loaf

## VEAL

Boneless Stew
Shoulder Chops
Sirloin Steak
Sirloin Roast
Rump Roast
Leg Roast
Rolled Shoulder
Rolled Breast

Arm Steak
Patties
Ground for Loaf Breast
Shoulder Roast
Hind and Fore Shanks
Giblets
Stew

## CURED PORK

Picnic
Boneless Picnic
Regular Ham
Half-Ham Shank
Half-Ham Butt
Ground Ham
Bacon

Salt Pork
Jowls
Bacon Squares
Bacon Ends
Ham Shank
Ham Shank Slices

## FRESH PORK

Butt

Boneless Boston Butt

Blade Steak

Cushion Shoulder

Arm Steak

Shoulder End Chops

End Loin Chops

Fresh Ham Shank Half

Fresh Ham Butt

Ham Butt Slice

Picnic

Center Loin Chops

Loin End Roast

Rib End Roast

Rolled Loin

Country Backbones

Side Pork

Fresh Ham

Spareribs

Neck Bones

Fore Shanks

Ham Hocks

## SPECIALTIES

Beef Tongue

Beef Heart

Beef Brains

Beef Liver

Oxtails

Beef Kidneys

Tripe

Calf's Tongue

Calf's Heart

Calf's Brains

Pork Snouts

Pork Brains

Pork Kidneys

Pork Liver

Pork Tongue

Pig's Feet

Tails

Lamb's Brains

Lamb's Liver

Lamb's Heart

## SAUSAGE

Veal Loaf

Veal Sausage

Smoked Liver Sausage

Thuringer

Fresh Liver Sausage Rings

Pork Sausage Links

Blood Sausage

Summer Sausage

Kosher Salami

Salami

Polish Sausage

Minced Ham

Frankfurters

Bologna

Head Cheese

Garlic Sausage

Sulze

Knockwurst

Fresh Liver Sausage

Ring Bologna

Pork Sausage Meat

## CANNED, FROZEN AND FRESH FOOD

The "fresh" spinach on your favorite vegetable stand may be ten days old when you buy it. It was probably raised in Texas—60 percent of our spinach is—spent a number of days in transport, some time in the hands of the produce exchange and the wholesaler, and finally arrived at your retailer's, where it possibly remained for several days before you bought it.

Truer freshness is one advantage of canned and frozen foods. The canners process fruits and vegetables immediately after harvesting, pack them in cans and cook them shielded from light and air, with strict control of the cooking temperatures. Since they start with fresh food and apply techniques which are unavailable to the housewife, they are likely to come out with a more nutritious food. Furthermore, because of their desire for a continued source of supply, the canners and freezers are likely to locate their plants where soils are fertile. This, in turn, will also be reflected in the nutritional value of their products. Some of the fresh produce which arrives in large cities may be derived from inferior soils, according to the United States Department of Agriculture, which has commented on deficiency diseases observed in animals grazing on the soils where truck farms supplying large urban areas are located.

Frozen foods are usually superior in flavor for, in the case of fruits and vegetables, the freezing process always starts with fully ripe produce. This is necessary, because freezing is a state of suspended animation, neither adding nor subtracting from the quality of the food.

It is more than probable that frozen foods will increasingly displace canned varieties and that our present system of food production and distribution will ultimately be revolutionized by the freezing industry. The system by which the housewife shops daily will disappear when the home food freezer is as universally adopted as the electric refrigerator. With this modern device, the housewife can store hundreds of pounds of choice frozen foods in her home and quick-freeze the "buys" she picks up when foods are in season and consequently lower in price.

# CHAPTER 17

## A FORTNIGHT OF MEALS

THIS CHAPTER IS INCLUDED AS A "SAMPLER" OF THE KIND of menus you can feed your family in order to give them nutritional advantages without sacrificing variety, interest or savor. It is not suggested that you weary your housemates with a repetition of these same fourteen daily menus; but that, having introduced them to eating habits that are sensible as well as satisfying, you will continue with improvised meals of your own planning which will follow the pattern of good nutrition.

Throughout these menus, recipes are included for dishes whose ingredients may present a choice between good and poor nutrition. Also included are some useful variations of standard recipes. For dishes listed without instruction, refer to my cook book, *The Carlton Frederick's Cook Book.*

You will note that luncheon and dinner menus seldom include a first course. From the nutritional point of view, one is not necessary. When family preference makes first courses desirable, they may be added.

For salads not specified as green salads, the author assumes that a generous amount of greens will be used as a base, not just as garnish.

Vegetables should be used in season, as should fresh fruits. If frozen or canned fruit is used for breakfast, drain it and reserve the sweet juice for the drain. You have enough sugar . . . *too much.*

The luncheons given in the menus complete a well-balanced day's meal along with breakfast and dinner, but they are patterns rather than rules and need not be followed literally. For example, when eggs are indicated they may be used in any form, but should be included in the meal.

It is assumed that absent members of the family will make an effort to balance lunch with breakfast and dinner. School children who carry their lunches can of course be provided with properly balanced noontime meals.

## BREAKFAST

*Sunday*
Stewed Figs & Cream
Sizzled Beef & Scrambled Eggs
Whole Wheat Coffee Ring
Beverage

*Monday*
Citrus Juice
Soft Cooked Eggs
Whole Wheat Toast & Apple Butter
Beverage

*Tuesday*
Citrus Juice
Pettijohn Cereal—Brown Sugar
Beverage

*Wednesday*
Fresh Pears
Fried Eggs & Bacon
Whole Wheat Toast
Marmalade
Beverage

## LUNCH

*Quick Rarebit on Whole Wheat
   Toast Triangles
Finger Salad
Pineapple Chunks
Cookies
Milk

Banana & Peanut Butter Salad
   on Shredded Greens
Jelly Sandwich—Whole Wheat
   Bread
Milk

Deviled Egg Salad—
   Whole Rye Toast
Fresh Fruit
Milk

Liverwurst or Salami Sandwich
   —Whole Wheat Bread
Green Salad
Baked Apples
*Cocoa

## DINNER

Citrus Fruit Cup
Chicken Fricassee—Whole Wheat Biscuits
Crab Apple Jelly
Okra Squash
Mixed Green Salad
*Fruited Gelatin—Whipped Cream
Beverage

*Ragout of Heart
Mashed Potatoes
Wax Beans
Red Cabbage, Apple, Celery
   Salad on Chicory
Boysenberries
Beverage

Veal Chops
*Mexican Corn
Spinach
Fresh Fruit Salad
Whole Wheat Crackers & Cheese
Beverage

Beef Stew—With Vegetables
Cole Slaw
Hot Whole Wheat Rolls
Citrus Fruit Cup
*Oatmeal Cookies
Beverage

250

*Thursday*
Citrus Juice
Hot Cornmeal
Honey
Beverage

*Eggs Cooked in Tomato Sauce
Whole Wheat Bread
Watercress
Fresh Fruit
Milk

Boiled Tongue
—Horse Radish
Creamed Potatoes
Broccoli
Mixed Green Salad
Gingerbread—Applesauce
Beverage

*Friday*
Citrus Juice
Cod Fish Cakes
Whole Wheat Rolls—Jelly
Beverage

Waldorf Salad
Creamed Tuna Fish—Whole
Wheat Toast
Milk

*Baked Fish Turbot
Cauliflower
Mixed Vegetables
Raw Spinach, Romaine, Green
Peppers Salad, French
Dressing
Strawberry Shortcake—Whipped
Cream
Beverage

*Saturday*
Citrus Juice
Poached Eggs on Whole Wheat
Toast
Apple Butter
Beverage

Soup—Whole Wheat Crackers
Peanut Butter, Bacon & Romaine
Sandwich—Whole Wheat Bread
Fresh Fruit
Milk

Frankfurters *Baked Beans
Buttered Kale
*Brown Bread & Honey
Peach & Cottage Cheese Salad
Beverage

Note:
Dishes marked with an asterisk* are given in recipe form on
following page. Recipes will serve four. If your family is
smaller or larger, vary amounts accordingly. When preparing hot cereals, add ½ cup dried non-fat milk to each cup of
dry cereal before cooking.

# RECIPES

### Quick Rarebit

Shred yellow cheese. Add for each cup, 2 tb. mayonnaise, 1 tsp. mustard, 1 tsp. catsup, 1 tsp. brewer's yeast. Mix well. Spread on w.w. toast and place under broiler till melted. Garnish with pimentoes or chopped parsley.

### Fruited Gelatin

Using plain unflavored gelatin, follow recipe on package for quantity needed. Use any fruit juices on hand, canned or fresh (except pineapple). Use no sugar. Add as much fruit as liquid will take.

### Ragout of Heart

2 Veal Hearts
seasoned w.w. flour
3 Green Peppers
2 tb. smoked brewer's yeast

Cut hearts in small pieces, dredge with flour. Brown in fat in heavy kettle. Add pot liquor, vegetable juices or water to cover. Cook till nearly done. (About 1 hr. in pressure cooker, 2½ hrs. in heavy kettle.) Add chopped peppers; simmer till tender. Just a few minutes before serving add yeast and a few tablespoons of Julep or Sherry.

### Oatmeal Cookies

½ cup shortening
2/3 cup brown sugar, packed
1 egg
1 tb. milk
½ tsp. vanilla
¾ cup sifted w.w. flour
½ tsp. baking soda
½ tsp. salt
1½ cup quick cooking rolled oats
1 cup peanuts (may be salted)

Cream shortening and sugar. Beat in egg, milk and vanilla. Mix well the dry ingredients and add. Drop by spoonful on greased cookie sheet. Bake about 15 min. in moderate oven.

### Mexican Corn

Saute in a little margarine 1 tb. minced onion, ¼ cup chopped green pepper and 2 tb. chopped pimento. When done add frozen corn or succotash (soybean preferred). Cover tightly and cook till done. Watch carefully and stir when needed. Add salt, pepper and a bit of garlic salt. When serving with meat which is to be broiled, spread half done vegetable in pan under meat and broil, allowing meat juices to drip on vegetables.

### Eggs in Tomato Sauce

Butter individual serving dishes or muffin pans. Put in each 2 tb. tomato soup or sauce. Drop egg carefully in each. Season, top with a little shredded cheese and buttered crumbs. Bake in mod. oven till eggs are set.

### Baked Fish Turbot

| | |
|---|---|
| 6 tb. margarine | ½ tsp. salt |
| 3 tb. w.w. flour | pepper |
| 1 tb. brewers' yeast | 2 cups warm milk |

Melt margarine. Add dry ingredients which have been well blended. Stir till smooth and gradually add milk. Cook till thick, stirring. Add 2-3 cups cooked fish. Pour into buttered casserole, cover with buttered crumbs and grated cheese. Bake ½ hr.

### Brown Bread

B. and M. Brand and A. & P. Brand are made with w.w. flour.

### Baked Beans

To each can of beans (oven baked style) add 1 tsp. chopped onion, 1 tsp. prepared mustard, 1 tsp. brewer's yeast, 1 tb. blackstrap molasses, and 1 tsp. hon. Heat thoroughly and allow to stand for a few min. before serving.

### Cocoa

For each cup allow 1 rounded tsp. cocoa, 2 tsp. brown sugar, 1 tb. powdered milk, few grains of salt, and a drop or two of vanilla. Mix well, add warm liquid milk, heat well.

| BREAKFAST | LUNCH | DINNER |
|---|---|---|
| *Sunday*<br>Minted or Honeyed Grapefruit<br>Scrambled Eggs<br>Smoked Salmon<br>Cream Cheese<br>Whole Wheat Rolls-Jelly<br>Beverage | Fresh Fruit Salad<br>Assorted Cheese Tray<br>Whole Wheat Crackers<br>Whole Rye Bread<br>Milk | Baked Ham   Cranberry Sauce<br>Candied Sweet Potatoes<br>Buttered Kale<br>Green Salad<br>Chocolate Nut Sundae<br>Beverage |
| *Monday*<br>Citrus Juice<br>Oatmeal<br>Honey<br>Beverage | Cottage Cheese, Green Pepper<br>& Watercress Salad<br>Deviled Ham Sandwich— Whole<br>Wheat Bread<br>Fresh Fruit | *Veal Fricassee<br>Brown Rice<br>Asparagus Tips Vinaigrette<br>(generous Greens)<br>Baked Custard<br>Beverage |
| *Tuesday*<br>Baked Apples<br>Fried Eggs & Bacon<br>Whole Rye Toast<br>Orange Marmalade<br>Beverage | Sliced Pineapple, Grated Carrot<br>& Raisin Salad<br>Peanut-butter Sandwich— Whole<br>Wheat Bread<br>Milk | Pan Fried Liver & Bacon<br>Baked Potatoes<br>Turnip Greens<br>Mixed Green Salad—French<br>Dressing<br>Citrus Fruit Cup<br>*Nut Cake<br>Beverage |
| *Wednesday*<br>Citrus Juice<br>Buckwheat (Whole) Griddle<br>Cakes & Syrup<br>Sausage<br>Beverage | Toasted Deviled Ham & Cheese<br>Sandwich— Whole Wheat Bread<br>Fresh Fruit<br>Nut Cake<br>Milk | Cheese Souffle<br>String Beans<br>Cole Slaw with Celery Seeds on<br>Greens<br>Apple Brown Betty<br>Beverage |

254

## Thursday
Grapes
*Eggs Poached in Milk
Whole Wheat Toast
Beverage

Soup
Whole Wheat Crackers
*Pear Waldorf Salad
Milk

Roast Pork—Apple Sauce
Pan Browned Potatoes
*Broccoli Broil
Mixed Green Salad
*Orange Surprise
Beverage

## Friday
Citrus Juice
Jelly Omelet
Cinnamon Toast
Beverage

Tuna Fish Salad
Whole Wheat Rolls
Fresh Fruit
Milk

Baked Halibut-Egg Sauce-
    Slivered Almonds
Lima Beans
Stewed Tomatoes
Mixed Vegetable Salad—
    Roquefort Dressing
Sliced Peaches
Cookies
Beverage

## Saturday
Citrus Juice
Hot Ralston
Molasses Butter
Beverage

Cream Cheese & Green Pepper
Sandwich—Whole Wheat Bread
Fresh Fruit
Cookies

Tomato Juice
*Hawaiian Hamburg
Peas & Carrots
*Wilted Greens
*Raisin Rice Pudding & Cream
Beverage

Note: Dishes marked with an asterisk* are given in recipe
form on following page.
Recipes will serve four. If your family is smaller or
larger, vary amounts accordingly.
When preparing hot cereals add ½ cup dried non-fat
milk to each cup of dry cereal before cooking.

### Eggs Poached in Milk

Bring to a boil enough milk to cover bottom of small pan to depth of about 1". Add ½ tsp. salt, slip eggs in one at a time. Cook slowly, spooning milk over eggs. When firm enough transfer to a warm deep platter. Into the milk break a little quick melting cheese and a few w.w. bread crumbs (enough cheese to suit taste and bread to thicken a little.) Pour over eggs; add w.w. toast triangles and a little currant jelly to garnish.

### Pear Waldorf Salad

In usual Waldorf salad, substitute sliced unpeeled pear for apple.

### Veal Fricassee

2 lbs. veal stewing meat
4 tb. w.w. flour
2 tb. fat
2 tsp. salt
¼ tsp. pepper
1 cup celery stalk and leaves cut in 1" pieces
1 small onion
1 cup peas (optional)
1 cup hot water
1 tb. brewer's yeast

Dredge meat in 2 tb. flour. Brown in hot fat. Season, add vegetables and hot water. (Vary if desired by substituting tomato juice for part or all of the water or ½ of the water for Cherry Julep.) Cover tightly and simmer till done—about 1½ hrs., or simmer for ½ hr. and pressure cook ½ hr. Thicken liquid with 2 tb. w.w flour mixed with a little cold water.

### Nut Cake

2 cups sifted w.w. flour
2½ tsp. double acting or 4 tsp. tartrate baking powder
1 tsp. salt
1 1/3 cup brown sugar, packed
1/3 cup margarine at room temperature
¾ cup milk

1½ tsp. vanilla
2 eggs, unbeaten
¾ cup nut meats, broken
Sift together salt, baking powder and flour. Add sugar and mix well. Add margarine, milk and vanilla. Beat 200 strokes or 2 min. by hand or at slow speed with mixer. Add eggs and beat same time or till smooth. Stir in nut meats. Pour into greased pan. Sprinkle with chopped nuts. Bake in moderate oven 35-40 min.

## Broccoli Broil

About 2 min. before serving, spread the following sauce over broccoli and place under broiler till hot.
½ cup mayonnaise
1 tb. chopped onion
3 tb. chopped pickle or relish

## Orange Surprise

1¾ cup orange juice
¼ cup water
1 envelope plain gelatin
2 oranges, sliced or sectioned
Soften gelatin in water. Dissolve over hot water. Peel and section or slice oranges. Squeeze any juice from skins and pulp. Add enough canned juice to make 1¾ cup. Add this to completely dissolved gelatin. When it has begun to thicken, pour into serving dish or individuals, arranging oranges attractively around edges. When firm, arrange more pieces of orange over surface. Garnish with sweetened whipped cream and sprinkle whole with coconut.

## Hawaiian Hamburg

Prepare hamburg patties seasoned with salt and pepper. Wrap with a strip of bacon, fasten with toothpick. Press chunks of pineapple into meat. Grill. Take your Vitamin C after any meal which contains nitrates or nitrites. It protects you against the nitrosamines which may form from such foods and which are carcinogenic.

## Wilted Greens

To every quart of greens, measured after washing, allow ¼

cup bacon fat, ½ cup vinegar and a small onion, chopped. Cook onion in fat till it turns yellow. Add vinegar. When hot add greens. Cover and cook just till wilted. Season and serve hot.

*Rice Pudding*

1 cup cooked brown rice
2½ cups milk
2 eggs
¼ cup raisins
1/3 cup powdered milk
¼ tsp. salt
¼ cup brown sugar

Combine milk and rice in double boiler, cook till hot. Blend dry ingredients; add to beaten egg yolks. Add gradually to rice. Add raisins. Cook a few minutes till thick. Remove from heat. Fold in stiffly beaten whites and flavor with vanilla or lemon rind. Serve with light cream and a sprinkling of nutmeg.

An important afterthought for any guide to foods and meals for good nutrition: Remember that no form of sugar is good food; that man has no physiological need for sugar; that ancient man was filled with energy though he had no sugar bowl; and that any cook can learn to reduce the sugar content of recipes, if it is done gradually. Though my recipes usually specify brown sugar, it is important that you know that this is not a good food, either, its only virtues being a small content of iron and a little chromium, missing from white sugar, but not useful enough to warrant rash use of the brown product, either. It is true that there are some recipes where the sugar content is important to texture, more than to flavor. These are a minority, and the average recipe is sweet in a degree which reflects nothing more than the degeneration of our tastebuds, numbed by an endless tide of sugar. Taste before you sweeten, an excellent rule: You'll use less. Abuse of the artificial sweeteners is likewise a journey into the unknown and into known dangers. The task at hand: Reeducation of our palates.

# CHAPTER 18

## DIET WITHOUT DROOPING

THE CONSTRUCTIVE REDUCTION DIET WHICH FOLLOWS IS one which creates no deficiency, except in calories. In this diet, every effort has been made to keep vitamin-mineral intake as high as possible, protein intake more than adequate, with enough fat and carbohydrate to achieve a ratio which will not invite fatigue from what your physician calls "ketosis," a kind of acidosis.

Nonetheless, any diet below 2,400 calories risks vitamin-mineral deficiencies, no matter how careful the food selection, for this is a hazard inherent in reducing the gross intake of food, and the hazard increases as the calorie intake decreases. It is recommended that this diet, therefore, be supplemented with multiple vitamins and minerals, as a safeguard. You can do more than this, if you'd like to explore what supplements can do in helping you to distribute your weight loss more equitably, so that your problem areas may respond, and your face not sink in, leaving you looking cadaverous. To try to accomplish all this, add to your supplements lecithin, Vitamin B Complex (high in choline and inositol); and Vitamin E, in the form of mixed tocopherols. (And don't write to me to tell me I'm quoting Mary Ann Crenshaw, for it's the other way around: years ago, I performed controlled research in redistribution of body fat toward the normal, both by diet and by use of supplements. What you have just read, then, isn't theory: It derived from practical application, and it works beautifully in about one quarter of those who try it.)

By the code system employed, and the lists of foods, the need for set menus is eliminated and there is no need for counting calories. Thousands of overweight persons have followed this diet safely, without weakness, deficiency or hunger.

# CONSTRUCTIVE REDUCTION DIET

**BREAKFAST**
  One serving of fruit
  One egg or egg substitute
  ½ slice (thin) whole wheat toast with ½ level teaspoonful
    butter
  One glass of skimmed milk
  One cup of coffee or tea (optional)
    (no sugar; no cream or milk)

**LUNCH**
  One helping of lean meat, fish, fowl or meat substitute
  One vegetable from Vegetable List "A"
  One salad (from Salad List)
  One serving of fruit or dessert
  One glass of skimmed milk or buttermilk
  One cup of coffee or tea (optional)
    (no sugar; no cream or milk)

**DINNER**
  One cup of soup (optional)
  One helping of lean meat, fish, fowl or meat substitute
  Two vegetables from Vegetable List "A" *plus* one from
    Vegetable List "B"
                        or
  One vegetable from Vegetable List "A" *plus* one from
    Vegetable List "B" *plus* one helping of salad (from Salad
    List)
  One portion of fruit or dessert
  Coffee or tea (no sugar; no cream or milk)
  Choose foods from the following lists:

**SOUP LIST**
  Consomme
  Clear Vegetable Soup
  Beef Broth
  Mutton Broth

Chicken Broth
other clear soups
*Note: No creamed soups, none with milk or content of vegetables, meat, or cereals.*

## FRUIT LIST

Orange (small)
Grapefruit (half, medium size)
Apple, (one, small)
Pineapple (two average slices)
Peach (one)
Cantaloupe (one half, medium size)
Melon (two-inch section of average size melon)
Tangerine (one, large)
Berries (one half cup)
Apricots (two, medium size)
Grapes (twelve)
Cherries (ten)
Pear (one, medium size)
Plums (two)
Nectarines (three)
Persimmon (one half, small)
Fruit juices: grapefruit, orange (unsweetened) 6 oz.
　(¾ water glass)

## MEAT LIST

Lean Beefsteak (¼ lb. about one inch thick, 2½ inches square)
Roast Beef (two slices, about three inches square, ¼ inch thick)
Beef Liver (one slice, three inches square, ½ inch thick)
Beef Tongue (two average slices)
Beef Kidney (¼ lb.)
Hamburger (¼ lb.)
Calf's Liver (¼ lb.)
Lamb Kidney (two, average size)
Lamb Chop (one, about two inches square, ½ inch thick)

Roast Lamb (one slice, 3½ inches square, ¼ inch thick)

Mutton Chop (two, medium size)

Boiled Mutton (one slice, four inches square, ½ inch thick)

Roast Veal (one slice, three inches by two inches, ¼ inch thick)

Veal Cutlet (one, average size)

Veal Kidney (two, average size)

Chicken, White Meat (two slices, four inches square—cut very thin)

Chicken, Broiler (½ medium size)

Chicken, Gizzards (two, average size)

Chicken, Livers (two whole, medium size)

## FISH LIST

Sea Bass (¼ lb.)

Bluefish (¼ lb.)

Cod, fresh (¼ lb. to ½ lb.)

Cod, salt (¼ lb. to ½ lb.)

Flounder (¼ to ½ lb.)

Haddock (¼ lb. to ½ lb.)

Halibut (¼ lb.)

Kingfish (¼ lb.)

Pike (¼ lb.)

Porgy (¼ lb.)

Red Snapper (¼ lb.)

Scallops (⅔ cup, raw measurement)

Shrimp (⅔ cup)

Smelt (¼ lb.)

Weakfish (¼ lb.)

Clams, round (10 to 12)

Crab Meat (one crab or ¾ cup flakes)

Lobster (½ small lobster or one cup flakes)

Mussels (four large or eight small)

Oysters (twelve large)

## MEAT SUBSTITUTES

Cottage chees (⅔ cup)

Eggs (two)
Buttermilk (two cups)
Whole milk (one cup)
Skimmed milk (two cups)

## EGGS AND EGG SUBSTITUTES

*Prepare your egg in one of the following ways:*
Plain omelet
Poached
Soft boiled
Hard boiled
Raw

## SUBSTITUTES FOR ONE EGG

Cottage cheese (four tablespoonfuls)
Lamb chop (one small, lean)
Lamb kidney (one)
Calf's liver (two ounces)
Mutton chop (one small, lean)
Buttermilk (one glass)
Skimmed milk (one glass)

## VEGETABLE LIST "A"

Asparagus (fresh or canned: eight)
String beans (½ cup)
Wax Beans (½ cup)
Beet Greens (two heaping tablespoonfuls)
Broccoli (one five inch stalk)
Brussels Sprout (½ cup)
Cabbage, cooked (½ cup)
Cabbage, raw (¾ cup, shredded)
Cauliflower (½ cup)
Celery (five stalks)
Chard (½ cup)
Chicory (½ cup)
Egg Plant (½ cup)
Endive (ten medium stalks)
Green Pepper (one, medium size)

Kohlrabi (two heaping tablespoons)
Leek, chopped (one-third cup)
Lettuce (ten leaves)
Radishes (five, medium size)
Sauerkraut (½ cup)
Spinach (½ cup)
Tomatoes, fresh (one)
Tomatoes, canned (½ cup)
Tomato Juice: four ounces (½ cup)
Watercress (ten pieces)

## VEGETABLE LIST "B"

Beets (two heaping tablespoons)
Carrots (two heaping tablespoons)
Chives (six)
Dandelion Greens (three heaping tablespoons)
Kale (two heaping tablespoons)
Onion (one, small size)
Parsnips (two heaping tablespoons)
Peas (two heaping tablespoons)
Pumpkin (three heaping tablespoons)
Rutabaga (two heaping tablespoons)
Squash (two heaping tablespoons)
Turnips (two heaping tablespoons)

## SALADS

Tossed Greens
Watercress and Lettuce
Radish and Watercress
Celery and Cabbage
Pimento and Greens
Baked Stuffed Tomato (cottage cheese, chopped celery)
*If butter is omitted from vegetables at lunch, one
teaspoonful of salad dressing may be used. Divide between
lunch and dinner, if salads are eaten twice daily; use
vinegar or lemon juice to augment.*

# DESSERTS

Fruit Cocktail (fruits from fruit list; small portion)

Cantaloupe Cocktail

Orangeade (one and one-half oranges; one-half lemon; egg white saccharin for sweetening)

Milk and Ginger Ale (half and half)

*Low calorie desserts don't exist; will power is the best dessert.*

## SPECIAL NOTES

*Extra Butter Allowance:*

At luncheon *or* dinner, one level teaspoonful of butter may be used on your vegetables. If you prefer, you may use a teaspoonful of salad oil as a dressing on salad (at lunch and dinner). If you use the salad oil—it replaces the butter. Lemon juice may be substituted for salad dressing, if you elect to use your fat allowance as butter on your vegetables.

*Appetite Cheaters:*

If your appetite is hearty—and dieting annoying because of hunger pangs, do the following:

*Avoid soups—they are optional anyway, and they tend to stimulate appetite.*

*Drink a glass of cold water when appetite presses you.*

*Choose salad instead of one vegetable, at meal.*

## DIET TO GAIN WEIGHT

Persistent underweight may be a symptom of serious disease. This possibility should be ruled out by a visit to your physician or clinic before experimenting with diet.

Weight gain is ordinarily a simple problem in mathematics. In body activity, you expend so many calories daily. If your intake of calories from food is less than your expenditure, you lose weight. If it is more, you gain. This is true even if your family has always been thin. It is true even though you have an overactive thyroid.

The way to achieve extra calories is not via pie, cake, cookies, candy and sodas. These average only 120 calories to the ounce, whereas *fatty* foods average 270. You need not stuff yourself with food if you select enough of the fatty ones—and, on that basis, the following recommended diet is built.

The first few days may be uncomfortable; a slender stomach is being stretched. Force yourself to eat. You will digest it. If you find that you can tolerate still more food, increase the size of the portions in the following manner: *Double* the starches, but increase the fatty food quotas by only half as much—50 percent. Too much fat may lead to acidosis or other serious condition. Stick to the suggested amounts.

The supplements which are recommended with this diet are—first—the Vitamin B Complex syrup (to increase appetite); multiple vitamins and minerals, and calcium supplements. Always take your supplements before or after a meal.

## CONSTRUCTIVE GAINING DIET
### *(2600 calories)*

**BREAKFAST**

| | |
|---|---|
| Fruit | 1 serving |
| Cereal (cooked) | 2/3 cup |
| Bacon | 2 slices |
| Egg | 1 |
| Bread (toast) | 1 slice |
| Butter | 2 squares |
| Honey | 3 tablespoons |
| Cream, 20% | ½ glass |
| Milk | ½ glass |
| Beverage—Coffee, tea or coffee substitute | |

**LUNCH**

| | |
|---|---|
| Egg or egg substitute | 1 serving |
| Potato substitute | 1 small serving |
| Vegetables | 2 servings |
| Bread | 1 slice |
| Butter | 2 squares |
| Fruit | 1 serving |
| Cream, 20% | ¼ glass |
| Milk | ¾ glass |

DINNER

| | |
|---|---|
| Meat | 1 serving |
| Potato | 1 small serving |
| Vegetable | 1 serving |
| Fruit salad | 1 serving |
| Bread | 1 slice |
| Butter | 2 squares |
| Dessert | 1 serving |
| Milk | ¾ glass |
| Cream, 20% | ¼ glass |

*(Plus Multiple vitamins and minerals, Vitamin B Complex, and Calcium Supplements.)*

A final and an astonishing suggestion for would-be weight gainers: There are numerous beverages on the market which are sold as aids to reducing. They are advertised for use instead of regular meals. I don't like substitutes for regular meals, however good nutritionally—which many of these products are *not*—but have you ever thought of using them as aids to weight gain? They usually supply about 900 calories in the daily usage suggested. And an extra 900 calories per day—6,300 per week, *in addition to* one's meals—must, if you're in normal health, produce weight gain. The fact that these products are liquid is an asset, for many who vow they can't eat another mouthful of solid food will find they *can* drink a beverage.

If this number of extra calories doesn't yield weight gain, your thyroid and your digestive tract, among other areas, invite a careful medical check-up. I hope it isn't necessary—and that your friends will see more of you.

We reach the end of our journey. If you're an average consumer, and you apply what you've learned, nothing but good will accrue to you and yours. I wish it to you all.

# INDEX